D1563080

WOMEN'S ROLES IN EIGHTEENTH-CENTURY AMERICA

WOMEN'S ROLES IN EIGHTEENTH-CENTURY AMERICA

Merril D. Smith

Women's Roles through History

 GREENWOOD

AN IMPRINT OF ABC-CLIO, LLC
Santa Barbara, California • Denver, Colorado • Oxford, England

Library of Congress Cataloging-in-Publication Data

Smith, Merril D.
　　Women's roles in eighteenth-century America / Merril D. Smith. — 1st ed.
　　　　p. cm. — (Women's roles in American history)
　　Includes bibliographical references and index.
　　ISBN 978-0-313-35552-3 (hard cover : alk. paper) — ISBN 978-0-313-35553-0
(e-book)
　 1. Women—United States—Social conditions—18th century. 2. Women—United
States—Legal status, laws, etc.—History—18th century, 3. Women's rights—United
States—History—18th century. I. Title.
　　HQ1416.S65 2010
　　305.40973'09033—dc22　　　　2009051084

14 13 12 11 10   1 2 3 4 5

This book is also available on the World Wide Web as an eBook.
Visit www.abc-clio.com for details.

Greenwood
An Imprint of ABC-CLIO, LLC

ABC-CLIO, LLC
130 Cremona Drive, P.O. Box 1911
Santa Barbara, California 93116-1911

This book is printed on acid-free paper ∞
Manufactured in the United States of America

For my mother-in-law,
Sandra W. Smith,
and in memory of my father-in-law,
Walter H. Smith

Contents

Series Foreword

Women's history is still being reclaimed. The geographical and chronological scope of the Women's Roles through History series contributes to our understanding of the many facets of women's lives. Indeed, with this series, a content-rich survey of women's lives through history and around the world is available for the first time for everyone from high school students to the general public.

The impetus for the series came from the success of Greenwood's 1999 reference *Women's Roles in Ancient Civilizations,* edited by Bella Vivante. Librarians noted the need for new treatments of women's history, and women's roles are an important part of the history curriculum in every era. Thus, this series intensely covers women's roles in Europe and the United States, with volumes by the century or by era, and one volume each is devoted to the major populated areas of the globe—Africa, the Middle East, Asia, and Latin America and the Caribbean.

Each volume provides essay chapters on major topics such as

- Family Life
- Marriage and Childbearing
- Religion
- Public Life
- Lives of Ordinary Women
- Women and the Economy
- Political Status
- Legal Status
- Arts

Country and regional differences are discussed as necessary.
  Other elements include

- Introduction, providing historical context
- chronology
- glossary
- bibliography
- period illustrations

The volumes, written by historians, offer sound scholarship in an accessible manner. A wealth of disparate material is conveniently synthesized in one source. As well, the insight provided into daily life, which readers find intriguing, further helps to bring knowledge of women's struggles, duties, contributions, pleasures, and more to a wide audience.

Acknowledgments

I love writing acknowledgments. It means I've completed a book, and I get to thank all of the people who have helped me along the way. Perhaps some writers write in isolation—I'm not one of them. Like an eighteenth-century housewife, I'm centered in my kitchen where my domestic and professional worlds overlap and occasionally collide (sometimes literally, as when one of our kittens jumped onto the kitchen table, knocked over my cup of coffee, and drenched my computer. I spent a day anxiously waiting for it to dry).

Because she understands so well that a moment like this happens, and that one cannot choreograph everyday life, I want to thank my editor, Wendi Schnaufer. This has truly been a year of wonders filled with both death and celebrations. Wendi has been so understanding, and she has offered encouragement at just the right times. Thank you, Wendi. I hope we will have another opportunity to work together.

I also want to thank, once again, my dear friend, Else Hambleton. Else has read chapters for me, and she has offered me cogent suggestions on how to improve them. The mistakes are my own. As a kindred spirit and history nerd, Else shares my fantasy of wanting to be able to travel back in time to talk to the women we've studied and find out what they *really* thought of their lives. Else's probably more stalwart than I am; my time-traveling device would have to be climate controlled and include running water, coffee (in a spill-proof mug), and chocolate.

My husband, Doug, has had his own trials this year, but he has offered me love and support, especially during the "have to finish this book" stage. Together this past year, we've once again experienced teenage angst, the college application process, and have celebrated our younger daughter's high school graduation. He and our daughters have put up with books all over the kitchen table, which then migrate to the dining room table. Because they tend to leave their own belongings all over the house, they probably have not been too perturbed, but I appreciate the fact that they have not complained about my mess.

Our daughters, Megan and Sheryl, are truly wonderful. I thank them for just being them. They make me laugh, and sometimes they make me cry, but I always love them. They've become intelligent, poised, charming, and accomplished young women. I hope they've learned from me; I know I've learned from them.

My mom, Sylvia Schreiber, is always ready to listen to me, whether it's to report on her granddaughters' activities, or to hear me complain. I know she's proud of me, and I love her.

To my niece, Hannah Tighe, your phone calls make me laugh and bring me back to reality (albeit a sometimes Hannah alternate reality). Keep being you. I love having you as my "sister."

I've dedicated this book to my mother-in-law and my late father-in-law. Because Doug and I met when we were both in ninth grade, I've known them for a long time. They both welcomed me into their family, despite not always understanding what I do, and have always given me, Doug, and their granddaughters unconditional love and support. In the past few months since my father-in-law's death, I think Sandy and those around her have come to realize just how strong, smart, and capable she is. Like the eighteenth-century widows I've studied, she has held her home and heart together through faith and action, and the help of her family and friends.

Finally, a shout-out to my friends and the rest of my family—you know who you are. You ask me how "the book" is coming along, and you actually want to know! You call me and e-mail me, and you show me you care. Thanks so much.

Introduction

History, real solemn history, I cannot be interested in . . . I read it a little as a duty, but it tells me nothing that does not either vex or weary me. The quarrels of popes and kings, with wars or pestilences in every page; the men all so good for nothing, and hardly any women at all.

—Jane Austen, *Northanger Abbey* (1818)

Women's Roles in Eighteenth-Century America is real history, but unlike the histories read by Miss Morland in *Northanger Abbey,* it is filled with women. Although this volume includes discussions of wars and pestilence, its aim is to examine how women were involved, how they reacted, and how they were expected to react to wars, pestilence, and a host of other situations they encountered in eighteenth-century America. Like Jane Austen's novels, this volume also focuses on marriage, family, and domestic life—and the books women read. The primary goal of *Women's Roles in Eighteenth-Century America* is to consider, describe, and explain how women and girls lived during this time and place. What was everyday life like for a wealthy white woman living in Boston or Philadelphia? What was life like for her servants? How did the mistress of a southern plantation live? How did the enslaved women around her live? What kind of work did a farm housewife do? How did life change for Native American women as European settlers encroached upon their tribal lands? How were their lives changed by war, religious revivals, education, and epidemics, as well as by marriage, childbirth, and widowhood? What opportunities were available to any of these women? These are some of the questions that I explore in this book, while also considering how perceptions *about* women changed during this century.

Women, of course, were not passive agents. They chose who to love, and, when they could, whom to marry. Some of them chose to limit the number of children they had. Some women fought to defend their homes or families from attack. Some ran away from abusive masters, or abusive husbands. Some went to court to defend their own rights. Many decided to convert to a different faith, and a few even created new religions.

Eighteenth-century America changed immeasurably over the course of the century, as it transformed from a group of colonies situated along the eastern coast to a new nation that spread much further inland (and would gain more territory with the Louisiana Purchase in 1803). This new nation was home to men and women of many different ethnicities, religions, and races. Yet it was a nation filled with contradictions. At its creation, men spoke and wrote of liberty and equality. Nevertheless, even Abigail Adams's famous admonition to her husband, John, to "Remember the Ladies," in writing a new code of laws was met with some ridicule by her usually admiring spouse.[1]

Women's Roles in Eighteenth-Century America explores the lives of white, black, and Native American women between 1700 and 1800. In the eighteenth century, these groups connected due to a number of factors, such as immigration and migration, the growth of transatlantic commerce and ideas, the African slave trade, and religion. These factors and others affected women living throughout British America, and they connected women to each other. To give just one example, nearly every woman experienced some aspect of war, or knew others who had.

During the colonial period, the British colonies were frequently involved in wars. Many of these conflicts were extensions of European wars that extended across the Atlantic. For example, Queen Anne's War in 1702 continued the War of the Spanish Succession. The French and English brought their battles to their colonies, and each tried to make alliances with various Native American tribes. In 1754, British, French, and Indian tribes fought at Fort Duquesne (now Pittsburgh, Pennsylvania) beginning the American portion of the Seven Years War. Conflicts continued to take place in the northern and southern borderlands throughout the colonial period and into the early national period. During these wars, white, black, and Native American women faced possible capture, rape, the destruction of homes and farms, or even the death of themselves or their loved ones. Women of different races met in these frontier locations, and occasionally they formed a connection with one another as women and mothers.

But wars also affected those living in cities and towns, as it did during the American Revolution. In Philadelphia, some Whigs became concerned that many of the city's socially prominent women were too interested in the British soldiers who occupied the city. In British-occupied Charleston, Frances Sheftall took in needlework to make ends meet. The British had captured her husband and son, and after their release they went to Philadelphia. The Revolution was a civil war that divided families and communities. In Connecticut, Mary Silliman lived in such a community. Tories who had once lived nearby broke into their home in the middle of the night and kidnapped her husband, Selleck, who was a colonel in the militia. Pregnant again at age forty-four, she took charge of the household, while trying to arrange a prisoner exchange for her husband.[2]

In the post-Revolutionary period, most women's lives remained centered in the domestic realm, although new opportunities for education and for careers in teaching developed after the Revolution. Nevertheless, throughout the eighteenth century, marriage was considered the ideal for both women and men. The concept of marriage, however, varied among the different populations of British North America. Among white Anglo-Americans, beliefs about marriage, marital roles, men, and women were all evolving in the eighteenth century. In previous centuries, women were perceived as sexually aggressive and lustful. They were the daughters of Eve, constantly tempting men to sin. It was commonly believed that marriage helped to confine the licentiousness of women and men, but many also believed marriage placed the weak and gullible minds of women under the control and guidance of husbands. Within the confines of marriage, sexual relations were both necessary and appropriate. Boston minister Samuel Willard, for example, proclaimed "conjugal love" should be revealed through "conjugal union, by which [husband and wife] become one flesh.[3]

Marriage thus created both a physical and spiritual bond between husband and wife, and it was the initial step in the creation of families, the key element in the formation of stable and orderly societies. Early modern philosophers called the family "the little commonwealth," comparing the father, who was head of the household, to the monarch, who was head of the state. Women who questioned authority, spoke out, or were unruly threatened the stability of both their households and society.[4]

By the mid-eighteenth century, the older image of women as sexual temptresses was in the process of transformation. White women began to be viewed as virtuous beings who could restrain the sexual passion of men. (Black women and Native American women continued to be perceived as licentious.) At the same time, Anglo-Americans were exposed to numerous conflicting and competing beliefs and conditions. In some areas, premarital sexuality increased as young couples hoped that pregnancy might force their parents to approve a marriage. In cities, such as Philadelphia, an urban sexual pleasure culture developed.

Moreover, a growing transatlantic trade that brought luxury goods, slaves, books, and ideas to the colonies induced some eighteenth-century Anglo-Americans to see women, along with marriage and marital roles, somewhat differently than previous generations had. Young women were now perceived as possible victims of seduction and warned about giving in to the ploys of lecherous rakes, rather than as the instigators of immoral behavior. Within marriage itself, changes developed as the colonies became more stable and established. For some, luxury goods were available and wealth could be displayed through elaborate displays within their homes. This changed the nature of women's household work, but did not necessarily decrease it. (See Chapter 3 for more on women and work.) Finally, the desire to have a true companion as a spouse influenced some eighteenth-century women to delay marriage until they found such matches, or even convinced them to never marry at all. By the late eighteenth century, many, though not all, viewed marriage more as a partnership between husband and wife rather than as a hierarchical structure. Women became the guardians of the home, although they remained legally subordinate to their husbands.

This ability to instill and inspire moral behavior carried over to women's roles as mothers. The image of the virtuous and moral mother, capable of raising future virtuous citizens, became one of the dominant images of the new republic. In a typical explanation of this image that linked colonial goodwife to republican mother, Virginian Frances Bland remarked to her daughter, Frances, that a married woman should be a "Virtuous tender and affectionate wife and parent, a humain [sic] mistress and a kind Neighbor."[5]

Neither the changes in marital expectations nor the evolution in how Anglo-Americans viewed women happened overnight. Older notions of women as sexual temptresses and older beliefs about marriage overlapped with the newer emerging beliefs. Deborah Read Franklin and Benjamin Franklin lived in a common-law marriage because Deborah was legally married to another man who had deserted her. If Deborah and Benjamin had sought a marriage before a minister or magistrate, they could have been prosecuted for bigamy, if Deborah's previous husband appeared. The Franklin's common-law marriage was accepted in pre-Revolutionary Philadelphia, but it probably would not have been by the next century, at least among the leaders of society, nor would it have been tolerated in seventeenth-century New England.[6]

Whether a woman was married or not, as well as to whom she was married, helped to determine both her status and her duties in eighteenth-century America. Yet marriage was not nearly so inevitable for women in the eighteenth century, as it had been in the seventeenth. As the size and population of the colonies grew, young women in some areas found it more difficult to find partners. In New England, for example, by the end of the seventeenth century, many young men were forced to move to frontier areas to find available farmland, leaving a surfeit of single, young women in the settled towns. Furthermore, as urban and commercial areas developed in British North America, they filled with young men and women, many of whom were not able or inclined to marry. Nevertheless, marriage remained the ideal, if not always the reality, for eighteenth-century women. As one young woman in New York wrote to a friend, "the thought of being Do[o]med to live alone I Cant yet Reconcile." She then declared the designation "old Made" was one "I don't believe one of our Sex wou'd voluntarily Bare."[7]

Some women, however, chose to remain single. One such woman was the Philadelphia Quaker writer Hannah Griffitts. She stated her opinion very clearly in a letter to a married cousin, noting "There are many of you weded ones who I believe are Placed in your Proper Sphere and I sincerely wish you encrease of Hapiness in it—without envying you one atom." She went on to say, "Everyone is not fitted for the single life—nor was I ever moulded for The weded on."[8]

In theory, single women had more freedom than married women; that is, they could earn money and own property in their own names. In reality, however, "respectable" single women generally lived in the households of others, and thus did not have the respect and authority accorded a wife in her own household. Women could not go into careers, such as law, medicine, or the ministry. Although some owned businesses, or inherited wealth and property, the choice for white women was often—but not always—marriage or a marginal existence. Young, single women frequently worked as servants, sometimes living in the homes of others until they married. Others lived more precariously as day or seasonal workers in both urban and rural areas, or in less savory work in the taverns and brothels of the cities.

Upon marriage a woman became a *feme covert,* with her legal identity subsumed by her husband. Unlike a single woman, a married woman could not own property in her own name, except under special conditions, and her husband could take charge of any wages she earned or money she inherited. In addition to changing her legal status, marriage could also alter a woman's social position.

Most of these topics are covered in the first three chapters of *Women's Roles in Eighteenth-Century America.* Chapter One examines marriage, the family, and the changes that took place during this time. Chapter Two looks at how laws affected women by determining their legal status, as married women, single women, and widows, and how and why women came before the courts as plaintiffs, defendants, and witnesses. Chapter Three considers the variety of work that women did in the eighteenth century. Most women were involved in some aspect of domestic work, but this could encompass a variety of jobs, including cooking and childcare, nursing sick family members, preserving food, spinning, and making and mending clothing—to name just a few. Women's work was determined in part by where they lived, their race, and their legal and social status. Women toiled in fields, owned shops, delivered babies, took in boarders, and taught school, in addition to other occupations.

Chapter Four describes how and why women traveled. Women immigrated and sailed across the Atlantic Ocean. Others came in chains from Africa. They also traveled on horseback, carriage, and sleigh to visit friends or attend to business. Some walked over cobblestones to church or shops in urban areas, ignoring the animals in the street and the filth around them.

Chapter Five explores how women were involved in and coped with the many wars and conflicts of the eighteenth century. Chapter Six analyzes women and religion. Religion played a major role in both colonial American and the new republic. The series of revivals, known as the Great Awakening, brought more women into churches, encouraged some to join other churches, and inspired a few to create new sects.

Chapter Seven focuses on how opportunities for women's education changed during the century. As women's role became centered in the domestic sphere, the education of women became a priority, as they were now thought to be the best suited to educate the future citizens of the new nation. Teaching, then, also became viewed as a suitable career for women. Increased literacy, along with a new availability of books, led more women to read, and more women to write, as well. A few women supported themselves and their families by writing, and an even smaller number became musicians and artists. Nevertheless, women's education often included music and dance instruction, and many women attended dances, concerts, and the theater.

Women's Roles in Eighteenth-Century America focuses on only part of British North America, the area that became the new United States. Readers should be aware that Great Britain held valuable colonies in the West Indies and received Canada from France under the Treaty of Paris that ended the Seven Year's War in 1763. After the Americans won the Revolution in 1783, the new United States was surrounded by British Canada, Spanish Florida, and Louisiana, which passed from France to Spain to France again, and then to the United States in 1803.

Because the aim of this volume is to focus on the many roles of women in the eighteenth century, it is not a book about "famous" women. Readers will find some women mentioned whose names are familiar, but when possible I have tried to include the names of women who may not be as well known. In both cases, the women discussed often serve as examples for the number of women whose lives they typify.

NOTES

1. Abigail Adams to John Adams, March 31, 1776, in Margaret A. Hogan and C. James Taylor, eds., *My Dearest Friend: Letters of Abigail and John Adams* (Cambridge, MA: Harvard University Press, 2007), 110. The correspondence of John and Abigail Adams is available online at the Adams Family Papers: An Electronic Archive, hosted by the Massachusetts Historical Society, http://www.masshist.org/digitaladams/aea/.

2. Kate Haulman, "Fashion and the Culture Wars of Revolutionary Philadelphia," *William and Mary Quarterly*, 62 (October 2005): 651; Jacob R. Marcus, *The American Jewish Woman: A Documentary History* (New York: Ktav Publishing, 1981), 28–31; Joy Day Buel and Richard Buel, Jr. *The Way of Duty: A Woman and Her Family in Revolutionary America* (New York: Norton, 1984), Ch. 6.

3. Samuel Willard, *A Complete Body of Divinity* (Boston, 1726), 609, quoted in Richard Godbeer, *Sexual Revolution in Early America* (Baltimore: Johns Hopkins Press, 2002), 56.

4. For more on women's roles in the seventeenth century, see Merril D. Smith, *Women's Roles in Seventeenth-Century America* (Westport, CT: Greenwood Press, 2008).

5. Frances Bland to Frances Bland Randolph, ca. 1770–71, Tucker-Coleman Papers, Earl Gregg Swem Library, College of William and Mary, quoted in Joan R. Gunderson, *To Be*

Useful to the World: Women in Revolutionary America, 1740–1790, rev. ed., (Chapel Hill: University of North Carolina Press, 2006), 60.

6. Gunderson, *To Be Useful*, 7–10. Among those of lower status and non-English groups, extralegal marriages were more acceptable, see Clare A. Lyons, *Sex Among the Rabble: An Intimate History of Gender and Power in the Age of Revolution, Philadelphia, 1730–1830* (Chapel Hill: University of North Carolina Press, 2006), 33–36.

7. Sarah Hanschurst to Sally Forbes, 1762, Sarah Hanschurst Letterbook, Miscellaneous Manuscripts, Library of Congress Manuscripts Division, quoted in Mary Beth Norton, *Liberty's Daughters: The Revolutionary Experience of American Women, 1750–1800*, With a New Preface by the Author (Ithaca, NY: Cornell University Press, 1996), 41.

8. Hannah Griffitts to "My Dear Cousin," n.d., Edward Wanton Smith Collection, Quaker Collection, Haverford College, quoted in Karin A. Wulf, *Not All Wives: Women of Colonial Philadelphia* (Ithaca, NY: Cornell University Press, 2000), 16.

SUGGESTED READING

Buel, Joy Day, and Richard Buel, Jr. *The Way of Duty: A Woman and Her Family in Revolutionary America.* New York: Norton, 1984.

Gunderson, Joan R. *To Be Useful to the World: Women in Revolutionary America, 1740–1790.* rev. ed. Chapel Hill: University of North Carolina Press, 2006.

Norton, Mary Beth. *Liberty's Daughters: The Revolutionary Experience of American Women, 1750–1800.* With a New Preface by the Author. Ithaca, NY: Cornell University Press, 1996.

Smith, Merril D. *Women's Roles in Seventeenth-Century America.* Westport, CT: Greenwood Press, 2008.

Wulf, Karin A. *Not All Wives: Women of Colonial Philadelphia.* Ithaca, NY: Cornell University Press, 2000.

Chronology

1749	Elizabeth Murray decides to remain in Boston and open a shop rather than live as a dependent in her brother's household.
1754–1763	Seven Years War in Europe and North America, it is sometimes called the French and Indian War in the United States.
1759–1761	Cherokee War in South Carolina.
1760	The Bray School for African American children (slave and free) is established in Williamsburg, Virginia. Ann Wager is the teacher and continues in the position until her death in 1774.
1761	John Wheatley purchases an African girl from a slave ship in Boston. He calls her Phillis. She will become a poet.
1763	Under the Treaty of Paris ending the Seven Years War, France cedes Canada to Britain.
1764	Parliament passes the Revenue Act (known as the Sugar Act) to raise funds. Parliament passes the Currency Act, preventing colonies from issuing paper money.
1765	Parliament passes the Stamp Act (which places taxes on newspapers, legal documents, playing cards, pamphlets, and other items) and the Quartering Act (which requires colonists to provide housing and supplies for British soldiers).
1767	Townshend Acts place duties on tea, glass, lead, paint, paper, and oil.
1770	Boston Massacre.
1771	Ann Lee, who will form the Shakers religious group, emigrates from England to America.
1773	Parliament passes the Tea Act and repeals duties on other items. The Boston Tea party protests the tea tax by dumping chests of tea into Boston Harbor.
	Phillis Wheatley's book of poetry *Poems on Various Subjects, Religious and Moral* is published. She is the first African American woman to publish a book.
1774	Intolerable Acts passed. The first act closes Boston Harbor until tea dumped in the harbor is paid for.
	Fifty-one women in Edenton, North Carolina, sign a petition to support their husbands and endorse the Nonimportation Resolves, the First Continental Congress's "resolves" against importing tea and other British goods.
	Ann Lee establishes the Shakers' first permanent settlement in New York.
	First Continental Congress is held in Philadelphia.
1775	The women of Pepperell, Massachusetts, hold a town meeting and organize a militia after the men of town march away to war. Paul Revere makes his midnight ride to warn colonists in Massachusetts that the British are arriving.

	The Second Continental Congress meets in Philadelphia.
1776	Declaration of Independence is adopted and signed.
	Abigail Adams reminds her husband, John, to "Remember the Ladies," as Congress begins to write new laws.
	New Jersey gives female property owners the right to vote, until the wording of the law is changed to "free, white males" in 1807.
1777	Sybil Ludington rides nearly 40 miles throughout Putnam County, New York, to gather the militia after her father receives word of a planned attack on Danbury, Connecticut.
	British troops occupy Philadelphia.
1778	France signs a treaty with the United States.
1779	Spain declares war on England.
1780	Pennsylvania begins gradual abolition of slavery.
	British capture Charleston.
	Esther DeBerdt Reed publishes *Sentiments of an American Woman* saying women should give up luxuries and donate money to the troops instead.
1781	English General Cornwallis surrenders at Yorktown.
	Articles of Confederation are ratified.
	Jury in Massachusetts decides in favor of "Mum Bett" (Elizabeth Freeman) and grants her freedom.
1783	The Treaty of Paris ends the Revolutionary War; Continental Army disbands.
1785	Martha Ballard, a midwife in Maine, begins her diary.
	Nancy Ward, the War Woman of Chota, is an official negotiator at talks in Hopewell, South Carolina.
	Pennsylvania passes a new divorce law as part of republican reforms.
1787	Benjamin Rush publishes "Thoughts on Female Education."
	The Young Ladies Academy of Philadelphia opens.
1788	The Constitutional Convention is held in Philadelphia.
1789	George Washington is inaugurated as the first president of the United States.
	The French Revolution begins.
1790	Judith Sargent Murray's *On the Equality of the Sexes,* written in 1779, is published.
1792	George Washington is reelected president.
1793	Yellow fever epidemic hits Philadelphia.
1796	John Adams is elected the second president of the United States.

1

---⌘⌘⌘---

Women, Marriage, and the Family

The lives of most white women in eighteenth-century British America were entwined with the lives of their families and with the duties and concerns of their households. Marriage changed a woman's name and legal status, but it also changed her economic status and her role within her family and the community. After marriage, a woman generally assumed the responsibility of running the household, bearing and caring for children, and nursing the sick—skills she may have practiced as a single woman, but without the authority or responsibility of being the mistress of the household. Marriage, of course, brought other changes for a woman, as she moved from her parents' home to her husband's. In addition to being in charge of domestic matters, she might also assist her husband in his business, or even run the business while he was away. Marriage also legitimized her role as a sexual being and mother.

When twenty-year-old Esther Edwards wed thirty-six-year-old Aaron Burr in 1752, after a courtship of less than two weeks, she found herself in a new role, that of wife and mistress of the household. Her husband was pastor of the Presbyterian church in Newark, New Jersey, and president of the newly created College of New Jersey (now Princeton). Esther was far away from her family and friends in Massachusetts as she adjusted to her new responsibilities. She was the daughter of the famous minister Jonathan Edwards, but her family had suffered both financial losses and decreased social esteem when her father lost his position in Northampton after years of acrimony between him and the church. Esther's marriage to Aaron Burr elevated her socially and quickly shifted her role from that of a daughter assisting her mother to a wife in charge of entertaining; feeding; and lodging visiting parents, ministers, college trustees, and sometimes students, as well as taking care of her own family and household. In addition, Esther coped with the added stress of having to be careful about her words and actions so as not to antagonize her husband's parishioners, parents of students, or college trustees.[1]

Marriage, family, and home formed the foundation of most white women's lives in eighteenth-century British North America. White women, for the most part, married and spent the majority of their lives married; however, by mid-century population growth and changing social and economic conditions meant there were also more single women living in Anglo-America. Of course most women did not marry college presidents, but they would have understood Esther Burr's fears and her desire to succeed in the transition from daughter to wife. Marriage was an important and significant step. Once a daughter married and "went to housekeeping," her position within her family and community was altered forever.[2]

Thus, the choice of a suitable spouse weighed heavily on the minds of men and women of marriageable age and their parents. A formal courtship often began with parental inquiries about the economic prospects of the young man or woman. Parents and guardians sought to determine the financial assets of their offspring's potential mates, or at least whether they had the possibility of inheriting money or property. Despite a new emphasis on romantic love and companionate marriages in eighteenth-century popular culture, a suitor's economic assets and background were often of more concern to parents than how much in love the young couple might be. As one historian notes, "the trick was to distinguish between marrying up, which was honorable and prudent, and fortune hunting, which was despicable." In other words, the wealth of a prospective marital partner was only one factor, albeit an important one, in determining whether a couple should wed.[3]

Religion was another factor that might determine whether a suitor was appropriate. From the beginning, Quakers attempted to ensure the formation of Quaker households and developed an elaborate procedure for marriage. Young men and women first had to obtain their parents' or guardian's consent to begin a courtship. In an attempt to keep young people from becoming too involved with one another before permission had been granted, committees of elders were occasionally sent to spy on them during market days and fairs in Chester and Philadelphia. Finally, permission to marry had to be granted by their parents or guardians, and approved by the men's and women's monthly meetings. Committees within the monthly meetings investigated the couple to make certain that they were free of prior entanglements and that they loved each other with a holy love. Occasionally, the meeting withheld approval of a marriage until a condition had been met. For instance, in 1713 the Chester women's meeting told Hannah Vernon to "acknowledge the sin of speaking with [Caleb Harrison] about marriage before she had consulted her parents." Hannah did so, and the couple married.[4]

In 1796, Philadelphia Quaker Molly Drinker did more than speak about marriage with Samuel Rhoads. The couple wed without telling Molly's parents, Elizabeth and Henry Drinker, because they feared Henry would not approve the match. On August 10, Elizabeth described in her diary what had occurred two days before. "Molly was gone, as I thought, and as she said, with Sally Large Shoping." Later that night, a man delivered a letter from Molly to her parents. Elizabeth and Henry did not know that their daughter had been seeing Samuel, and Henry was extremely angry when he heard about the marriage. On August 9, the couple learned some more details about the wedding: that the couple had been married by a magistrate, but "according to friendly order" and that after the ceremony the couple and friends had set off for an acquaintance's house two miles outside of the city. Elizabeth was relieved to know where her daughter was, but was still upset, and wrote, "little did I think that a Daughter of mine would or could have taken such as step, and she always appeard to be one of the last girls that would have acted such a part—to leave her fathers house, and go among strangers to be *married*!"[5]

Two months later, on October 9, Molly came to see Elizabeth. Elizabeth recorded that it had been nine weeks since she had seen Molly, but she "was pleased to see her, and heartily wish an Amicable meeting would take place between her father and her." Her wish came true on November 1 when Henry and Molly met unexpectedly at the Drinker's house, after he left meeting early. Molly and her father reconciled, although Elizabeth did not listen to what was said, because, as she recorded, she had "feelings of my own at the time."[6]

In her haste to marry and begin her new role in life, Molly Drinker violated Quaker practices. She actually made-up with her parents several months before the Quaker women's monthly meeting decided to accept her written apology on May 23, 1797. Molly had to meet again with the women's monthly meeting, and Samuel had to meet again with the men's monthly meeting a few months later. Finally on November 17, after a public reading of the couple's statements, the Quaker monthly meeting reinstated Molly and Samuel Rhoads.[7]

Molly and Samuel's experience was not all that unusual. After the mid-eighteenth century, the Pennsylvania Society of Friends disowned a significant number of its members for marrying "out of unity." Young people, especially in the rural areas surrounding Philadelphia, went against their parents' wishes and married men or women who were not Quakers. Like Molly and Samuel, the women and men had to publicly acknowledge their wrongdoing; those who would not do so were not pardoned. After 1762, even when a woman was pardoned by the meeting for marrying a non-Quaker, her children were not automatically accepted into the meeting. Thus, Pennsylvania's Quaker community lost members in the eighteenth century.[8]

Furthermore, marriage contributed to the loss of Quaker membership in another way. A reform movement was taking place in the 1750s and 1760s in which Quakers attempted to reconnect to the original teachings of George Fox,

the founder of the Society of Friends. One reform measure was aimed at preventing marriages between close relatives. Colonial Quakers had long permitted
such marriages, and in fact, many elite Quakers were bound by intermarriage. It
has been noted that "for many, these family ties were extremely important to
their sense of identity and the Quaker prohibition against marrying non-
Quakers was so strong that to marry kin was an obvious solution, especially if
potential marriage partners were limited by requirements of social and economic
status as by religion."[9]

When Milcah Martha Hill married Charles Moore of Philadelphia in 1767,
the Quaker meeting disowned them because of their close family ties. They were
both first and second cousins. Yet, Milcah Martha's sister, Hannah, had married
Samuel Preston Moore, Charles's brother twenty years before, and the couple
only received a reprimand from the Meeting. The Meeting permitted Hannah
and Samuel to return after the couple wrote a letter of apology. Milcah Martha
and Charles, however, were not allowed to return. Milcah Martha did rejoin the
Quaker Meeting after Charles died in 1801.[10]

Most parents would not force a mate on their child, and if child or parents felt
a suitor was wrong, even a fortune and high social rank could not assure a match.
For example, although there were a limited number of suitable Jewish men in
eighteenth-century New York, Abigail Levy Franks rejected wealthy David
Gomez as a possible suitor for her daughter, Richa, calling him "a Stupid
wretch." In a letter to her son, Naphtali Franks, in 1742, Abigail declared,
"[even] if his fortune was much more and I a beggar noe child of Mine . . .
Should Never have my Consent and I am Sure he will never git hers."[11]

Richa Franks did not find a suitable spouse until after the death of her parents, when she moved to England and married there. In Europe, Jewish sons and
daughters generally married a person chosen by their parents. Moreover, Spanish
and Portuguese Jews (the Sephardim) seldom married those who came from
Central Europe (the Ashkenazim). In America, however, young people often
chose their own mates, and because the Jewish population was not very large,
Sephardim and Ashkenazim intermarried. (Religion is discussed more fully in
Chapter 6.)[12]

Two of Abigail Franks' children, her daughter Phila and her son David, married Christians. The news of Phila's secret marriage to Oliver DeLancey in 1752
came as a shock to Abigail, although she socialized with the elite Christian families of New York. Abigail expressed her grief to her son Naphtali, whom she
called Heartsey, noting:

> the severe affliction I am under on the conduct of that unhappy girle [Phila]. Good
> God, wath a shock it was when they acquainted me she had left the house and had
> bin married six months. I can hardly hold my pen whilst I am writing it. Itt's wath
> I never could have imagined . . . I gave noe heed [to rumors about the marriage]
> further than a generall caution of her conduct wich has allways bin unblemish'd,

and is soe still in the eye of the Christians whoe allow she had disobliged us but has in noe way bin dishonorable, being married to a man of worth and character.

She continued to express her grief, "My spirits was for some time soe depresst that it was a pain to me to speak or see any one. . . . I shall never have that serenity nor peace within I have soe happyly had hittherto." Abigail never reconciled with Phila.[13]

Parents who were among the elite in eighteenth-century America often made a conscious effort to ensure that their offspring made advantageous marriages. This was particularly true in eighteenth-century Virginia, where the sons and daughters of wealthy planters married each other, forming an elite group knit together by marital and family ties. This group dominated social and political life in Virginia throughout the century. For example, the wealthy and powerful Virginia planter Robert "King" Carter maintained and strengthened his holdings by helping his children make advantageous marriages with the richest and best connected families in Virginia. Upon marriage, his sons received plantations and slaves, thus keeping land and slaves within the family. Carter gave his daughters cash settlements, however, which made them attractive to other wealthy landholding families, but permitted the family lands to stay intact.[14]

Parents desired their offspring to marry men or women of similar backgrounds and wealth so that they would be able to live as comfortably after marriage as they had in the parental home. Ideally, parents and children agreed on potential mates, but parents or other relatives stepped in if it appeared likely that a young man or woman might be considering someone unsuitable. Virginia planter William Byrd II opposed several of his daughters' suitors because he believed the men would not be able to adequately provide for them.[15]

Daughters of the planter elite generally followed the advice of their parents, and most seemed to agree with the planter marriage ethos. Maria Carter, who was the granddaughter of both Robert "King" Carter and William Byrd II, copied into her commonplace book advice she read in books and magazines about marriage. For example, she recorded this counsel on happy marriage from the *Spectator*, "A happy marriage has in it all the Pleasures of Friendship, all the Enjoyment of Sense and Reason, and indeed all the Sweets of Life. A marriage of Love is pleasant; a marriage of Interest easie; and a marriage where both meet, happy."[16]

It was not only the planter gentry, however, that desired their children to make advantageous matches. When Eliza Selden traveled from Petersburg, Virginia, to Richmond in 1791 in search of a husband, she soon found one. Shortly after she returned home, a relative of hers wrote her to say he did not think the man would be able to provide for her. Eliza noted that "want of fortune is his only fault," but she agreed that it was important and promised not to marry him until he could support her.[17]

But as the examples of Molly Rhoads and Richa Franks indicate, some daughters did not wait for parental approval. In New England, population growth and inheritance patterns led to changes in how and when couples married. Because most New England towns were already densely settled, in many cases fathers could not increase their holdings in order to leave the land to all of their sons. In some families then, all or most of the family's property went to the oldest son. Younger sons went into trade or moved to frontier areas. Some of these young men married at a younger age because their parents no longer had any hold on them. Some older sons, in response, also began to marry at a younger age.[18]

Young men and women were also influenced by republican ideology espousing individual freedom, and they benefited from advice literature that advocated a more tender and permissive approach to child rearing. The Reverend Nicholas Collins of Gloria Dei Church in Philadelphia frequently refused to marry young couples who came to him without proof of parental approval. In July 1797, after refusing to marry a couple he thought were runaways, he wrote," similar cases happen not seldom: young girls, some 15, coming with improper men, as strangers, etc., insisting on their capacity and right of choosing for themselves; young persons being, or appearing to be, apprentices or servants; persons demanding secrecy."[19] Earlier in the century, Jonathan Edwards condemned the growing youth culture, as many youths in his Northampton, Massachusetts, parish were "very much addicted to night-walking, and frequent the tavern, and lewd practices, wherein some by their example exceedingly corrupted others." Furthermore, Edwards condemned parents who declined to exert their authority, as he noted that "indeed family government did too much fail in the town," while young people gathered together in frolics and engaged in lewd behavior. This position did not endear him to his parishioners.[20]

Young men and women had opportunities to mingle and socialize in many settings and at many different activities. In northern New England, young men and women gathered at taverns, went to dances, and socialized during group working parties called "frolics." Quilting bees, barn raisings, and harvest gatherings were usually followed by socializing, eating, drinking, and dancing.[21] Young men and women were free to attend these frolics, often without much parental supervision. The practice of "bundling," in which a courting couple spent the night together in a bed, may have been a way for parents to keep some control over their offspring. Although ministers condemned the custom, it gave couples a chance to get to know one another and engage in some sexual intimacy while also holding them accountable for their actions.[22]

Premarital pregnancy rates increased in the eighteenth century. In the 1730s, Benjamin and Deborah Franklin's household in Philadelphia included his illegitimate son, William. After the Revolution, however, there was a new emphasis on feminine virtue. Daughters from elite Philadelphia who became pregnant were hidden and sent away until after they delivered. Often these young women were said to be at one of the new academies that educated women.[23] (See

Chapter 7 on education.) Premarital pregnancy also increased in New England. In late eighteenth-century Maine, midwife Martha Ballard delivered the first babies of 106 women between 1785 and 1797. Although most of these women were married by the time of delivery, forty of the babies (38%) had been conceived before the wedding. Sometimes the nuptials came just in time. On August 25, 1799, Martha Ballard wrote in her diary, "Was calld by Mr Young to go and see the wife of John Dunn who was in Labour. She was safe delivered at 7 hour 30 Evening of a fine son. . . . Mr. Dunn was married last Thursday. He was 20 years old last July."[24]

In the seventeenth century, both women and men were prosecuted for fornication, but by the mid-eighteenth century, men were seldom prosecuted for the crime. Yet in towns such as Hallowell, Maine, community pressure often forced the young men of the town to marry or provide for women they impregnated. Permitting courting couples to spend the night together might have made it easier and more comfortable for them to engage in sexual relations, but it also meant that the woman's parents knew whom to blame if their daughter became pregnant. Local men generally did not want to face community sanctions and the threat of jail and fines for their actions, and most often they settled matters outside of court—either by marrying the young woman or by agreeing to pay her a settlement. An eighteenth-century woman in New England did not usually face social ostracism in these cases, nor did she have a problem finding a husband if she did not marry her child's father. (For more on fornication and bastardy, see Chapter 2.)[25]

In frontier regions where clergymen were scarce, couples often decided to live as husband and wife until a minister could be found to officiate. Other couples "self-divorced" and then married again, with or without the benefit of a clergyman or magistrate. In the early to mid-eighteenth century even somewhat prominent couples could live in common-law relationships without public outcry. Benjamin Franklin and Deborah Read lived together as husband and wife for forty-four years in a common-law marriage. Deborah had previously married a man who soon deserted her, but divorce and remarriage were not possible at that time under Pennsylvania law. Rather than face bigamy charges, Deborah and Benjamin simply set up housekeeping together in September 1730.[26] (For more on marriage and divorce laws, see Chapter 2.)

Clergymen or magistrates could perform eighteenth-century weddings, depending on the couple's religion and the laws of the particular colony. Quaker couples married before their meeting without a religious authority officiating. For the most part, wedding celebrations were not too lavish until the mid-eighteenth century. In seventeenth-century Puritan New England, for example, both weddings and funerals were simple and solemn affairs because Puritans opposed the Church of England's sacraments and rituals. In fact, in early New England marriages were civil contracts officiated by magistrates, rather than ministers. By the mid-eighteenth century, however, wedding celebrations began to be more elaborate affairs, even for ministers and their families. Westfield, Massachusetts, minister John Ballentine wrote of his daughter's wedding, "I gave a general invitation, some stayed away because they thought some had a more particular invitation, some stayed away because they thought there would be too many for comfort." Gifts included items to eat and drink, such as rum, joints of mutton, pigs, fowl, apples, potatoes, and flour. Guests from the groom's home in Sheffield stayed for a day after the wedding, eating and drinking with the Ballentines. A party of friends and family then traveled with the bride and groom to Sheffield.[27]

In a letter to his wife, Julia, Benjamin Rush, the Philadelphia physician, described a Jewish wedding he attended in 1787. In the afternoon, "sixty or forty" men assembled in the parlor of the bride's father. There they were led in prayers by a rabbi. After that the groom signed a "deed of settlement," which gave his bride part of his estate if he died before her. Then they erected "a beautiful canopy composed of white and red silk in the middle of the floor." Four young men wearing white gloves held the four poles of the canopy. At this point, the bride, her mother, sister, and other female relations came downstairs. The bride wore a veil over her face. The ceremony involved prayers, wine, and breaking the wine glass, customs that are still followed in modern day Jewish weddings. Rush observed that the groom placed a ring on the bride's finger, "in the same manner as is practised in the marriage service of the Church of England." At the conclusion of the ceremony, "kisses and congratulations became general through the room." Benjamin Rush remained for wedding cake and wine before departing with a piece of wedding cake that the bride's mother insisted he take home for his own wife.[28]

In some places, however, weddings and wedding celebrations remained simple affairs. For example, on October 28, 1792, Martha Ballard of Maine recorded in her diary, "Thee Matrimonial writes were cellibrated between Mr Moses Pollard off this Town and my daughter Hannah this Evening. Esquire Cony performed the ceremony." It does not appear that the any members of the groom's family were there, nor were all of Hannah's brothers and sisters. Although she reported roasting a turkey two days later, Martha's account does not mention any special dinner or baking on the day of the wedding.[29]

After the wedding ceremony, the bride continued to live with her parents, while Moses occasionally slept and ate there. When Martha's niece Parthenia Barton married Shubal Pitt a few weeks later on November 18, the couple followed the same pattern. During the month to six weeks following the wedding, Martha and "the girls" were busy making quilts and gathering the items necessary to set up housekeeping together. The list of essential items seems absurdly small by today's standards, yet they were comparable to what other households in Hallowell, Maine, owned: a coffee pot, a frying pan, a kettle, pewter spoons, forks, and knives, and some plates and bowls. Some wealthy New England households did not even own forks in the latter part of the eighteenth century.[30]

After the couple finally moved into their own home and "went to housekeeping," their marriage truly began. This point is illustrated in Martha Ballard's diary, in which she continued to refer to Hannah and Parthenia as "the girls" while they continued to reside with her. Once they permanently left her home, however, they became "Daughter Pollard" and "Mrs. Pitts."[31]

Once married and settled in their own homes, parents and the community expected daughters to become wives. A wife's duties depended to some extent on several factors, such as her social class, whether she had servants or other women or girls who could help with household chores, and where she lived: in an urban area, a farm, or in a frontier settlement. In each of these situations, however, she was responsible for overseeing the household, as well as taking care of her husband and children. (Women's work is discussed more fully in Chapter 3.)

Eighteenth-century Anglo-Americans expected wives to obey and submit to their husbands. Indeed, under English law a married woman did not even have a separate legal identity. Hers was covered by her husband, and she was known as a *feme covert*. As the well-known English legal scholar Sir William Blackstone (1723–1780) expressed it:

> the husband and wife are one person in law: that is, the very being or legal existence of the woman is suspended during the marriage, or at least is incorporated and consolidated into that of the husband: under whose wing, protection, and cover, she performs every thing; and is therefore called in our law-french a feme-covert.

In general, a married woman could not own property in her name, and her dowry, belongings, and money all belonged to her husband.[32] (See Chapter 2 for more on married women and their legal status.)

This legal definition of a married woman united her identity with that of her husband's, but placed her under his protection and authority. Early in the century, Benjamin Wadsworth, a Boston minister and president of Harvard University, wrote an advice book called *The Well-Ordered Family*. In this work, which was reprinted several times, Wadsworth described the duties of husbands and wives within the ideal, hierarchical family. Wadsworth accepted that husbands should be at the head of the family and that wives should obey them. Yet husbands were not supposed to mistreat their wives or treat them cruelly. He wrote:

> The husband is called the head of the woman. It belongs to the head to rule and govern. Wives are part of the houses and family, and ought to be under the husband's government. Yet his government should not be with rigor, haughtiness, harshness, severity, but with the greatest love, gentleness, kindness, tenderness that may be. Though he governs her, he must not treat her as a servant, but as his own flesh; he must love her as himself.

Wadsworth believed both husbands and wives should be loving and tolerant. "You, therefore, that are husbands and wives, do not aggravate every error or mistake, every wrong or hasty word, every wry step as though it were a willfully designed intolerable crime."[33]

Parents gave similar advice to their daughters. Cadwallader Colden, the New York physician, botanist, and politician, wrote an eight-page letter to his daughter, Elizabeth DeLancey, in 1737, telling her that he knew she would be "Dutyfull" to her husband and thus enjoy a happy marriage. "Let your Dress your Conversation & the whole Business of your life be to please your Husband & to make him happy & you need not fail of being so your self." Even in the later part of the century, many still subscribed to these ideals. In 1790, Thomas Jefferson wrote to his newly married daughter, Martha (Patsy) Randolph, "The happiness of your life depends now on the continuing to please a single person." He then continued, "to this all other objects must be secondary."[34]

These were ideals, however, and most women—and men—recognized this. In close-knit colonial communities, it was difficult to keep secrets from family, friends, and neighbors, who saw and heard the best and worst of many marriages. If a woman was happily married and generally agreed with her husband, it was probably easier for her to "submit" to him. By the mid-eighteenth century, however, many women were more likely to expect their husbands to be partners and loving companions. If their husbands adhered to a traditional patriarchal view of marriage—regardless of whether or not they loved their wives—it could cause problems for the couple.[35]

In 1758, John Adams noted in his diary a huge argument that he witnessed between his parents. Susanna Adams was upset because her husband had agreed to take in a young girl to board at their house without consulting her. Another boarder increased Susanna's work without increasing the family income by very much, so she was understandably angry. The younger John Adams reported his father "uttered not a rash Word, but resolutely asserted his Right to govern." Meanwhile, his mother raged, "I wont have all the Towns Poor brought here, stark naked, for me to clothe for nothing. I wont be a slave to other folks folk for nothing."[36] Even in a happy marriage, some husbands asserted their authority as head of the household.

Many men valued their wives and believed them to be their best friends. In a letter to his "lovely Sally," Tapping Reeve, the well-known lawyer and educator from Connecticut, wrote about his "Pleasure of reflecting that I have one friend in you that will be ever an unshaken friend." A Massachusetts educator, Eliphalet Pearson wrote to his new bride in 1785, "You will excuse my just hinting at, the happiness your friend would enjoy in the company & converse of his other Self. . . . I never wished so much to see my friend. Shall have many matters to communicate, on which I shall wish for your advice."[37]

Once married, for better or for worse, women usually began childbearing. On average, eighteenth-century American women became pregnant within their first year of marriage. After that, they gave birth approximately every two years while they remained fertile. Thus, most white women, if they married in their early twenties, could expect to have five to ten pregnancies and to have three to eight surviving children. For example, Mary Holyoke, the wife of a physician in Salem, Massachusetts, gave birth to twelve children in twenty-two years. Of the twelve, only four survived past infancy.[38]

As might be expected, repeated childbearing took its toll on a woman's body and health, and even family and friends commented on it. One Virginia woman wrote in 1791 about her daughter, "My Poor Dr Polly is again in ye way to increase her Family." She then continued and commented that she wished her daughter "did not have 'em so fast" because "breeding has alter'd her very much."[39] After the birth of her fifth child in 1776, Molly Carroll, who married into the wealthiest family in Maryland, began taking laudanum (an opium based preparation) to ease the pain. Molly had endured complicated pregnancies before this one; out of her seven pregnancies, only three children survived.[40]

Nearly all eighteenth-century Americans knew at least one woman who had died after giving birth. Consequently, most people probably perceived the chance of a woman dying during childbirth as higher than it actually was. Nevertheless, one can understand the apprehension with which John Coalter and his third wife, Fanny Tucker, greeted her first pregnancy, because John's first two wives died following their first pregnancies.[41]

In fact, it was not unusual for a husband to feel anxiety during his wife's pregnancy, especially as the time of her delivery approached. In 1760, Benjamin Bangs wrote in his diary about a night when he and his wife both had difficulty sleeping:

My Dearest friend is much Concern'd being in and near a time of Dificulty & Dreamd a Dream that troubl'd Her much I put it off Slightly for fear of Disheartning Her but Directly upon it Dreame'd much ye Same my Self of Being Bereft of Her & Seeing my Little motherless Children about me which when I awoke was Cutting to think of.[42]

Some women relied upon their strong religious faith to get them through "travail." Seventeenth-century Anglo-Americans believed the ordeal of childbirth was God's curse on women, the daughters of Eve, and many in the eighteenth century continued to feel this way. Yet childbirth was also a way in which women redeemed themselves. Mary Cleaveland of Ipswich, Massachusetts, recorded the birth of each of her children. In October 1751, she wrote: "[T]he Lord apeard for me and maid me the liveing mother of another liveing Child." After she gave birth to her seventh child, she recorded the event, noting, "The Lord was better to me than my fears."[43]

Yet even the faithful knew God did not work without the help of those on Earth, and when a woman went into labor, the midwife and other women were summoned to help. More than once, Ebenezer Parkman, a minister in Westborough, Massachusetts, had to go out in snow and bad weather to get the midwife when his wife went into labor. During one of her deliveries, he noted in his diary, "I resign my Dear Spouse to the infinite Compassions, allsufficiency and soverign pleasure of God and under God to the good Women that are with her, waiting humbly the Event."[44]

After bringing or sending for the midwife and other women, husbands generally waited for news and updates somewhere outside the bedchamber. In 1709, when Lucy Bryd went into labor, her husband, the Virginia planter William Byrd, sent for several women and the midwife. He then went to bed leaving "the women full of expectation with my wife."[45] Other men, however, did remain with their wives through childbirth. Joseph Reed, the Pennsylvania statesman, would not leave his wife, Esther, when she went into labor with their first child. He also remained nearby for subsequent births.[46]

Throughout most of the eighteenth century, midwives attended most women when they went into labor. Toward the latter part of the century, some women began to call in doctors, especially if the birth did not seem to be progressing or if the labor was expected to be particularly difficult. In Philadelphia, physicians attended the births of many of the city's elite women. Charles Moore, the husband of Milcah Martha, received a certificate in midwifery in 1751 after studying medicine in Edinburgh, Scotland. Many of his and his wife's relatives became his patients. Yet even when doctors were consulted, women often had their female friends and relatives present. As the women arrived, and before labor got too intense, the laboring woman provided her attendants with food and drink. The women might also encourage the mother-to-be to consume some of the "groaning beer" or "groaning cakes." During birth, women often gave the mother physical support, as well as emotional support. The mother might lean against another woman as she gave birth, or women might support her as she crouched over the midwife's birthing stool.[47] (For more on midwives, see Chapter 3.)

After the baby was born and swaddled tightly, it was usually fed by one of the women assisting at the birth. Anglo-Americans believed colostrum, the clear fluid produced by the new mother's mammary glands before her milk "came in," was harmful to the newborn. They did not know that it actually helped give the newborn immunity to diseases, or that the sucking of the infant helped the new mother to heal by causing contractions in her uterus. Early modern medical authorities considered both menstrual blood and the blood discharged after birth to be impure, even dangerous. Cultural taboos about engaging in sexual intercourse with a menstruating woman were similar to those advising new mothers not to nurse until the impurities were gone from her system.[48]

Seventeenth and eighteenth-century Anglo-Americans considered breast milk to be whitened blood. Thus they believed when women nursed their infants, they literally gave their own blood. Unlike menstrual blood, however, breast milk was pure. It was a powerful, life-sustaining fluid. It was even recommended as a cure for ailing adults and was considered an essential ingredient in many medicinal recipes. When the Reverend Ebenezer Parkman was ill in 1752, his wife, Hannah, sent their one-year-old son off to be weaned. She then fed her husband with her own breast milk for several nights until he was better.[49]

FRONTISPIECE.   *Vol. VI*

In this print, Minerva has given up her battle attire, and she nurses a baby. Similarly, American women were urged to forget war and nurture their children. Breastfeeding was considered to be the ultimate expression of motherly love. Mentor is holding an olive branch. He is teaching two children the "advantages of peace." Courtesy Library of Congress.

To eighteenth-century Americans, breastfeeding imbued women with an aura of maternal love and self-sacrifice. It represented all that was good and virtuous in women. Even women of questionable virtue could be transformed through the act of nursing their children. Elizabeth Wilson, an unmarried mother who was executed for the murder of her twin sons in 1786, was one such woman. She would not speak in her own defense when first arrested after the bodies of her sons were found, and therefore, under the law in Pennsylvania, the court had to sentence her to death. Eventually, she told her tale to her brother and some ministers, claiming that the father of babies had ruthlessly murdered them while holding her at gunpoint. Her brother sought to obtain a pardon for her, but after encountering several delays, he arrived too late.

Elizabeth had been hanged. According to the legend based on her story, Elizabeth's brother was overcome by grief and became a hermit, living in a cave near Harrisburg, Pennsylvania. The narrative of her tragic tale of seduction and betrayal—purportedly in her own words—was published immediately after her execution, and it proved popular reading with both men and women.[50]

Elizabeth Wilson was the mother of illegitimate babies—she had given birth to other children before the twins, although it is not known what happened to them. She could not claim to be virtuous and pure. She was executed for infanticide. Why then did she become a sympathetic figure? The comments Charles Biddle, vice-president of the Supreme Executive Council of Pennsylvania, made in his autobiography provide a clue. Biddle noted that he believed Elizabeth Wilson was innocent because "it appeared highly improbable that a mother, after suckling her children for six weeks, could murder them."[51] By breastfeeding her babies, Elizabeth Wilson was transformed into an unselfish and nurturing mother, although it was not enough to save her life.[52]

Yet some women could not, or chose not, to breastfeed their infants. A severe illness or injury could prevent a woman from nursing her baby. Stress and fatigue could inhibit the "let-down reflex" and prevent the release of the mother's milk. Sometimes these conditions were temporary, and the mother found friends or relatives who would nurse the baby until she could do so again. At other times, mothers paid wet nurses to nurse their infants. Some well-to-do eighteenth-century Bostonians believed that the city was unhealthy. They sent their infants to wet nurses in rural areas outside of the city.[53]

The inability to nurse their own children caused great distress in some women. Philadelphia Quaker Betsy Rhoads Fisher could not breastfeed any of her children because of a recurring condition in her breasts. Her husband, Samuel, noted this was "a Source of trouble to her delicate Mind, & seemed a greater trial of her fortitude than her own bodily pains."[54] Elizabeth Drinker, another Philadelphia Quaker, nursed her babies when she could, but she also paid wet nurses.

In August 1781, Elizabeth Drinker's son Charles was born. In October, she reported that he "appears to be thriving," and that she had finally recovered enough "so as to be able with the help of feeding to Nurse my little one." She had two nurses who stayed with her for several weeks as she recovered, but feeding him was a problem. When Charles "was 5 days old he was taken with a sore mouth which prevented him from sucking for nine days: in which time my capacity for Nursing him was much lessen'd—agree'd with Rachel Bickerton a shoemakers wife next door to come in 4 or 5 times a Day to suckle him: which she did for 4 weeks—and with what little I could do in that way me made out for that time." Rachel became ill, and Elizabeth tried a series of nurses who did not work out. Finally she concluded, "it is a favour to be able to do that offece oneself—as there is much trouble with Nurses."[55]

For the next two years, Elizabeth reported on Charles's health, noting each time he (and other members of the household) became ill. In March 1784, she made the following sad entry:

> Our dear little one after dilegint nursing had out grown most of his weeknees and promissed fair to be a fine Boy, became much oppres'd with phlegm, insomuch that Docr. Redmans oppinion was that unless we could promote some evacuation he could not live, he ordred what he thought might a prove a gentle vomittt, agatated him much, but did not work, and in little more then 20 minits from the time he took it, he expired aged 2 years 7 months and one day—about a week before he was fat, fresh and hearty—he cut a tooth a day before he dyed—thus was I suddenly depried of my dear little Companion over whome, I had almost constantly watchd, from the time of his birth, and his late thriving state seem'd to promise a [reward] to all my pains—he dy'd the 17 march, fourth day.[56]

The death of children was a sad, but not unusual occurrence for eighteenth-century Americans. Of the nine children born to Elizabeth and Henry Drinker, five reached adulthood. Having many children living at one time must have been unusual enough that Elizabeth Drinker mentioned it in her diary on January 1, 1782, "Isey Pleasants came this morning to acquaint us, that his mamy was brought to Bed, at 6 this morning of a Son—who they call James—their 10th Child; all living."[57]

As the population of the American colonies grew and farmland became less available in already settled areas, it became more difficult for landowners and their wives to pass land on to their offspring. In addition to marrying later or not at all, some women may have consciously attempted to limit the number of children they had. Quaker women in the eighteenth century delayed marriage *and* limited the number of pregnancies they had. Quaker husbands and wives may have cooperated in this effort by choosing to abstain from sexual intercourse or by using coitus interruptus. Some women may have extended breastfeeding to delay conception.[58] This method of delaying conception seems to have been a technique that Elizabeth Drinker used, and she advised her daughters, who nursed their babies for longer periods of time, to do the same thing. In 1799, while her oldest daughter, Sally, was in the midst of a long and difficult labor on her own birthday, Elizabeth told her, "the time of her birth was over by some hours, she was now in her 39th year, and that this might possiably be the last trial of this sort, if she could suckle her baby for 2 years to come, as she had several times done heretofore."[59] In addition to breastfeeding, there is also evidence suggesting that some wives of elite Virginia planters deliberately took trips away from their husbands to avoid getting pregnant, or at least to increase the time between pregnancies.[60]

Nonetheless, middle-class white women began to reflect more upon their responsibilities as mothers in the mid-eighteenth century. Women certainly loved their children and spent time caring and worrying about them in previous centuries, but in the mid-eighteenth century there were more women who were educated and able to write about their concerns and fears. They were influenced by current thoughts on motherhood because they had the time to read and had access to advice manuals, and they discussed childrearing with other women. Sally Logan Fisher believed she was not qualified for the "great task" of motherhood. Abigail Paine Greenleaf noted that "even we the weaker Sex may be Servicable to the Society where we live and to the world in general by bringing up our Children in Such a manner as to abhor Vice and act Virtuously from a principle early inculcated which is the most likely to be lasting."[61] By the time of the American Revolution, and in the early years of the new nation, motherhood assumed a political caste, as mothers became seen as instrumental in the raising and educating of future virtuous citizens.[62] (For more on women's education and reading, see Chapter 7.)

Women spent a substantial portion of their lives pregnant, breastfeeding, and caring for their children, but they could not neglect their household duties simply because they were pregnant or caring for young children. Women continued their activities throughout their pregnancies, with only slight adjustments. Generally, eighteenth-century clothing was adaptable, and women did not purchase or make maternity clothes. Many gowns laced, and the lacings could be let out as needed. Petticoats, which usually had ties at the sides, could also be adjusted. If a woman continued to wear stays (a corset) through her pregnancy, she could have them fastened in the front, instead of the back. This made nursing more convenient, as well. In the late seventeenth and into the eighteenth century, women often wore long aprons tied over their clothing to hide their pregnancies. At the turn of the century, high-waisted, uncorseted gowns became popular. They were more comfortable and convenient for women during pregnancy, because they could adjust them by loosening the drawstrings.[63]

In addition to bearing and caring for children, wives were responsible for feeding, clothing, nursing, and overseeing household servants and slaves, boarders, and guests. Although luxury items become more commonplace in the eighteenth century, it did not mean women spent less time in housekeeping—only that the type of work they did changed or even increased. For example, Mary Holyoke had tea with her friends, hung pictures on her walls, and wore fashionable clothing. Yet her work did not lessen; instead her standards increased. She could purchase clothing, instead of making it, but she embroidered her husband's cravats. She had silver on her table, but it had to be polished. Instead of "plain" cooking, she tried more sophisticated techniques and "Dressed a Calves Head turtle fashion." Moreover, she continued to perform traditional duties, such as sowing peas, cauliflower, and beans; preserving quinces, plums, and meat; and washing, ironing, and mending clothing.[64] (See Chapter 3 for more information on women's work.)

In the eighteenth century, those who could afford to do so built bigger houses, or remodeled older ones. Instead of living and working in one room on the first floor, people performed specific tasks, such as eating, sleeping, or working in specific rooms. One study of houses that were built between 1750 and 1775 in Worcester, Massachusetts, found fifty-one out of eighty-eight houses were two rooms deep, instead of only being one room deep, as most houses built earlier were. Many of the houses had two stories, and they had lean-tos added on to them. Older houses in rural areas were often expanded, too. The majority of the houses in the Worcester study were not central hall, Georgian-style houses, but they did include some Georgian features, such as more and bigger windows, higher ceilings, and stairs instead of ladders.[65] The housing changes occurred throughout the British American colonies. Deborah and Benjamin Franklin's new home in Philadelphia—built in the 1760s—featured a basement kitchen, separate bedrooms for the members of the household, a dining room, a library, and a parlor. The house held three rooms on each floor. Eliza Farmer noted in 1774 that her new house in Philadelphia had a "little Hall with a Parlour on each side & a Kitchen behind." In both the Franklins' and Farmers' houses public activities took place on the first floor. Most eighteenth-century Philadelphians, however, continued to live in smaller homes and continued to combine public and private functions on the ground floor, which often contained a shop and a sitting area, as well as the kitchen.[66]

Entertaining in the eighteenth century became more formal and elaborate. Diners ate from individual plates with their own fork and knife instead of eating from a common pot with a carved spoon. Homeowners began to replace wooden dishes with those made of pewter, or even china. Groceries, such as tea, coffee, chocolate, and sugar also became more common, even in middling households. The drinking of tea, coffee, and chocolate, however, required the purchasing of additional items. To serve tea, one needed a kettle in which to boil the water, covered teapots for brewing, a slop bowl for the discarded tea leaves, sugar and cream containers, tea cups, saucers, spoons, and a serving tray.[67] Individual place settings, tea sets, and more elaborate meals meant there was more food to be prepared and dishes and pots to be washed or polished by the women of the household, whether it was done by the mistress, or her daughters, servants, or slaves.

Tea drinking also inspired new customs, as men and women sat and drank together, and even ordinary farm wives could sit down and participate in conversation as they poured the tea for guests. For the well-to-do of the urban areas and among the southern planter gentry, tea drinking was also a time for female socializing and gossiping, especially as more and more the business and social activities of men began to take place outside of the home. For example, women held tea parties, whereas men went to coffee houses. The drinking of tea, however, became politically charged in the years immediately preceding the American Revolution. Supporters of the patriot cause often drank coffee or herbal teas instead of regular tea during this time.[68]

For members of the southern gentry, a display of wealth in the size and design of their houses, their furnishings, and their clothing symbolized their gentility and social position. In the 1730s, wealthy planters began to demonstrate their wealth by building new brick houses, and remodeling older wooden homes. Often planters built new houses to begin lives with their brides. William Byrd II is one such example. After he married his second wife in 1726, he began to construct a brick mansion to replace the wooden house built by his father. The building of new brick mansions continued throughout the 1750s and 1760s. The mansions were two-story structures with center halls, permitting privacy, between the bedrooms on the second floor and other private areas of the household. On the first floor, there were rooms set aside specifically for dining and entertaining.[69]

In general, the plantation houses of the elite were set carefully in scenic locations. Most often, the homes were located near waterways to make the transportation of goods and people easier, but sometimes the houses were situated on bluffs or terraced hills overlooking the water. This first impression of a planter's home made a dramatic and commanding statement on his visitors. By land, the homes were reached by traveling a long drive until the house suddenly came into view, flanked by formal gardens and smaller buildings called "dependencies." These smaller buildings kept the service areas such as kitchens and laundries, as well as the slave quarters, separate from the plantation house of the white family. This division between grand mansion and service buildings also indicated that a planter was wealthy enough to have slaves who cooked, cleaned, and even helped with childcare, so that his wife did not have to engage in manual labor, but instead could be a gentlewoman. Thus, the mansion with the dependencies represented class, gender, and racial divisions that were only possible for the wealthiest planters. As one historian notes, "the plantation celebrated the triumph of the male planter over nature, his household, and colonial society."[70]

Both men and women of the gentry wore fancy clothing as another indication of wealth. Fashionable clothing indicated that the wearer was sophisticated enough to know the latest styles and did not have to worry about the cost, or worry about having to perform chores that would soil the finery. For women, however, clothes assumed more importance, because they were items that belonged to them, unlike their houses and estates. In addition, clothing permitted genteel women to display their knowledge of current fashions. Although male planters frequently complained about the time, effort, and money their wives and daughters spent on dressing fashionably, they were also pleased when their women received favorable attention. William Byrd grumbled in 1711, "Mr. Dunn and I played at billiards and then we read some news while the ladies spent three hours dressing, according to custom." That same year, however, he was quite pleased when the governor chose his wife, Lucy Parke Byrd, to open a ball held in Williamsburg.[71]

Fashionable clothing had to be kept clean. Cleanliness was another sign of gentility, as only people of lower status wore grease-stained or dirty clothing. Farmwife Mary Cooper of Long Island seems to have been chronically tired and overworked. Although there were other women in the household, as well as slaves, her days were often spent cleaning, cooking, or involved with the domestic production of items such as dried apples and sausages. In several diary entries she mentions cleaning clothes. On December 24, 1768, she wrote, "I am drying and ironing til almost brake of day." On the evening of January 7, 1769, she wrote, "O, I am tired almost to death waiteing on visseters. My feet ach as if the bones was laid bare. Not one day's rest have I had this weeke. I have no time to take care of my cloths or even to think my [ ] thoughts." On May 7, 1769, she noted, " Sabbath. I am much distrest. No cloths irond, freted and tired almost to death and forst to stay at home." Mary Cooper wanted to have clean clothing for meeting. Whether it was a sign of respect, or whether it was because others would see her there, is unknown, but not having the clean or proper clothing to wear was something that upset her greatly, and as the wife of a well-to-do farmer she would have been expected to dress appropriately.[72]

Looking clean was a sign of gentility, but actually having a clean body was not a necessity for most Americans, even the most genteel. In his book *The School of Good Manners*, the Boston schoolmaster Eleazar Moody counseled his readers to "Come not to the Table without having your Hands and Face washed, and your Head combed." Washing hands and appearing neat and clean was important to keep from looking "Sordid and Clownish." Toward the end of the eighteenth century, being clean became fashionable in England, due to people such as George Bryan ("Beau") Brummell, who spent two hours each day washing and scrubbing himself, shaving, and cleaning his teeth. The fashion of cleanliness traveled across the Atlantic to the United States.[73]

Nevertheless, bathing all over was not something that was done by everyone even in elite households. When Henry Drinker installed a shower box in the backyard of his home in Philadelphia in 1798, his wife, Elizabeth, did not use it until the following year, noting, "I bore it better than I expected, not having been wett all over at once, for 28 years past." [74] Elizabeth Drinker was considered a woman of refinement, and no one seemed to think it was odd that she did not bathe all over. Without a doubt, she washed her hands and face and kept herself neat and presentable in clean clothing, as befitting the wife of a wealthy merchant.

Like other well-to-do women, Elizabeth Drinker was mistress of a household that included a number of servants, and it was part of her role as mistress to supervise them. The number of servants in the Drinker household varied over the years, but most of the time there were at least five or six and often more. There were both indentured servants and free servants. The indentured servants were generally bound as children. The free servants included long-term live-in workers and short-term live-in workers who just came for a particular job, such as nursing or wet nursing. Others did not live there, but instead came on daily basis and performed such tasks as sewing, laundry, or whitewashing. The long-term free servants were usually single women who lived in the Drinker home and worked as maids whose duties included cleaning, cooking, or taking care of the children. In the eighteenth century, servants were considered part of the household, and to the Drinkers they were members of the family. Elizabeth Drinker took care of sick servants and even gave money and clothing to former servants. She considered them her responsibility, and, as if they were her children, she also supervised them, commented on their behavior, and gave them advice on personal matters, which, understandably, many of them did not always appreciate.[75]

In the case of Sally Brant, a white servant in the Drinker household, Elizabeth Drinker's interference contributed to the loss of her baby. Sally began her life in the Drinker household when she was ten years old. Elizabeth seemed fond of her and thought she was a good servant. When Sally became a bit older she began to flirt with the young men she encountered, and apparently she did more. In 1794, Elizabeth discovered that sixteen-year-old Sally was pregnant, and that their black coachman, Joe Gibbs, was the father.[76]

Most likely, Elizabeth Drinker would have been upset if any young unmarried woman in her household became pregnant, but in this case, it appears she was even more disturbed because Sally was white and Joe was black. The Drinkers fired Joe, and they would not let him communicate with Sally. Sally was sent to Clearfield, the Drinkers' summer home in Germantown, outside of Philadelphia, for the remainder of her pregnancy. Sally gave birth to a little girl and named her Hannah Gibbs. When Elizabeth came to visit, she promptly changed the child's name to Catherine Clearfield, even though it upset Sally. Sally was brought back to Philadelphia, but the child was kept from her and nursed by a series of women, until she died at seven months old. Fearing that having her baby with her would remind Sally of Joe and perhaps bring him back to the Drinker household, Elizabeth Drinker determined that keeping Caty Clearfield in Germantown was for the best. Little Caty was given a funeral, and though Elizabeth might have felt a little guilty, she believed she had done her duty and had acted responsibly in her capacity as Sally's mistress.[77]

Elizabeth Drinker may also have been particularly upset by the whole incident because she was fond of Sally Brant. When Sally was caught flirting and kissing another young man, the Drinkers were ready to let her go back to live with her own mother, but they concluded that if they released Sally from her indenture "upon her mothers terms, she would be in the high road to further ruin." Henry Drinker gave Sally a stern warning to mend her behavior or they would turn her away. Sally cried, but she did not promise to reform. Elizabeth Drinker commented, "How it will end, or what we shall do with her, I know not—set aside this vile propensity, she is one of the most handy and best servant we have ever had—and a girl of very pritty manners."[78]

Despite the problems, Sally continued a relationship with the Drinkers even after she left service with them. On January 12, 1798, Elizabeth Drinker noted that Sally Brant had been there to visit, and that she had been married to a barber for three or four months. For the next several years, Sally Brant Shearer made occasional visits to Elizabeth Drinker, usually with one of her children, and sometimes took tea with her or other family members. For example, on March 1, 1799, Elizabeth reported "Sally Brant and child took tea here, Shearer is her name," and on June 24, 1806, "Sally Sherer with her 4th, child of 6 months were here, I have not seen her since she lay-in—poor girl she has enough to do."[79]

Although Sally Brant became a "respectable" mother, her life was still difficult. Pregnancy and caring for young children compounded the already shaky financial situation of poor women. Many former servants returned to Elizabeth Drinker's house to ask for assistance for themselves or their families, especially when a family member became sick, was injured, died, or was about to give birth. Other Quaker women also provided aid to former servants. Sally's life could have been far worse than it was—poor and desperate women who did not have previous employers who were willing to help them could end up in the poorhouse. (See Chapter 2 on women and the law.)

Sally Brant's interracial relationship is one example of many such unions. The topic of interracial sexual relationships concerned many Americans in the eighteenth century. In Philadelphia, such unions were common, but not necessarily accepted. For example, in July 1800, Reverend Nicholas Collins, the minister at Gloria Dei (Old Swede's Church) in Philadelphia noted in his "Remarkable Occurrence Concerning Marriage":

> A negro came with a white woman, said that he had had a child with her which was dead, and was uneasy in his conscience for living in such a state. I referred him to the negro minister, not willing to have blame from public opinion, having never yet joined black and white. Nevertheless these frequent mixtures will soon force matrimonial sanction. What a particoloured race will soon make a great portion of the population in Philadelphia.[80]

Sexual relationships between blacks and whites were also common in the slaveholding regions, but they were more likely to be coerced relationships between white masters and black slave women. In the seventeenth century, many English women who came to the southern colonies were forced by economic conditions to work in the fields, although it was considered to be men's work. As slavery became established, slave women could take the place of white women in the fields and also take over the most unpleasant household tasks. By the mid-eighteenth century in Virginia, the term "wench," which had been used to refer to lower class English or African women, began to be used almost exclusively as a term for black women. Moreover, as white women began to be viewed as chaste and virtuous, instead of lewd daughters of Eve, black women continued to be perceived as promiscuous and sexually insatiable. Furthermore, sexual practices that existed within some African societies—such as polygamy—were considered by some Europeans to be the product of innate depravity in those of African descent. Many Europeans believed that black slaves could not be faithful to one spouse, and this opinion was strengthened when they observed the instability of slave family life. This instability existed, however, because most slaves were not permitted to marry legally; because husbands, wives, and children could be separated and sold at any time; and because slave women could be forced to have sex at any time with white masters and overseers.[81]

In addition to not having legal status, the marriages of slave women contrasted with those of white women in other ways. Slave couples had to endure the constant threat of being separated if one of them was sold, and they had to accept it if a white man made sexual advances towards the wife. Slaves on smaller plantations, or in areas in which there were few slaves, were not always able to find a spouse. In a comparison of enslaved women and white women in King William Parish in Virginia, enslaved women gave birth to fewer children than white women, were more likely to have miscarriages, and had a larger number of infants die. Enslaved women performed heavy labor right up until the time of birth, increasing their chances of miscarrying. Moreover, enslaved women with children had to take care of them around their other duties. They could not put their husbands or children before their tasks. Although free servants often had little choice about doing their jobs if they wanted to survive, they did not usually have to fear being sold, punished, or raped if they did not work.[82] The newer perception of women as virtuous wives and mothers generally excluded black women, whether they were slaves or not, just as it did many poor white women.

Life for both enslaved and free black women in the north was somewhat different from that of black women on southern plantations. The production of tobacco in the Chesapeake and sugar in the West Indies, and the demand for workers to produce these labor-intensive crops, helped to embed slavery in these regions. In contrast, slavery existed in places like Philadelphia, but slaves were never a large part of the workforce there because large numbers of white servants immigrated to the colony in the early part of the century, and antislavery reform movements developed in the later part of the century.[83]

In Philadelphia, slave families did not usually live together, as most owners had only two or three slaves. In an examination of the records of Christ Church and St. Peter's Church in Philadelphia, one historian found sixty-four black couples who married between 1727 and 1780, most of them after 1765. Both partners were free in 25 percent of the marriages; one partner was free and one partner was a slave in 14 percent, and both partners were slaves in 45.3 percent (twenty-nine) of the marriages. Only seven of twenty-nine couples, or less than one quarter of the slave couples, were owned by the same master. Yet because Philadelphia was a small city in area with a fairly large black population (approximately 1,500 black residents out of a total population of approximately 15,000 in 1750), it is likely that spouses lived near one another.[84]

Most slave women in Philadelphia did not live with their children. In Chester County, however, a rural area outside of Philadelphia, most slave mothers did live with their children. Still, there were fewer slaves in the rural Pennsylvania counties, and they often lived far apart on distant farms. Conditions for slave women did change in Philadelphia by the 1770s because of the large free black population living there. By the 1790s, the free black population increased because of the Pennsylvania Abolition Act of 1780, which mandated that slaves born after 1780 were to be freed—once they became twenty-eight years old. In addition, slaves from other states came to Philadelphia seeking freedom, as did mixed-race and black slaves from Haiti who arrived with their French masters. Most slave women and free black women in Philadelphia probably worked in domestic tasks such as cooking, cleaning, and laundry. A few black women, however, owned property in the city and left estates for their offspring.[85]

The situation of Native American women differed from those of both white Anglo-American women and black women. By the eighteenth century, thousands of Native Americans had died in wars and from exposure to diseases brought by Europeans. For example, as a result of King Philip's (Metacom's) War of 1675–76, the lives of New England Indians underwent enormous changes. Communities were destroyed as Indian survivors were captured and sold as servants. Often families were split apart, and husbands, wives, and children were parted forever.[86]

Throughout eighteenth-century North America, Native Americans often lived lives that intersected with, and were frequently profoundly changed by, the white communities around them. Members of some Indian nations devastated by disease and war joined other tribes and reorganized. Others became Christians, and lived as "friendly" Indians. Still others moved farther west. Most of the Lenape of Pennsylvania, for example, were forced to move west as more and more Europeans settled there. As Hannah Freeman reported in her brief autobiography, "the Country becoming more settled the Indians were not allowed to Plant Corn any longer," that is, in the summer they could no longer follow their traditional way of life as foragers along the Delaware because of European farms, settlements, and dams along the river.[87] Although many Lenape did move to western areas, some stayed in Pennsylvania and married white spouses, but they continued to practice their traditional ways in secret, and passed these traditions and crafts down through the centuries.[88] Hannah Freeman lived in Chester County and never married. She lived as many poor, single women did in Chester County, as an itinerant domestic laborer. (For more on women's work, see Chapter 3.)

The perception of Native American women by white Americans varied according to time and place. Early explorers of the southeastern Indian tribes generally regarded them as lustful and promiscuous because they did not always fully cover their bodies as Europeans did. As fur traders and other Europeans settled in America, some of them began to view the women as noble and as princesses. Some traders saw the commercial and diplomatic advantages of marrying Native American women, although some were dismayed by Native American gender roles and views on marriage, divorce, and child rearing. Southeastern Native American women also saw an advantage in marrying Europeans. Women were in charge of food production and distribution. Wives of white traders were among the first to receive items such as metal hoes and axes and copper pots, which made their lives easier and gave them status within their villages.[89]

Most of the Native American tribes that early Americans encountered were matrilineal. Women owned the houses, and sisters and their families often lived together. Clan affiliation was passed on through the mother, not the father, and it was the mother's brothers and sisters who were the child's "little mothers" and "little fathers." In many Native American tribes, such as the Mahican and Delaware, marriage was "flexible," and either husband or wife could end it if unhappy or dissatisfied.[90] This was also true of the southeastern tribes. Because women owned the houses and controlled the fields, men simply removed their personal belongings from the house when a couple divorced. Children remained with their mothers and belonged to their mother's clan.[91]

By the 1760s, white settlers were viewing Indians as a threat to expansion for the white population. References to Indian women became more derogatory, and they were often referred to as "wenches," just as black women were. After the French and Indian War and its brutal fighting in frontier areas, "savagery was associated with Indianness." Those Indians who had adapted to English culture were perceived to be merely hiding their savagery behind a facade of polite behavior.[92]

White, black, and Indian women all nursed their babies. Most slave women gave birth to their first child at a younger age than did white women. Infant mortality rates were higher among slaves because pregnant slaves often had to work at heavy agricultural chores right up to the time they gave birth. Although some mistresses might supply their favorite slaves with special childbed linens, slave mothers did not have the luxury of an extended "lying in" period after the birth, as their mistresses and other middle-class and upper-class women did. Enslaved women who worked in the fields took their nursing infants with them. Women in Africa often breastfed their babies for several years, and many enslaved women also nursed their infants as long as they could. Slave mothers and nursing infants were usually treated as a single unit. No doubt the mothers extended nursing as long as possible to prevent their babies from being sold away. Moreover, extended lactation helped to prevent conception and provided their babies with nutrients. Native American women also generally nursed infants for a longer period of time than did white mothers. This helped to ensure the survival of both mother and child because many Indian tribes migrated to different summer and winter areas.[93]

As the thirteen British colonies became the United States of America, new ideas about women, marriage, and families emerged. White women were recast as virtuous wives and republican mothers, while women of color were frequently perceived as "wenches." As women's roles changed and racial hierarchies became more explicit over the course of the eighteenth century, so did the laws that concerned them.

NOTES

1. Carol F. Karlsen and Laurie Crumpacker, eds., *The Journal of Esther Edwards Burr, 1754–1757* (New Haven, CT: Yale University Press, 1984), 12–15.

2. Laurel Thatcher Ulrich, *A Midwife's Tale: The Life of Martha Ballard, Based on Her Diary, 1785–1812* (New York: Knopf, 1990), 142.

3. Suzanne Lebsock, *The Free Women of Petersburg: Status and Culture in a Southern Town, 1784–1860* (New York: W.W. Norton, 1984), 21.

4. Barry Levy, *Quakers and the American Family: British Settlement in the Delaware Valley* (New York: Oxford University Press, 1988), 132–133. Quote, p.134, is from Chester Women's Monthly Meeting Minutes, 7th month, 28th day, 1713, Friends Historical Library, Swarthmore, Pennsylvania.

5. Elaine Forman Crane, ed., *The Diary of Elizabeth Drinker* (Boston: Northeastern University Press, 1991), v. 2, 829–830.

6. Crane, *Diary of Elizabeth Drinker*, 850, 857.

7. Crane, *Diary of Elizabeth Drinker*, 921.

8. Joan M. Jensen, *Loosening the Bonds: Mid-Atlantic Farm Women, 1750–1850* (New Haven, CT: Yale University Press, 1986), 12–14.

9. Catherine La Courreye Blecki and Karin A. Wulf, eds., *Milcah Martha Moore's Book: A Commonplace Book from Revolutionary America* (University Park: Pennsylvania State University Press, 1997), 15–16.

10. Blecki and Wulf, *Milcah Martha Moore's Book*, 16–19. These pages include a family tree and an explanation of the complicated family relationships.

11. Abigail Franks to Naphtali Franks, December 5, 1742, in Ellen Smith, "Portraits of a Community: The Image and Experience of Early American Jews," in Pamela S. Nadell, ed., *American Jewish Women's History: A Reader* (New York: New York University Press, 2003), 17.

12. Hasia M. Diner and Beryl Lieff Benderly, *Her Works Praise Her: A History of Jewish Women in American from Colonial Times to the Present* (New York: Basic Books, 2002), 25–27.

13. Quoted in Jacob R. Marcus, *The American Jewish Women: A Documentary History* (New York: KTAV Publishing, 1981), 3–5. Also see Diner and Benderly, *Her Works Praise Her*, 24.

14. Kathleen M. Brown, *Good Wives, Nasty Wenches, and Anxious Patriarchs: Gender, Race, and Power in Colonial Virginia* (Chapel Hill: University of North Carolina Press, 1996), 256–258.

15. Brown, *Good Wives, Nasty Wenches*, 258.

16. Maria Carter Copybook, folder 30, Carter Family Papers, Special Collections, College of William and Mary Archives, Swem Library, Williamsburg, Virginia, quoted in Brown, *Good Wives, Nasty Wenches*, 257.

17. Lebsock, *Free Women*, 19–20.

18. Richard Godbeer, *Sexual Revolution in Early America* (Baltimore: Johns Hopkins Press, 2002), 237.

19. Under Pennsylvania law, parental permission to marry was required for applicants under twenty-one years old. Servants and apprentices needed the permission of their master to marry. Susan E. Klepp and Billy G. Smith, "The Records of Gloria Dei Church: Marriages and 'Remarkable Occurrences,' 1794–1806," *Pennsylvania History* 53.1 (January 1986): 126, 135.

20. Jonathan Edwards, "A Faithful Narrative," in C.C. Goen, ed., *The Great Awakening* (New Haven, CT, 1972), 146, quoted in Godbeer, *Sexual Revolution in Early America*, 238–239.

21. Ulrich, *A Midwife's Tale*, 145–147.

22. Laurel Thatcher Ulrich, *Good Wives: Image and Reality in Northern New England, 1650–1750* (New York: Oxford University Press, 1983), 122–123.

23. Godbeer, *Sexual Revolution in Early America*, 314.

24. Ulrich, *A Midwife's Tale*, 156.

25. Ulrich, *A Midwife's Tale*, 148–157.

26. Clare A. Lyons, *Sex Among the Rabble: An Intimate History of Gender and Power in the Age of Revolution, Philadelphia, 1730–1830* (Chapel Hill: University of North Carolina Press, 2006), 33–36; Joan R. Gunderson, *To Be Useful to the World: Women in Revolutionary America, 1740–1790*, rev. ed., (Chapel Hill: University of North Carolina Press, 2006), 7–10.

27. John Ballentine Journal, October 17, 1769, American Antiquarian Society, Worcester, MA, quoted in Gloria L. Main, *Peoples of a Spacious Land: Families and Cultures in Colonial New England*, (Cambridge, MA: Harvard University Press, 2001), 79–80.

28. Marcus, *The American Jewish Woman*, 37–39.

29. Ulrich, *A Midwife's Tale*, 134, 138–140.

30. Ulrich, *A Midwife's Tale*, 143, 389 n.10.

31. Ulrich, *A Midwife's Tale*, 141.

32. William Blackstone, *Commentaries on the Laws of England*, chap.15, bk.1. Available at The Avalon Project at Yale Law School, http://avalon.law.yale.edu/18th_century/blackstone _bk1ch15.asp.

33. Benjamin Wadsworth, *A Well-Ordered Family*, 2nd ed., (Boston 1719), 22–59, quoted in Nancy Woloch, *Early American Women: A Documentary History, 1600–1900* (Belmont, CA.: Wadsworth Publishing, 1992), 17.

34. Cadwallader Colden to Elizabeth DeLancey, [c.1739], Delancey Papers, Museum of the City of New York; Edwin M. Betts and James A. Bear, Jr., eds., *The Family Letters of Thomas Jefferson* (Columbia, MO, 1966), 50, both quoted in Mary Beth Norton, *Liberty's Daughters: The Revolutionary Experience of American Women, 1750–1800* (Ithaca: Cornell University Press, 1996), 61.

35. Merril D. Smith, *Breaking the Bonds: Marital Discord in Pennsylvania, 1730–1830* (New York: New York University Press, 1991), Chap. 2.

36. John Adams, *Diary and Autobiography of John Adams*, L. H. Butterfield, ed., (Cambridge: Harvard University Press, 1961), vol. 1, 65–66, quoted in Wilson, *Ye Heart of a Man*, 89–90.

37. [Tapping Reeve] to Sarah Reeve, September 25, 1773, Reeve Family Papers, Yale University Library, New Haven, CT; Eliphalet Pearson to Mrs. Pearson [Sarah Bromfield], October 15, 1785, Park Family Papers, Yale University Library, New Haven, CT, both quoted in Lisa Wilson, *Ye Heart of a Man: The Domestic Life of Men in Colonial New England* (New Haven, CT: Yale University Press, 1999), 76–77.

38. Ulrich, *Good Wives*, 70, 134.

39. S[arah] Cary to Betsy Whiting, March 30, 1791, Blair-Banister-Braxton-Horner-Whiting Papers, Box 1, Earl Gregg Swem Library, College of William and Mary, Williamsburg, VA, quoted in Norton, *Liberty's Daughters*, 75.

40. Joan R. Gunderson, *To Be Useful to the World: Women in Revolutionary America, 1740–1790* (Chapel Hill: University of North Carolina Press, 2006), 63.

41. Norton, *Liberty's Daughters*, 77.

42. Benjamin Bangs Diary, April 25, 1760, vol. 2, 65, Bangs Collection, Massachusetts Historical Society, Boston, MA, quoted in Wilson, *Ye Heart of a Man*, 83.

43. Diary of Mary Greenland Cleaveland (1742–1762) in Cleaveland Family Papers, The Essex Institute, Salem, MA, quoted in Ulrich, *Good Wives*, 131.

44. Ebenezer Parkman, *The Diary of Ebenezer Parkman, 1703–1782*, Francis G. Walett, ed., (Worcester: American Antiquarian Society, 1974), 150, quoted in Wilson, *Ye Heart of a Man*, 84.

45. William Byrd, *The Secret Diary of William Byrd of Westover, 1709–1712*, Louis B. Wright and Marion Tinling, eds., (Richmond, VA, 1941), 77, 79–82, quoted in Brown, *Good Wives, Nasty Wenches*, 302.

46. Norton, *Liberty's Daughters*, 79.

47. Ulrich, *Good Wives*, 127–129; Blecki and Wulf, *Milcah Martha Moore's Book*, 15.

48. Gloria L. Main, *Peoples of a Spacious Land: Families and Cultures in Colonial New England* (Cambridge, MA: Harvard University Press, 2001), 99; Marylynne Salmon, "The Cultural Significance of Breastfeeding and Infant Care in Early Modern England and America," *Journal of Social History* 28.2 (Winter 1994), 252, 258.

49. Salmon, "Cultural Significance of Breastfeeding," 247, 250–252.

50. For more on Elizabeth Wilson, see Merril D. Smith, "'Unnatural Mothers': Infanticide, Motherhood, and Class in the Mid-Atlantic, 1730–1830," in Christine Daniels and Michael V. Kennedy, eds., *Over the Threshold: Intimate Violence in Early America* (New York: Routledge, 1999), 173–184.

51. Charles Biddle, *Autobiography of Charles Biddle* (Philadelphia, PA, 1883), 199–201.

52. The Pennsylvania law on infanticide was changed later in 1786, after Elizabeth Wilson's execution. Under the new statute, women were more likely to be imprisoned than executed.

53. Janet Golden, *A Social History of Wet Nursing in America: From Breast to Bottle* (Cambridge, MA: Harvard University Press, 1996), 19–22.

54. Samuel W. Fisher, Memoir of Elizabeth Rhoads Fisher, Samuel W. Fisher Papers, Historical Society of Pennsylvania, Philadelphia, PA, quoted in Norton, *Liberty's Daughters*, 90.

55. Crane, *Diary of Elizabeth Drinker*, vol. 1, 391.

56. Crane, *Diary of Elizabeth Drinker*, vol. 1, 420.

57. Crane, *Diary of Elizabeth Drinker*, vol. 1, 395.

58. Jensen, *Loosening the Bonds*, 28–29.

59. Crane, *Diary of Elizabeth Drinker*, vol. 2, 1227; Elaine F. Crane, "The World of Elizabeth Drinker," *The Pennsylvania Magazine of History and Biography* 107 (January 1983), 12.

60. Brown, *Good Wives, Nasty Wenches*, 302.

61. Sally Logan Fisher Diary, June 1, 1777, and January 1, 1786, Historical Society of Pennsylvania; Abigail Greenleaf to Robert T. Paine, March 18, 1755, Paine Papers, Massachusetts Historical Society, Boston, MA, quoted in Norton, *Liberty's Daughters*, 100–102.

62. On Republican Motherhood, see Linda K. Kerber, *Women of the Republic: Intellect and Ideology in Revolutionary America* (Chapel Hill: University of North Carolina Press, 1980).

63. Linda Baumgarten, "Fashions of Motherhood," www.colonialwilliamsburg.com/history/clothing/women/motherhood2..cfm.

64. Ulrich, *Good Wives*, 70–71.

65. Main, *Peoples of a Spacious Land*, 217–221.

66. The Franklins' house was demolished in 1812. An underground museum exists on the site. See, "The Electric Ben Franklin," http://www.ushistory.org/franklin/info/court.htm; E[liza] Farmer to Jack, May 18, 1714, Eliza Farmer Letterbook, 1774–1777, 1783–1789, Manuscripts, Historical Society of Pennsylvania, quoted in Gunderson, *To Be Useful to the World*, 157.

67. Main, *Peoples of a Spacious Land*, 222–226.

68. Main, Peoples of a Spacious Land, 226; Brown, *Good Wives, Nasty Wenches*, 283–285; Gunderson, *To Be Useful to the World*, 156–157.

69. Brown, *Good Wives, Nasty Wenches*, 260–262.

70. Brown, *Good Wives, Nasty Wenches*, 261–263.

71. William Byrd, *The Secret Diary of William Byrd of Westover, 1709–1712*, Louis B. Wright and Marion Tinling, eds., (Richmond, VA, 1941), 324–325, quoted in Brown, *Good Wives, Nasty Wenches*, 294. Also see the essays on clothing on the Colonial Williamsburg Web site, http://www.history.org/history/clothing/intro/index.cfm.

72. Field Horne, ed., *The Diary of Mary Cooper: Life on a Long Island Farm, 1768–1773* (Oyster Bay, NY: Oyster Bay Historical Society, 1981), 5, 6, 12.

73. Eleazar Moody, *The School of Good Manners* (New London, 1754), 1, 6–7, 9, 24, 25, quoted in Richard L. Bushman and Claudia L. Bushman, "The Early History of Cleanliness in America," *The Journal of American History*, 74 (March 1988), 1219–1220.

74. Crane, *The Diary of Elizabeth Drinker*, July 1, 1799, v. 2, 1185.

75. Crane, "The World of Elizabeth Drinker, 14–15," 18–19.

76. Alison Duncan Hirsh, "Uncovering 'the Hidden History of Mestizo America' in Elizabeth Drinker's Diary: Interracial Relationships in Late-Eighteenth Century Philadelphia," *Pennsylvania History: A Journal of Mid-Atlantic Studies* 68 no. 4 (Autumn 2001), 501–502.

77. Hirsh, "Uncovering," 502–503.

78. Crane, *Diary of Elizabeth Drinker*, vol. 1, 667, 672–673.

79. Crane, *Diary of Elizabeth Drinker*, vol. 2, 1141, vol. 3, 1941.

80. Susan E. Klepp and Billy G. Smith, "The Records of Gloria Dei Church: Marriages and 'Remarkable Occurrences,' 1794–1806," *Pennsylvania History* 53.1 (January 1986), 136.

81. Brown, *Good Wives, Nasty Wenches*, 369–370; Godbeer, *Sexual Revolution*, 152.

82. Gunderson, *To Be Useful to the World*, 5–7.

83. Jean R. Soderlund, "Black Women in Colonial Pennsylvania," *The Pennsylvania Magazine of History and Biography* 107 (January 1983), 51–52.

84. Soderlund, "Black Women in Colonial Pennsylvania," 55.

85. Soderlund, "Black Women in Colonial Pennsylvania," 59, 61, 63, 65–66; Hirsh, "Uncovering," 490.

86. Ann Marie Plane, *Colonial Intimacies: Indian Marriage in Early New England* (Ithaca, NY: Cornell University Press, 2000), 100–101.

87. Marshall J. Becker, "Hannah Freeman: An Eighteenth-Century Lenape Living and Working Among Colonial Farmers," *Pennsylvania Magazine of History and Culture*, 114 (April 1990), 251, 255.

88. This secret history has been revealed in an exhibit, "Fulfilling a Prophesy: The Past and Present of the Lenape in Pennsylvania," University of Pennsylvania Museum of Archeology and Anthropology, http://www.museum.upenn.edu/new/exhibits/FAP/index.shtml.

89. Eirlys M. Barker, "Princesses, Wives, and Wenches: White Perceptions of Southeastern Indian Women to 1770," in Larry D. Eldridge, ed., *Women and Freedom in Early America* (New York: New York University Press, 1997), 44–46, 48–49, 50.

90. Jane T. Merritt, *At the Crossroads: Indians and Empires on Mid-Atlantic Frontier, 1700–1763*, (Chapel Hill: University of North Carolina Press, 2003), 53–54.

91. Barker, "Princesses, Wives, and Wenches," 51.

92. Merritt, *At the Crossroads*, 12–13.

93. Gunderson, *To Be Useful to the World*, 62–64, 90.

SUGGESTED READING

Blecki, Catherine La Courreye, and Karin A. Wulf, eds. *Milcah Martha Moore's Book: A Commonplace Book from Revolutionary America.* University Park: Pennsylvania State University Press, 1997.

Brown, Kathleen M. *Good Wives, Nasty Wenches, and Anxious Patriarchs: Gender, Race, and Power in Colonial Virginia.* Chapel Hill: North Carolina Press, 1996.

Crane, Elaine Forman, ed. *The Diary of Elizabeth Drinker.* Boston: Northeastern University Press, 1991. 3 vols.

Diner, Hasia R., and Beryl Lieff Benderly. *Her Works Praise Her: A History of Jewish Women in America from Colonial Times to the Present.* New York: Basic Books, 2002.

Godbeer, Richard. *Sexual Revolution in Early America.* Baltimore: Johns Hopkins University Press, 2002.

Gunderson, Joan R. *To Be Useful to the World: Women in Revolutionary America, 1740–1790.* Chapel Hill: University of North Carolina Press, 2006.

Karlsen, Carol F., and Laurie Crumpacker, eds. *The Journal of Esther Edwards Burr, 1754–1757.* New Haven, CT: Yale University Press, 1984.

Levy, Barry. *Quakers and the American Family: British Settlement in the Delaware Valley.* New York: Oxford University Press, 1988.

Main, Gloria L. *Peoples of a Spacious Nation: Families and Cultures in Colonial New England.* Cambridge, MA: Harvard University Press, 2001.

Norton, Mary Beth. *Liberty's Daughters: The Revolutionary Experience of American Women, 1750–1800.* Ithaca, NY: Cornell University Press, 1996.

Ulrich, Laurel Thatcher. *A Midwife's Tale: The Life of Martha Ballard, Based on Her Diary, 1785–1812.* New York: Knopf, 1990.

2

⁘

Women and the Law

In eighteenth-century America, as in most of the Western world, men controlled the legal system. Only men were permitted to be lawyers and judges, and only men served on juries. Men wrote and voted on legislation, and men controlled most, though not all, church disciplinary systems as well.[1] Women, however, did come before the court as defendants and plaintiffs to testify, to answer complaints, to resolve questions about property or guardianship, and even, in the case of midwives, to serve as expert witnesses. Moreover, sometimes officials authorized panels of matrons to examine the bodies of and provide testimony about women or girls involved in cases of rape or infanticide.

Consequently, women as a group were not unfamiliar with courts or the law, though by the middle of the eighteenth century they were less likely to actually enter courtrooms than they were in previous decades. Seventeenth-century courts were somewhat informal with proceedings often held in taverns, meetinghouses, or the homes of magistrates. In the eighteenth century, colonies and states began to erect more permanent structures as they started to enforce a system that demanded the use of prescribed methods of pleading. This more formal legal system required the use of lawyers, or at least those who understand the law, and thus fewer women and fewer poor men brought civil suits before the courts.[2]

Still, the law was a constant in the lives of women, because among other things it defined their status: single, married, servant, or slave. Married women, for instance, lived within the framework of coverture, discussed in Chapter 1, but the restrictions of coverture were not absolute. Under this common law doctrine, wives generally could not own property, earn wages, or make contracts, and they were dependent on their husbands for economic maintenance. In reality, however, the economic well-being of many households depended upon husbands and wives working together, because the economy of early America was based on trade and bartering, as well as cash and credit. Rural households in particular often relied upon women to produce goods, which they then sold or traded for other products needed by the family. (See Chapter 3 for more on women and work.)

Some women found ways to circumvent the restrictions coverture placed on them. One method was through the use of prenuptial agreements. In this type of contract, a woman (or her male relatives) determined how much control her husband could have over property she brought to the marriage. Often the family of a woman initiated these contracts in order to keep lands in the family. Prenuptial contracts were settled in equity courts where cases were tried without a jury. Challenges to prenuptial agreements frequently came after the death of the husband when creditors sought money from the estate, or a widow sought to hold on to property. Prenuptial contracts necessitated a certain amount of sophisticated legal knowledge, and therefore they were usually written by and for wealthy people.[3]

In general, under common law the land a woman owned prior to her marriage remained her separate estate, but coverture gave her husband the right to use it as he wished. Husbands, however, were not permitted to destroy the property or sell it without permission from their wives. Although a man might attempt to force his wife to sell her property, most states at least attempted to address this problem by requiring judges to question wives in private to determine if they wished to sell or not.

Marrying a woman with property was one way a man could gain the qualifications needed to vote if he did not otherwise own enough land to meet the necessary property requirements. Thomas Roberts, for example, voted in the 1755 election in Elizabeth City County, Virginia, "by virtue of his interest" in his wife's estate. Thomas Roberts had married a widow who inherited a life interest of 100 acres from her previous husband. Before marrying Roberts, she put most of the land in trust for her children, but kept 25 acres for him to use until her son achieved majority. The 25 acres were enough to allow Roberts to vote.[4]

Laws regarding coverture and married women's property rights varied from state to state and over time. In Virginia, historians have found evidence that some women deliberately provided male family members with land to enable them to vote. Anne Holden stated this explicitly in deeds she made to relatives Joseph Boggs and Elijah Milbourne in 1787. Anne provided each man with 25 acres of land, noting that it would enable them to "vote at the Annual Elections for the Most Wise and Discreet men who have proved themselves real friends to the American Independance." After each man built a house and lived on the land for one year, he had the right to vote in Virginia. Anne made similar gifts of land to John and Frank Boggs. Although she could not vote, she used property law to indirectly participate in the political culture of eighteenth-century Virginia.[5]

Coverture, however, could leave a woman in a legal limbo—unable to sell land, collect debts, or earn a living—if her husband deserted her or refused to support her. When Ann Eyers Mifflin married the Norfolk, Virginia, merchant Humphrey Roberts, she was a widow with property. Humphrey was a loyalist who escaped Virginia in 1776, leaving Ann behind. During the early years of the Revolution, Ann and the son from her first marriage sought refuge on the property she had inherited from her father, an entailed estate that included slaves. In 1779, Virginia declared Humphrey Roberts an enemy alien whose land could be confiscated. Because the former colony had abolished entailment, Ann's property was subject to confiscation; however, Virginia's officials did not take it over. Still, Ann did not have power of attorney and so could not sell any property or collect debts. In 1783, after the war ended, Humphrey returned to Virginia for a short period. Before returning to England, he designated Ann's inherited estate as her dower, but left her still under coverture. Ann petitioned the Virginia legislature in 1786, but legislators refused to allow her to act independently, and she remained unable to collect debts owed to her husband or to sell any property.

In 1782, Ann freed her adult slaves and noted that their children should be freed as they came of age. She believed that she had control over the slaves as part of her inheritance. When Humphrey returned to Virginia in 1783, he challenged her right to free the slaves and disallowed the freedom granted to the children. He even sold one child, Tom. When Tom turned twenty-one in 1793, he sued for his freedom, and the case *Tom v. Roberts* came before the court. At issue was whether Ann had had the power to free her slaves. The suit argued that though she was a married woman she had remained loyal to Virginia, unlike her husband who fled to England as a traitor. The judge, St. George Tucker, ruled for coverture and against Ann Roberts having independent citizenship, and Tom lost his plea for freedom.[6]

Another post-Revolutionary case, this one in Massachusetts, explored the notion that "women might be citizens with their own responsibilities to the state."[7] James Martin's lawsuit asked that the properties that were confiscated from his mother, Anna Gordon Martin, during the Revolutionary War be returned. James's father, William Martin, was a British officer. He and Anna fled Boston along with the British troops during the Revolution, going first to Halifax and then to New York City when the British occupied it. William Martin took over as commander of artillery there until 1783, when the British evacuated. He and his family then went to England.[8]

Anna had inherited several substantial properties in Massachusetts and New Hampshire when her father died in 1770. Because she was a married woman, her husband, William, had the use of them during his lifetime, but the property would be passed to Anna's heirs. When William and Anna fled the country with the British, however, they lost the property, which Massachusetts and New Hampshire confiscated. James was suing Massachusetts to have the confiscated property returned to him.[9]

Massachusetts' confiscation law, passed in 1779, permitted the wife or widow of a loyalist to claim one third of his estate and her dower rights, but only if she remained in the state. James Martin was claiming the property that Anna Martin owned. "But because she had fled the revolution, the state of Massachusetts did not think the property should be returned to her estate." The Supreme Court of Massachusetts overturned the lower court's decision and ruled that James Martin did have a valid claim to his mother's property. Thus the court upheld the common law over women's ability to act independently as citizens of the state. As one of the four judges, Theodore Sedgwick, declared, a woman should not lose her property and her children's inheritance for permitting her husband to choose where they will live. "Was she to be considered a criminal . . . Because she did not in violation of her marriage vows, rebel against the will of her husband?"[10]

He then stated, "A wife who left the country in the company of her husband did not withdraw herself—but was, if I may so express it, withdrawn by him. She did not deprive the government of the benefit of her personal services—she had none to render." Judge Sedgwick and the other judges clearly denied the claim that women could act independently, that they were citizens of the republic. As one scholar of the case notes, "The paradox was that, in order to sustain the state's claim that Anna Martin had been a 'member' of the Commonwealth, she and her heirs would have had to forfeit their property."[11]

Coverture was also an issue when a wife left her husband because of his abusive behavior or infidelity. Hannah Pyle of Thornbury Township, Chester County, Pennsylvania, petitioned for a separate maintenance and alimony from her husband, William, in 1757. Hannah alleged that William had mistreated her and lived with "an Idle Strumpet" named Rose Linch who had "threatened to take away her life." Hannah was living with her brother when she filed the petition. She claimed she had brought a considerable estate to the marriage, which William was likely to "Squander away" along with his own estate and asked the court to take measures before she was "reduced to Poverty and distress." The court ruled that William should pay his wife three shillings per week in quarterly installments as long as they were separated. In addition, he was ordered to give her "one side saddle, one feather Bed, six of his best Chairs, one Iron pot, one tea table, half a dozen of Pewter plates and one dish [?], and that what part of the said William Pyle's household goods the said Hannah hath got into her possession."[12]

At some point, Hannah and William must have reconciled. In 1773, Hannah once again petitioned the court. In her petition, she noted that they had been living apart for about nine months, and that William "Refuseth me any support & will not alow me to live with him." The court ordered William to pay five shillings per week "into the Hands of Robert Mendenhall" for her support. Hannah outlived William, and in his will he bequeathed to her twenty pounds per year, "the House where Joseph Curten formerly lived," and a list of household furnishings, "in Lieu and full satisfaction & Barr of her Dower, of and in all the Lands and Tenements which I shall Die Seised of." The couple did not have children, and the bulk of William's estate was left to the children of his brothers. Because Hannah was elderly by that time, it was probably a better arrangement for her to have money and a place to live than to have to maintain a property.[13]

Divorce was another option for some women who were stuck in abusive marriages or who had been deserted by their husbands. In England, divorce was possible only through the ecclesiastical courts or through an act of Parliament. Few divorces were attempted or granted, and most were granted to noblemen whose wives had been unfaithful. A divorce prevented the adulterous wife or the offspring fathered by another man from inheriting the nobleman's land and fortune. In British North America, however, the New England colonies from the first years of settlement permitted divorce. Under the Puritans, marriage was a civil contract rather than a sacrament, thus making it easier to dissolve the marital bonds. Puritans did not believe divorces should be granted lightly, but did believe they were necessary at times. Granting a divorce to a woman who had been deserted by her husband, for example, meant the woman could remarry, which might prevent her from engaging in an extramarital sexual relationship and threatening the stability of the community.

Colonial Pennsylvania permitted divorce by legislative decree, although few were attempted or granted during the colonial period. In 1785, Pennsylvania enacted a new divorce law that authorized the Pennsylvania Supreme Court to grant divorces. In 1804, the authority to grant divorces was transferred to the county courts. Women's petitions for divorce under the Pennsylvania divorce act far outnumbered men's petitions. Between 1785 and 1815, 236 women petitioned for divorce in Pennsylvania, out of a total of 367 cases. Of these petitions, 114 (48 percent) were granted.[14]

As was true of other early divorce laws, the 1785 act listed very specific grounds for divorce. The grounds for an absolute divorce, which permitted the spouses, in most cases, to remarry, included adultery, bigamy, desertion for a period of more than four years, and impotence that existed at the time of the marriage. A wife who committed adultery was not allowed to marry her lover if a divorce was granted to her husband. If a man or woman remarried because of a reliable, but "false rumor" of the previous spouse's death, it would not be considered adultery. The first spouse could then choose to divorce or not.[15]

Petitioners under the 1785 act could also choose to petition for a divorce from bed and board, which did not permit remarriage. Only women could petition for a divorce from bed and board with alimony on the grounds of "cruel and barbarous treatment" by her spouse. That women applied for a divorce on the grounds of cruelty more often than other grounds suggests that they were more interested in being financially secure if they left an unhappy and possibly abusive marriage than they were in remarrying. That they did not win their suits very often suggests the difficulty in proving "cruel and barbarous treatment."[16]

Although cultural beliefs about white women were changing in the eighteenth century, many still believed that women had a propensity toward lewd or unseemly behavior. Authorities were not inclined to reprimand a husband who seemed to be merely "correcting" the unsuitable conduct of his spouse. Jacob Burkhart explained in his 1785 response to his wife's divorce petition that he had only given her "One blow with his open hand in such a Manner as to hurt her but very little," despite her "Lewd Conduct and abusive language."[17] There were limits to what most deemed acceptable correction by a husband, however, even if it was difficult to say exactly where the line should be drawn. "Cruel and barbarous" treatment went beyond the acceptable punishment a husband might give his wife.

Even when women did not receive alimony, they often benefited economically from a divorce because it released them from their status as a *feme covert*. In New England, it appears many women sought divorces, as least partly, to regain *feme sole* status. Even if a wife lived apart from her husband, he could claim her property and wages at any time, as long as they were married. Moreover, his creditors could seize her property and wages to pay his debts. A divorce prevented this from occurring, whether the woman received alimony or not. Still, most eighteenth-century women did not attempt to divorce their husbands, even in locations where divorce was legal. Most married women endured unhappy marriages with the hope that matters would improve, or they relied upon family and friends to help them.[18]

For most marriages, death, not the law, parted husband and wife. Widowhood was the next role for a woman who outlived her husband, and it often brought significant changes to a woman's life in addition to the grief of losing a spouse. Eighteenth-century American family law generally followed the English common-law practice of granting a widow her "thirds" or dower. If a man died intestate (without a will), his widow received one third of his personal estate. This included household furnishings, tools, and livestock, but not land. The widow was given the use of land and buildings, which were to be passed on to the children of the couple when she died. Husbands could write wills, however, and leave their widows more than their thirds and even give them outright claims to land.[19]

When a man died, the executor of his estate had to settle his debts. In Pennsylvania, unlike most places, a husband's debts were paid before his widow received her share. The widow received her share *after* all bills were paid. Pennsylvania law treated widows differently in another way, too, as one historian has noted. Beginning in the late eighteenth century, many states started to permit a widow "to obtain a cash equivalent for her life interest in a third of her husband's real estate. In this way a widow could convert her life interest to money and thus use or bequest her legacy as she wished." Pennsylvania law, however, did not permit a widow's life interest to be converted to cash.[20]

This treatment of widows in much of eighteenth-century America contrasts markedly with that accorded widows in the seventeenth-century Chesapeake colonies of Maryland and Virginia. In those predominantly immigrant societies, the unbalanced sex ratio meant there were many more men than women in the population. In addition, early deaths, brought on by the unhealthy environment, and marriages occurring only after the completion of indentures meant nearly all widows remarried. Yet husbands tended to trust that their wives would take care of their property and provide for their children. Far more often than not, husbands left their wives with more than their "thirds." For example, John Shircliffe left his entire Maryland estate to his wife in 1663 with the admonition that she would use it "towards the maintenance of herself and my children into whose tender care I do Commend them Desireing to see them brought up in the fear of God and the Catholick Religion and Chargeing them to be Dutiful and obedient to her."[21]

By the end of the seventeenth century, however, conditions in the Chesapeake were more stable, and the legal treatment of both married women and widows followed common law more strictly. In Virginia, married women who had appeared before the court on their own in earlier decades were later denied this privilege by justices who ruled that as *femes covert* they could not do so. The growth of slavery also led to challenges, especially the issue of how slaves were bequeathed. In the first half of the eighteenth century, widows generally inherited slaves as real estate. This meant that they had the lifetime use of these slaves. When the slaves had children, however, or when widows ventured to bequeath their inherited slaves, complications arose. In the eighteenth century, the choice of executors changed, too. Men in eighteenth-century Virginia began to leave their estates in the care of their eldest sons instead of making their wives executers of their estates. Yet men also lived longer and were more likely to have grown sons than they were in the seventeenth century, which might account for this change.[22]

By the eighteenth century, Virginia justices had become more suspicious of female-headed households. Widows were often suspected of sexual transgressions and accused of keeping "disorderly" homes. In particular, white widows who socialized or appeared to socialize with black men were a source of alarm to their neighbors and to justices. In 1742, Sarah McBoyd of Lancaster County, Virginia, was charged by the grand jury with not attending church and living a "Sole Loose life harbouring negroes and servants." Moreover, eighteenth-century Virginians apparently extended the suspicions they harbored about the immoral or criminal behavior of widows and women living without men to their slaves. Slaves owned by women were more likely to be accused of crimes, and they were more likely to be found guilty and to be executed than slaves owned by men.[23]

Early American laws helped to create a system that linked status to race, as well as to gender. Before the 1630s, African slaves made up only a small percentage of the population of Virginia. Slavery was a somewhat fluid system at first, and African slaves were not necessarily slaves for life. Some slaves were freed after a period of time, and some became landowners. As the cultivation and production of tobacco became increasingly important to Virginia planters, however, the demand for laborers increased. The English did not consider agricultural labor to be appropriate "women's work," but the demand for labor in the Chesapeake colonies was so great that many female servants had to work in the fields. As a native born white population became established and the population of African slaves grew, female slaves took over the fieldwork that the wives and daughters of white planters might otherwise have been forced to do.

Further distinguishing the differences between white women and black women, Virginia law made African slave women "tithable," that is, they were subject to a tax to be paid by their master. Free white men, African American men and women, and Native American servants, male and female, over sixteen years old, were all tithable. Free white women were not. Black women were considered field laborers and subject to be taxed, unlike "English" women. For a time, free black women were excluded from tithing, but by 1723, under Virginia law, free black women were again considered tithable, as were the "wives of negroes, mullattoes, or indians."[24]

By the 1660s, Virginia law had begun to define slavery. Under law, the children of enslaved mothers were slaves, and slavery, unlike indentured servitude, was lifelong. In 1667, Virginia lawmakers clarified the law to indicate that baptism did not guarantee freedom for a slave. A law passed three years later limited perpetual slavery to Africans. Native Americans captured during war were considered to be servants who were freed after serving their time. Thus, by the eighteenth century, African and African American women in Virginia were clearly set apart by law from white women and from Native American women, as well.[25]

Perceptions about race and gender also separated white and black women. Many Europeans throughout British North America viewed black women as lascivious and sexually insatiable. Furthermore, both black men and women were often thought to be incapable of sexual fidelity. Although it was difficult—and sometimes impossible—for slaves to maintain a stable marriage and family life when they could not legally marry in most areas and family members could be sold at any time, many whites took this very instability as a sign that Africans and African Americans were savage and wanton.[26]

One example from New York reveals how perceptions about race and gender were changing in the eighteenth century and how this affected civil law and religious policies. Until the mid-eighteenth century, Lutherans in colonial New York and New Jersey welcomed free and enslaved African Americans into their church community, and Lutheran ministers performed marriages for them. Lutheran clergymen also performed marriage ceremonies for mixed race couples. By the 1720s, however, Lutherans, like many other Protestant groups, were beginning to question whether it was right to enslave Christians. Many who were slaveholders believed that slaves should not be baptized. In 1745, a scandal concerning the pastor of the Zion Loonenburg, New York, Lutheran church helped to turn public opinion against interracial unions and led African Americans to leave the Lutheran church.[27]

In 1745, Margareta "Grit" Christiaan, who had been a servant in Pastor Wilhelm Christoph Berkenmeyer's household from the age of seven until her dismissal at age twenty-one, arrived at the pastor's home and informed him that she was pregnant with his child. When Pastor Berkenmeyer accused her of lying, Grit told him that he would be sorry, and then began to tell others her story. The gossip quickly swept through the congregation and then to other areas in New York. Facing public dishonor, the pastor went before the church elders and declared "the prostitute" to be a liar.[28]

Pastor Berkenmeyer was more than the pastor of a small town in New York. He was also the superintendent of Lutheran churches in the mid-Atlantic region. As one historian notes, "his power paralleled and sometimes exceeded that of the civil magistrates." He was the spiritual and moral leader of the community, and he kept order along with the church court, called the consistory, and the sheriff. When the pastor decided to publicly address the rumors about him and Grit Christiaan, he reminded the congregation that he could only be removed from his position by the ruling of a consistory in Germany. Thus, he suggested instead that he lead an ecclesiastical inquiry.[29]

Grit came from a mixed-race family. Both her mother and her sister had given birth to illegitimate children, and her sister had faced public opprobrium after the birth of her third illegitimate child. It is not surprising then that the court declared the pastor innocent of the charge of fornication with Grit. When Grit gave birth to a son with very dark skin, the women present at the birth, including Grit's mother, also concluded that the pastor could not be the father. Moreover, Grit refused to name the father of the child while in labor, despite being questioned by the midwife.[30]

Neither Grit nor the pastor appeared before a secular court. Pastor Berkenmeyer publicly forgave Grit and her supporters, but refused to allow them back into the church for a year and one month. They were to be readmitted only after they could prove to the satisfaction of the congregation that they had repented and improved their morals. The pastor also refused to baptize the child if any of the family were present. The pastor called Grit a "lying prostitute," and he stated, "much evil is rooted in this race." Previously Berkenmeyer had welcomed black members into the church, but his angry slander of Grit and African Americans echoed the sentiments of the congregation who agreed with his characterization of black women as lascivious and interracial sex as wrong. Ultimately, the Christiaan family and other black families left the Lutheran church and joined the Methodists.[31] (For more on religion, see Chapter 6.)

In eighteenth-century British North America, the evidence of interracial sex could be seen in the number of mixed-race babies born. The degree to which interracial sexuality was tolerated, however, varied from region to region. Many colonies, and later states, passed miscegenation laws (some remained extant until the 1960s). Beginning in the 1660s, Maryland and Virginia passed laws prohibiting interracial fornication and marriage. There, as in other colonies, lawmakers were primarily concerned with the possibility of white women bearing the children of black men. Even northern colonies passed legislation outlawing interracial unions. Massachusetts passed one such law in 1705, and Pennsylvania passed one in 1725–26. In other colonies without statutes explicitly banning the practice, interracial unions were frowned upon.[32] As noted in Chapter 1, Quaker Elizabeth Drinker was particularly upset when her white servant, Sally Brant, became pregnant as a result of a relationship with a black man. In contrast, New York Lutherans were willing to accept legitimate interracial unions until mid-century, and may even have tolerated premarital pregnancies that were later legitimized. Many interracial unions in British North America, however, involved white men and enslaved women. In the West Indies, such relationships were carried out quite openly, whereas in the Chesapeake region they were typified by "stealth" and "whispers."[33]

The status of Native American women involved in interracial unions varied depending on when and where they took place and with whom. In eighteenth-century New England, marriages between Indian women and African American men became more common. Women outnumbered men in the Native American population because many Native American men had died during the numerous wars with Europeans. Within the African American population of New England, however, men outnumbered women because more men were brought as slaves to address the labor shortage. Moreover, many colonies (and later states) prohibited marriage between whites and blacks or Indians. As a consequence, Native American women frequently married African American men.[34]

Such marriages took a variety of forms. Some were English-style ceremonies performed by a minister or other authority. Other couples married according to Indian customs. Still others "solemnized" their commitment to each other in an extra-legal ceremony. Many interracial couples lived together in a common-law marriage. A scholar notes that "a two-tiered system of marriages emerged during the late colonial period, as legal forms and rituals became more prominent and prevalent in Anglo-American society, while folk customs continued among Indians, blacks, and poorer whites."[35]

These unions were seldom recorded. Most references to interracial, Indian, black, and poor white couples that appear in historical records do so because the couples experienced legal or marital problems. For example, in 1709, the Plymouth, Massachusetts, court found a Native American man, Josiah, guilty of murdering his wife, Margaret, who was also Native American. After beating and kicking her, Josiah "took a firebrand in Right hand & strook the sd Margaret on her head so mortal a blow that She then & there Instantly dyed." The court sentenced Josiah to be hanged.[36]

The marital status of Sarah Mukamugg was a concern to her because she did not have a husband who could support her or their children financially, but it became a legal issue only after her death: her children fought over who had the right to her share of clan land. Sarah Muckamugg was a Nipmuc from the Indian village of Hassanamisco, which became the town of Grafton, Massachusetts. In 1728, she and Aaron, an African American slave, solemnized their union in Providence, Rhode Island, where Sarah was living. After several years and a couple of children, their marriage fell apart. Most likely, the couple had never actually cohabited, because Sarah was a servant in one household, and Aaron was a slave in another.[37]

Sarah left Providence, taking the children with her. In doing so, she may have been falling back on Native American customs that placed women in control of the land and permitted them to leave their husbands. Nevertheless, Sarah was distraught, and when Mary Wilkinson first saw her sitting at the side of the road near the Wilkinson's Smithfield, Rhode Island, farm, she noticed that Sarah was crying. Sarah told Mary her story, saying that she and Aaron had never married, but "that he Promised to do well by me & . . . that she would then be marryd but he would not." Aaron had told Sarah that he had "another Squaw," and that he would not live with her, "neither would he help maintain the Children." The Wilkinsons allowed Sarah to build "a hut" on their land.[38]

Sarah lived there for a time before moving back to Grafton. She bound out two of her children, including a son, Joseph, to Richard Brown in Providence— again following Native American custom and taking charge of the children. For Anglo-Americans, the father was head of the household. In general, he would have been the person who signed indenture contracts for a couple's children.[39]

In Grafton, Sarah married another African American man named Fortune Burnee. The couple had a daughter, Sarah Burnee. Sarah Muckamugg died in 1751, and her clan lands in Hassanamisco went to her daughter Sarah Burnee, who had been raised there. Her half-brother, Joseph Aaron, had spent much of his life in Providence. Nevertheless, he demanded his share of the land. Because he was an outsider, his parents' marital status became a subject of debate. Witnesses, such as Mary Wilkinson, reported that Sarah and Aaron had never married. Hallelujah Olney, the midwife who helped to deliver Sarah's children, first stated that Sarah was Aaron's wife, but later said the couple was not married. William and Mary Page, however, testified that the couple had wed in their house according to the laws of the colony. Joseph Aaron eventually won his claim. He was also accepted as a full member of the Hassanamisco community.[40]

Just as the toleration of interracial relationships depended on where and when they took place and the status of the people involved, so too did the toleration of premarital sexuality. Officials rigorously prosecuted men and women for fornication and bastardy throughout the seventeenth century, especially in the New England colonies. In seventeenth-century New England, authorities demanded that even married couples whose first child arrived too soon after the marriage took place confess their crimes and submit to the court. In the eighteenth century, however, fornication was less likely to be prosecuted, and for the most part the courts stopped pursuing men and married couples who might have engaged in premarital sexual relations.

By the 1740s in Connecticut, and probably elsewhere, a "prosecutorial dou-ble standard for sexual behavior" was firmly in place. Seventeenth-century Puritans had held both women and men accountable for the sin of fornication and other immoral behavior and demanded that they publicly confess. Eighteenth-century New England, however, was a more commercial and secular place. There seemed little value in men confessing to behavior that might hurt their business interests and connections. Moreover, authorities seemed to believe more strongly by the mid-eighteenth century that a woman might falsely accuse a man of seduction. By the 1750s and 1760s, in keeping with the values of Anglo and Anglo-American popular culture, those in authority, as well as the general public, expected women to guard their own virtue and held them responsible for the results if they did not. This was especially true of women who were strangers in a town, or who were of questionable status or background. In the early decades of the eighteenth century, Connecticut women still came before the court and confessed their sins, but men in positions of authority, as well as those of the middling ranks, began to feel uncomfortable with having their daughters confessing to fornication in public. Consequently, "the range of women prose-cuted narrowed in large part to marginal figures—poor women, domestic ser-vants, women in interracial relationships, women who repeatedly bore children without marrying."[41]

As discussed in Chapter 1, premarital sex in New England became much more common in the eighteenth century as Puritan controls and values declined. In the first half of the century, premarital sexuality and illegitimate births occurred in all levels of society. When a young woman became pregnant, her family mem-bers often exerted pressure on the reputed father to marry her. The young man's family frequently urged the same thing, and the wedding took place. The use of community controls often were most effective for the daughters of "respectable" families whose lovers were not strangers in the town. Even when a man refused to marry a woman he had impregnated, he could often be compelled to acknowledge paternity.[42]

For example, in the 1730s in New Haven, Connecticut, Bathsheba How's two sisters accosted Benjamin Robinson and accused him of committing fornication with their sister. Robinson admitted his guilt and promised to pay maintenance for the child. Although he later denied fathering Bathsheba's child, Bathsheba's accusation, along with the testimony of her sisters and an eyewitness to the couple's sexual encounter, led to the court's decision that he pay maintenance.[43]

In fact, throughout British North America, the number of men prosecuted for fornication declined greatly after the first couple decades of the eighteenth cen-tury. In southern frontier areas, there were very few ministers. New England was generally settled in an orderly system of towns that usually included a minister. Schools such as Harvard were founded in the early years of settlement to produce ministers. The southern frontier areas consisted of scattered farms, and Anglican ministers had to be brought from England. As a consequence of this lack of ministers, couples frequently lived together without being legally married. When a minister came to their area, couples who had been cohabiting for years often asked to be formally wed and to have their children baptized. Charles Boschi, a parson in South Carolina from 1745 to 1747, reported that most of the brides he married were already pregnant. He sometimes had "to call for a chair to make the woman to sit down in the time of marriage because they were fainting away."[44]

When couples cohabited without being legally wed, their children were illegitimate. In many situations, these couples lived as if they were married. Their situations were only brought before the courts when the man could not, or did not, support his offspring. In late colonial Philadelphia, as in other urban seaports, bastardy also became quite common. Sometimes churches took over disciplining the members of their congregations. They had no legal standing, but did exert pressure on individuals who wanted to remain within the church community. For example, within the Quaker meetings, premarital sexuality—as well as bastardy—was disciplined, and sinners were expected to confess or forced to leave the Quaker community. In contrast, the Second Presbyterian Church of Philadelphia only disciplined its African members for sexual misbehavior.[45]

Unlike the counties surrounding it, the Philadelphia courts generally did not punish premarital sexuality in men or women. Women who required child support could go before a judge or alderman to swear an oath of paternity. If the father could be found, he was required to post a bond for the child's support. The bond was held by the Overseers of the Poor, who would hold it until the child could be bound out for service at age five for girls or age seven for boys. Cases only came before the court if a father disputed paternity.[46]

Similarly, a Massachusetts law passed in 1786 allowed women to bypass an appearance at the Court of General Sessions. Instead, the woman was permitted to confess to fornication before a justice of the peace and pay a small fine. A similar act was passed in Connecticut. If the woman named the man who impregnated her at the time of this confession and then again named him while in labor, he could be prosecuted. If the man chose to settle out of court or the charges were dropped, however, his name would not appear in the records. As one historian has discovered, often these cases were settled out of court. The man was not acquitted of his crime, but the charges were dropped because he married the mother or agreed to pay maintenance for the child. It is likely that the threat of a lawsuit was enough to make some men take action.[47]

Nevertheless, young men could not always be compelled to marry the women they impregnated, but in the eighteenth century they were no longer whipped or fined, as they would have been in the seventeenth. For men, fornication was decriminalized, whereas in some areas women continued to be prosecuted for the crime. In general, young men who fathered children out of wedlock did not have a problem later finding a spouse, but young women who bore illegitimate children were not always so lucky. In addition, women, of course, actually bore the children. They had to cope with the physical discomforts of pregnancy, as well as the possibility of dying during childbirth.

One unusual Connecticut example brings many of these issues to light. In September 1742, Sarah Grosvenor of Pomfret, Connecticut, died as the result of complications from an abortion. Historians can discuss this case only because three years later two magistrates decided to investigate what happened and brought the matter to court. The justices were not so much concerned with the abortion, which was not illegal at the time, but rather with the death of Sarah. If the abortion had come to light while Sarah was still living, she might have been charged with fornication.[48]

When Sarah Grosvenor and Amasa Sessions began their relationship, she was nineteen, and he was twenty-seven. They both came from leading families in the village, and their fathers both held high local offices and sizeable farms. The families appeared to have had a cordial relationship and most likely would have approved a marriage between Sarah and Amasa. Yet when Sarah became pregnant, Amasa did not want to marry her and coerced her into taking an abortifacient. According to the testimony of Sarah's friends, she wanted to marry Amasa, but rather than pressure him into it, she pleaded with him not to compound their sins. She even told him that "she was willing to take the sin and shame to her self, and to be obliged never to tell whose Child it was, and that she did not doubt but that if she humbled her self on her Knees to her Father he would take her and her Child home."[49]

Amasa would not agree to her suggestion, so Sarah began "taking the trade," as she later confessed to her sister Zerviah. It is clear that both Sarah and Zerviah understood the term to mean ingesting an abortifacient, and that the idea of taking an abortifacient to eliminate a pregnancy that resulted from premarital sexual activity was known to the young people in the community. Unfortunately for Sarah, the powder that Amasa obtained from Dr. John Hallowell did not have the desired result, and the doctor decided he had to operate. Operating on Sarah in secret at the nearby home of Sarah's cousin John, Hallowell attempted to abort her in a long and painful episode that resulted in a miscarriage two days later. Sarah's sister and her cousin's wife, Hannah, buried the fetus and kept Sarah's secret. About ten days after the miscarriage, Sarah developed a fever and pain, and died shortly thereafter. Before dying, Sarah recounted the whole sordid tale to her good friend, Abigail Nightingale.[50]

Throughout the whole ordeal, Sarah's father and stepmother remained unaware of what was going on. Indeed, no older adults were even overseeing the courtship of Sarah and Amasa. Traditionally, older, married women monitored the love lives and sexual problems of the young. An older female relative might give a young woman advice on courtship, while a pregnant, single woman might go to the midwife for help. Yet aside from Dr. Hallowell, the only people who knew what was going on with the couple and who later knew about the abortion were young adults ranging from nineteen to thirty-three. Hallowell, however, was the only person convicted of a crime—and he escaped punishment by flee-ing to Rhode Island.

The court depositions revealed another interesting aspect of the whole incident—how differently the men and women involved reacted to the events. Sarah and Zerviah were haunted by guilt—not because they believed abortion was a sin, but because Sarah had the abortion to cover up the sin of fornication. The culture and traditions of Puritan New England dictated to the women the proper response to sin: confession and repentance. Only through confession and admitting her sins could a person hope to escape God's judgment on herself and her community. Instead, the women concealed Sarah's pregnancy, her attempt at "taking the trade," her surgical abortion, and the burial of the fetus. Ultimately both women did con-fess. Sarah gave her deathbed confession to her friend Abigail. Zerviah kept the secret for three years before deposing to the court. According to legend, Sarah's ghost haunted Zerviah night after night and urged her to reveal the story.[51]

In contrast to the guilt felt by the sisters after Sarah miscarried, Hallowell and Amasa boasted of their actions. Hallowell bragged about his surgical techniques, and Amasa portrayed himself as a lover who could successfully deal with an unwanted pregnancy and move on to another conquest. Only when Sarah appeared near death did Amasa appear to feel remorse. Unlike the women, how-ever, neither man wanted to take responsibility for his own actions. Instead, they blamed each other.[52]

It is impossible to know how common abortion was in eighteenth-century America. Examples sometimes appear as part of other court cases, such as in the investigation of Sarah Grosvenor's death. Yet the idea that it was possible to take an abortifacient to end a pregnancy seems to have been commonly known to young women in both urban and rural areas. In rural Chester County, Pennsyl-vania, in 1739, Margaret Kain reported that Martin Rierdon had wanted her to take the "Botle of Stuff" he obtained from a doctor "in order to Make me Mis-carrie." Margaret refused to take it, believing as Sarah Grosvenor did, that it compounded the sin of fornication. Martin, however, told her "it was no Sin being it had not Quickened." More remarkable, in 1771, Margaret Rauch of Philadelphia actually made up a story about drinking tea made of pennyroyal in order to induce an abortion. In fact, she was covering up the birth and murder of her illegitimate child.[53]

A woman who bore a child out of wedlock could face severe economic obsta-cles. In some instances, as noted, her family or community might successfully compel the father of her child to marry her. In other cases, the woman's family supported both her and the child. Some women, however, did not have families able to support them, and they were unable to find spouses. Although the citi-zens of late colonial Philadelphia tolerated premarital sexuality, this sexual free-dom came at a cost for many young women who found themselves pregnant and alone. Support payments were minimal and usually not enough to provide all the needs of the child, and they did not cover the mother at all.[54]

A few women found the burden too heavy to bear, and they abandoned or killed their infants. The British colonies generally followed English law, which designated infanticide a capital crime. The law presumed that if a woman concealed the birth of a child, and it was found dead, then she must have killed it. In other words, the mother was presumed guilty and had to prove her innocence. In Pennsylvania, only a few women were convicted under this law, and fewer were executed. Philadelphia prosecuted fewer cases of infanticide than other counties in Pennsylvania.[55] Over time, as one scholar notes, "prosecutorial standards became increasingly lenient as standards of evidence changed. The woman would not be convicted if she told anyone of her pregnancy, if she had assistance in childbirth, or if she had collected baby linen. These were taken to be proofs that she had not intended concealment."[56]

Historians disagree over how many women in Philadelphia (or elsewhere) actually murdered their infants. Infanticide probably occurred more frequently than the court records reveal. Newspapers and diaries note instances when the bodies of dead infants were discovered in the city, but it is likely that there were other bodies that were never found. In the 1980s, archaeologists excavated an eighteenth-century privy in Philadelphia and uncovered the remains of two new-born infants. According to a historical archaeologist who participated in the excavation and examination of the remains, women of means, or of good character, were rarely convicted of infanticide, but female servants needed to have good characters in order to get and keep a job. Consequently, they may have been more willing or desperate enough to commit infanticide in order to stay employed."[57]

Changing ideas about premarital sexuality may have influenced some female servants. Some may have decided to participate in a more permissive sexual culture and then became pregnant. Pregnancies in single women, however, were not always the result of looser morals, or even of a seduction. They also occurred as a result of sexual coercion. Seventeenth-century Anglo-Americans believed that conception could not occur as the result of rape because they thought a woman needed to enjoy the sexual act in order to conceive.[58]

By the mid-eighteenth century, these beliefs were beginning to wane, although they did not completely disappear. Gynecological manuals, folk beliefs, and court papers continued to articulate the belief that if she was pregnant, the woman must have consented. For example, a petition arguing for the commutation of a convicted rapist came before the Virginia courts in 1817. The petitioner argued that because the woman became pregnant, "the connection called a rape was by *consent*."[59]

The concept of marital rape did not exist in the eighteenth century. By consenting to marry, wives agreed to make their bodies available to their husbands. According to *A Treatise of the Pleas of the Crown*, "a husband cannot by law be guilty of ravishing his wife, on account of the matrimonial consent which she cannot retract."[60] Agreeing to the sexual demands of one's husband was implicit in the role of being a wife. Only when a man went beyond what was considered "proper" marital sexuality—that is, if he physically abused her or committed an actual crime (because marital rape was not a crime)—could it be brought before the court. Even so, such cases were extremely rare.

In any case, rape was difficult to prove. In the early eighteenth century, women who brought rape charges before the court were often punished for lewdness. Later in the eighteenth century, a court was not as likely to discipline a woman who claimed to have been raped. Yet her reputation might be ruined if she admitted to having had a sexual encounter and then the court dismissed her claims of rape. Rape was believed to be a crime of passion. It was up to women to control their own passions and not to excite those of men. At the same time, women were still perceived as temptresses who eagerly desired sex.[61]

Because popular culture portrayed women as both seductresses and the ones placed in control of sexual encounters, some men believed a woman's refusal to have sex was just a ploy. This theme was common in eighteenth-century newspapers and almanacs. For example, a song included in Alexander Hamilton's *The History of the Ancient and Honorable Tuesday Club* proclaimed that coy maidens "swear if you're rude they will bawl,/ But they whisper so low, / By which you may know/'Tis artifice, artifice all, all, all."[62]

Some rapists asserted that their victims had given consent, or at least did not completely oppose having sex. Emmanuel Lewis admitted to having sex with his mistress's five-year-old grandchild, but he denied that he had raped her. He stated that the "child did not Cry when he lay with it, but asked him to do it more—that the child pulled up its coats—put his yard to its body." Other rapists believed the women they raped were concerned about getting pregnant, but not actually opposed to having sex. Rebecca McCarter's attacker "reassured" her that "he could work long enough and not get me with Child."[63]

Although a woman might have wished to remain silent, sometimes an untimely pregnancy forced her to make a rape charge. This may have been the case with Rebecca Foster, the wife of the minister of Hallowell, Maine. While her husband, Isaac, was away, Rebecca Foster claimed several men attacked her over a period of days. One of the men was the powerful Judge North. Martha Ballard, the midwife, had taken an interest in the young Mrs. Foster, who was about the same age as her daughter, Lucy Towne. When Rebecca came to Martha and cried, "they Could do nothing wors that they had unless they killed her," Martha listened, but did not ask questions. She later noted in her diary that she "Begd her never to mentin it to any other person. I told her shee would Expose & perhaps ruin her self if shee did." Judge North was not only one of the most powerful men in the county, he was also an employer of Martha's husband, Ephraim.[64]

Rebecca gave birth to a daughter about eight and a half months after the alleged attacks. The knowledge that she was pregnant—and that her husband had been away—may have spurned her to charge the judge and the other men with rape. Judge North was found not guilty, to Martha Ballard's surprise. By this time the Fosters had moved away. Almost from the time he began his tenure as minister there, Isaac Foster had had disagreements with some of the townsfolk, and he was eventually dismissed. Martha Ballard had attended church fairly regularly, but after Isaac Foster was dismissed she did not attend church for nearly four years.[65]

Women were conditioned and expected to defer to men. Rebecca Foster knew the men who she claimed had attacked her. Any one of them, including the judge, might have stopped by her house for a number of reasons, and Rebecca might have let them in. It might have been even more difficult for a young woman to deny hospitality to a man of authority, such as the judge.[66] If a man had additional power over a woman (or girl)—as head of the household or as master—then the woman could find it difficult to resist. Yet only women who maintained that they were willing to die rather than be raped were guaranteed to be believed in the courts.[67] As dependents within a household, servants were often at risk of sexual coercion from their masters or his sons. Fifteen-year-old Rachel Davis was an indentured servant in the Philadelphia County household of William and Becky Cress. She endured months of sexual assaults from her master before his wife, who suspected something was going on, demanded that Rachel be sent away. William appeared at her new residence and attempted to coerce her into having sex with him again. Ultimately, Rachel's father discovered that William had been sexually assaulting Rachel. William was charged with rape, convicted, and sentenced to ten years in prison.[68]

In many ways, rape and coerced sex were similar experiences for servants and enslaved women. Both faced pressure from their masters to engage in sexual acts. Often masters did not have to use physical force. Instead a master often attempted to manipulate a woman by promising to make her life better, if only she would give in to his sexual demands. Unlike servants, however, enslaved women could not turn to the law to help them if their masters raped them. The law defined slaves as chattel owned by their masters, who could do with them as they wished. As one study notes, "no historian has recorded a conviction of a white man for the rape of a slave at any point from 1700 to the Civil War, let along a conviction of a master for raping his own slave. Rape in early America was a crime whose definition was structured by race."[69]

Furthermore, many viewed enslaved women as promiscuous or immoral because in many cases their unions with other slaves were not legal. To some men this meant enslaved women were always available for sexual encounters. Moreover, such men would not have to fear retribution because an enslaved woman's reputation and honor were besmirched. Of course, masters could choose to recognize slave marriages, but they were under no legal obligation to do so.[70] For enslaved women, all sexual encounters were technically illicit and all births illegitimate. A baby born to an enslaved woman, however, meant another slave for her master, and so there would be no reason to prosecute the slave woman for fornication or bastardy.

In the years following the Revolutionary War, northern states began passing laws to eliminate slavery. In general, these laws permitted emancipation, but gradually and over a period of time. The Revolution and discussions of equality and freedom motivated some slaves, both men and women, to seek their own freedom. Elizabeth Freeman, known as Mum Bett, grew up as a slave in the household of John Ashley in Sheffield, Massachusetts. She listened to the conversations of the wealthy men who visited the household as they discussed the new Massachusetts Constitution and the Bill of Rights. This inspired her to visit the noted lawyer, Theodore Sedgewick (later a judge who heard the case brought by James Martin), and ask him to help her sue for her freedom. Another slave in the Ashley household, Brom, joined in the lawsuit. The jury ruled in Brom and Mum Bett's favor, awarding them their freedom and ordering John Ashley to pay them thirty shillings and court costs. Brom and Bett were the first enslaved people to win freedom under the new Massachusetts constitution of 1780.[71]

The post-Revolutionary period brought few legal changes for most women. Women entered eighteenth-century courts as both criminals and defendants. They encountered civil laws as they married and became widows. Some new states passed divorce laws that helped abandoned or abused wives who wanted to dissolve the marriage vows. Nevertheless, married women remained under coverture.

Laws in eighteenth-century America were based on English common law, but were infused with new ideas of freedom and equality after the Revolution. The law defined the roles of women in the eighteenth century and denoted their status as wife, widow, servant, or slave. New conceptions of womanhood helped to change the roles of women to some extent, but Native American and African American women were rarely able to take on the new roles of Republican wives and mothers. Even poor or single white women found it difficult to participate fully in the ideology of domesticity.

NOTES

1. Women voted for a brief time in New Jersey, and they were involved in extra legal political activities, particularly around the time of the American Revolution. Judith Apter Klinghoffer and Lois Elkis, "'The Petticoat Electors': Women's Suffrage in New Jersey, 1776–1807," *Journal of the Early Republic*, 12 (Summer 1992): 159–193. See Chapter 5 on Women and War. Women had major roles in some religions, most notably among Quakers, Shakers, and Moravians. See Chapter 6 on Women and Religion.

2. Joan R. Gunderson, *To Be Useful to the World: Women in Revolutionary America, 1740–1790*, rev. ed., (Chapel Hill: University of North Carolina Press, 2006), 154–155; Cornelia Hughes Dayton, *Women before the Bar: Gender, Law, and Society in Connecticut, 1639–1789* (Chapel Hill: University of North Carolina Press, 1995), 87–89.

3. Linda K. Kerber, *Women of the Republic: Intellect and Ideology in Revolutionary America* (Chapel Hill: University of North Carolina Press, 1980), 141–142.

4. John G. Kolp and Terri L. Snyder, "Women and the Political Culture of Eighteenth-Century Virginia: Gender, Property Law, and Voting Rights," in Christopher L. Tomlins and Bruce H. Mann, eds., *The Many Legalities of Early America* (Chapel Hill: University of North Carolina Press, 2001), 284.

5. Accomack County, Virginia, Deeds No.6, 1783–1788, 448–449, Library of Virginia, quoted in Kolp and Snyder, "Women and the Political Culture," 272.

6. Gunderson, *To Be Useful to the World*, 204–205.

7. Linda K. Kerber, "The Paradox of Women's Citizenship in the Early Republic: The Case of *Martin vs. Massachusetts,* 1805," *American Historical Review* 97 (April 1992): 355.

8. Kerber, "The Paradox of Women's Citizenship," 349, 355–356.

9. Kerber, "The Paradox of Women's Citizenship," 357.

10. *Martin v. Commonwealth*, 392–93, 391, quoted in Kerber, "The Paradox of Women's Citizenship," 373.

11. *Martin v. Commonwealth*, 390–92 quoted in Kerber, "The Paradox of Women's Citizenship," 373, 374.

12. *Hannah Pyle v. William Pyle*, Quarter Sessions Records, November 1757, Chester County Archives, West Chester, PA.

13. The Petition of Hannah Pyle, Quarter Sessions, Docket B, August 1773, Quarter Sessions Papers, August 1773, Chester County Archives, West Chester, PA; Will of William Pyle, #3992, Proven, January 12, 1789, Chester County Archives, West Chester, PA.

14. Merril D. Smith, *Breaking the Bonds: Marital Discord in Pennsylvania, 1730–1830* (New York: New York University Press, 1991), Chapter 1.

15. Smith, *Breaking the Bonds*, 23–27.

16. Smith, *Breaking the Bonds*, 26–28.

17. *Burkhart v. Burkhart,* Answer of Respondent, 1785, Pennsylvania Supreme Court Divorce Papers (1785–1815), Records of the Supreme Court, Eastern District, Pennsylvania Historical and Museum Commission.

18. Mary Beth Sievens, *Stray Wives: Marital Conflict in Early National New England* (New York: New York University Press, 2005), Chapter 6.

19. Dayton, *Women before the Bar*, 41.

20. Lisa Wilson, *Life After Death: Widows in Pennsylvania, 1750–1850* (Philadelphia: Temple University Press, 1992), 26–27.

21. Lois Green Carr and Lorena S. Walsh, "The Planter's Wife: The Experience of White Women in Seventeenth-Century Maryland," in Nancy F. Cott and Elizabeth H. Pleck, eds., *A Heritage of Her Own: Toward a New Social History of American Women* (New York: Simon and Schuster, 1979), 34–35.

22. Kathleen M. Brown, *Good Wives, Nasty Wenches, and Anxious Patriarchs: Gender, Race, and Power in Colonial Virginia* (Chapel Hill: University of North Carolina Press, 1996), 288, 290.

23. Lancaster Order Book 8, July 9, 1742, 350, quoted in Brown, *Good Wives, Nasty Wenches*, 289, 306–313, 290.

24. Brown, *Good Wives, Nasty Wenches*, 120–128; William Waller Hening, ed., *The Statutes at Large; Being a Collection of All the Laws of Virginia, from the First Session of the Legislature*, 13 vols., (1823; facsimile reprint, Charlottesville, VA, 1969, October 23, 1705, III, 258, quoted in Brown, 123.

25. Brown, *Good Wives, Nasty Wenches*, 108–109; 135–136.

26. Richard Godbeer, *Sexual Revolution in Early America*, (Baltimore: Johns Hopkins University Press, 2002), 151–152, 200.

27. Graham Russell Hodges, "The Pastor and the Prostitute: Sexual Power among African Americans and Germans in Colonial New York," in Martha Hodes, ed., *Sex, Love, Race: Crossing Boundaries in North American History* (New York: New York University Press, 1999), 60, 64–65, 69.

28. Hodges, "Pastor and Prostitute," 60.

29. Hodges, "Pastor and Prostitute," 66.

30. Hodges, "Pastor and Prostitute," 66.

31. Hodges, "Pastor and Prostitute," 66–69.

32. Peter W. Bardaglio, "'Shamefull Matches': The Regulation of Interracial Sex and Marriage in the South before 1900," in Hodes, *Sex, Love, Race*, 112, 144–16.

33. Godbeer, *Sexual Revolution*, 222.

34. Ann Marie Plane, *Colonial Intimacies: Indian Marriage in Early New England* (Ithaca, NY: Cornell University Press, 2000), 147; Daniel R. Mandell, "The Saga of Sarah Muckamugg: Indian and African American Intermarriage in Colonial New England," in Hodes, *Sex, Love, Race*, 73–74.

35. Mandell, "The Saga of Sarah Muckamugg," 75.

36. Quoted in Plane, *Colonial Intimacies*, 150.

37. Plane, *Colonial Intimacies*, 143–144; Mandell, "The Saga of Sarah Muckamugg," 72–76.

38. Plane, *Colonial Intimacies*, 143–144; Mandell, "The Saga of Sarah Muckamugg," 75.

39. Plane, *Colonial Intimacies*, 144.

40. Plane, *Colonial Intimacies*, 144–145; Mandell, "The Saga of Sarah Muckamugg," 82–83.

41. Dayton, *Women before the Bar*, 159–161.

42. Dayton, *Women Before the Bar*, 207–210.

43. Dayton, *Women Before the Bar*, 203–204.

44. Florence Gambrill Geiger, ed., "St. Batholomew's Parish as Seen by Its Rectors, 1713–1761," *South Carolina Historical and Genealogical Magazine* 50 (1949): 191, quoted in Godbeer, *Sexual Revolution*, 128.

45. Clare A. Lyons, *Sex Among the Rabble: An Intimate History of Gender and Power in the Age of Revolution, Philadelphia, 1730–1830* (Chapel Hill: University of North Carolina Press, 2006), 83–86.

46. Lyons, *Sex Among the Rabble*, 74–78.

47. Laurel Thatcher Ulrich, *A Midwife's Tale: The Life of Martha Ballard, Based on her Diary, 1785–1812* (New York: Knopf, 1990), 150–155.

48. An abortion before "quickening," or when the mother first felt the fetus move, was not viewed as a crime in Anglo-America. The Grosvenor-Sessions case is discussed in Cornelia Hughes Dayton, "Taking the Trade: Abortion and Gender Relations in an Eighteenth-Century New England Village," *William and Mary Quarterly*, 48 (January 1991), 19–49.

49. Deposition of Abigail Nightingale, *Rex v. John Hallowell et al.,* Superior Court of Connecticut Records, Book 9, 113, 173, 175, in Dayton, "Taking the Trade," 32.

50. Dayton, "Taking the Trade," 25–28.

51. Dayton, "Taking the Trade," 40–45.

52. Dayton, "Taking the Trade," 42–43.

53. *King v. Martin Rierdon*, Statement of Margaret Kain, Chester County Quarter Session Indictments, 5/1739, Chester County Archives, Westchester, PA. Margaret Rauch's case is discussed in Lyons, *Sex Among the Rabble*, 98–99.

54. Lyons, *Sex Among the Rabble*, 92–93.

55. G.S. Rowe, "Infanticide, Its Judicial Resolution, and Criminal Code Revision in Early Pennsylvania," American Philosophical Society, *Proceedings*, 135 (1991): 200–232.

56. Susan E. Klepp, "Lost, Hidden, Obstructed, and Repressed: Contraceptive and Abortive Technology in the Early Delaware Valley," in Judith A. McGraw, ed., *Early American Technology: Making and Doing Things form the Colonial Era to 1850* (Chapel Hill: University of North Carolina Press, 1994), 75.

57. Sharon Ann Burnston, "Babies in the Well: An Underground Insight into Deviant Behavior in Eighteenth-Century Philadelphia," *Pennsylvania Magazine of History and Biography* 106 (1982): 174, 185.

58. See Else Hambleton, "The Regulation of Sex in Seventeenth-Century Massachusetts: The Quarterly Court of Essex County vs. Priscilla Willson and Mr. Samuel Appleton," in Merril D. Smith, ed., *Sex and Sexuality in Early America* (New York: New York University Press, 1998), 89–115 for a seventeenth-century Massachusetts case in which a young woman was raped and became pregnant. Her attacker was not charged with rape, but he was ordered to pay expenses associated with the birth.

59. John Holloman, October 1817, Virginia Executive Papers, Box 3, Library of Virginia, Richmond, quoted in Sharon Block, *Rape and Sexual Power in Early America* (Chapel Hill: University of North Carolina Press, 2006), 141.

60. Sir Edward Hyde East, *A Treatise of the Pleas of the Crown,* vol. 1, (Philadelphia, 1806), I, 446, quoted in Block, *Rape and Sexual Power*, 78.

61. Block, *Rape and Sexual Power*, 38–39.

62. Alexander Hamilton, *The History of the Ancient and Honorable Tuesday Club*, 3 vols., Robert Micklus, ed., (Chapel Hill: University of North Carolina Press, 1990), I, 232n.1, 233, 269–270, quoted in Block, *Rape and Sexual Power*, 39.

63. Case of Emmanuel Lewis, Aug. 13, 1734, Massachusetts Superior Court of Judicature Records, Suffolk Files, no. 37793; *Republica v. David Robb*, Yeates Legal Papers, March-April 1789, fol. 2, Historical Society of Pennsylvania, PA, both quoted in Block, *Rape and Sexual Power*, 43–44.

64. This case is analyzed in Ulrich, *A Midwife's Tale*, Chapter 3. Also see the Web site Dohistory, which uses Martha Ballard's diary as a case study. On this site, http://dohistory.org/home.html, Martha's diary and the official documents of the case are presented side by side to permit readers to decide what happened. There are also clips from the movie *A Midwife's Tale*.

65. Ulrich, *A Midwife's Tale*, Chapter 3.

66. Ulrich, *A Midwife's Tale*, 124–125.

67. Block, *Rape and Sexual Power*, 44.

68. Sharon Block, "Lines of Color, Sex, and Service: Comparative Sexual Coercion in Early America," in Hodes, *Sex, Love, Race*, 142.

69. Block, "Lines of Color," 142–143.

70. Godbeer, *Sexual Revolution*, 200.

71. "Elizabeth Freeman (Mum Bett)," *Africans in America*, Part 2, http://www.pbs.org/wgbh/aia/part2/2p39.html.

SUGGESTED READING

Block, Sharon. *Rape and Sexual Power in Early America*. Chapel Hill: University of North Carolina Press, 2006.

Brown, Kathleen M. *Good Wives, Nasty Wenches, and Anxious Patriarchs: Gender, Race, and Power in Colonial Virginia*. Chapel Hill: University of North Carolina Press, 1996.

Dayton, Cornelia Hughes. *Women before the Bar: Gender, Law, and Society in Connecticut, 1639–1789*. Chapel Hill: University of North Carolina Press, 1995.

Gunderson, Joan R. *To Be Useful to the World: Women in Revolutionary America, 1740–1790*, rev. ed., Chapel Hill: University of North Carolina Press, 2006.

Plane, Ann Marie. *Colonial Intimacies: Indian Marriage in Early New England*. Ithaca, NY: Cornell University Press, 2000.

Smith, Merril D. *Breaking the Bonds: Marital Discord in Pennsylvania, 1730–1830*. New York: New York University Press, 1991.

Wilson, Lisa. *Life After Death: Widows in Pennsylvania, 1750–1850*. Philadelphia: Temple University Press, 1992.

3

◆◆◆

Women and Work

In 1795, Gulielma M. Smith from Burlington, New Jersey, wrote a letter to her mother, Margaret Hill Morris, then living in Philadelphia, Pennsylvania. This was not unusual, because the members of this large, extended Quaker family corresponded with one another on an almost daily basis. In this particular letter, Gulielma discussed the difficulty she was having in finding a woman to help her with her household work. She was eager to find someone before she went into confinement for the birth of one of her children. She tried to reassure her mother by telling her that her neighbors were also having trouble finding help. In fact, Gulielma believed she might actually be better off than most of them, because she did have "a black woman close by that washes every week for me, & that I can have at any time." She further noted that an acquaintance "has for many weeks past shut up her shop & put herself a good deal out of the way in order to come & help me Iron."[1]

A few months later, in another letter to her mother, Gulielma voiced her concerns that her husband might become overheated while haying, because he had lately been ill. She discussed the health of other family members and declined her mother's offer to provide her with help with her spinning. Gulielma told her mother that she was sending her a cheese, and then she closed the letter by noting "the Child is extremely tedious & can not sleep so that I have written this by scraps."[2]

These two letters touch on many of the daily routines and concerns of northern white women in late eighteenth-century America. For early American women, work meant many things. The constant cycle of pregnancy, nursing, and childcare brought joys and sorrows, but it also generated a great deal of work for

A New England Kitchen. A Hundred Years Ago. Although this is a nineteenth-century representation of an eighteenth-century New England kitchen, it clearly shows the range of activities that would occupy an eighteenth-century New England farm wife. Courtesy Library of Congress.

women, as well as stressing their bodies. The frequent burden of caring for sick family members and servants produced more work. At the same time, there were household chores, and, in rural areas, there were also farm chores to do. Cows had to be milked and people needed to be fed, even if the housewife was busy or babies were "tedious." There were enough tasks to be done in one household that it was difficult for one woman to complete them all. Thus, there was a great demand for servants or family members who could help with housework, particularly with the arduous jobs of washing and ironing clothing. Many eighteenth-century northern housewives struggled to find young women who could assist them with both their everyday duties and the occasional jobs that needed to be done.

Within Gulielma's letters, modern-day readers also get a glimpse into the female world of exchange and networking. For instance, there is Gulielma's reference to sending the cheese to her mother. Although this case may simply represent a fond daughter sending her mother some food, many women did exchange the goods they made for products or services that other women could provide. In Gulielma's world, the free African American laundry woman, the shopkeeper, and her own mother were among the women who helped her with goods and services.

The daily activities of most rural white women took place within the house, in the kitchen gardens, and in outbuildings such as breweries and milk houses. Yet, as the diary of the Maine midwife Martha Ballard reveals, housework might also include such tasks as chopping wood or carrying numerous buckets of water from a flooded basement, along with caring for livestock, knitting, carding wool, or even building a fence. Even with these duties, however, the midwife delivered almost 1,000 babies between 1778 and 1812 and provided treatment for the sick. Of course, most women did not deliver hundreds of babies in their life-times, but the daily chores of most women went beyond "housework."[3]

Midwives delivered the babies of most eighteenth-century American white and black women, although the presence of doctors at births increased by the latter part of the century. Many people perceived male doctors as more knowledgeable and better trained than female midwives. In some areas, the use of a male physician became fashionable toward the latter part of the eighteenth century. Moreover, physicians were able to use forceps during difficult births. Doctors generally charged a higher fee than midwives; therefore, in the eighteenth century, they mainly attended births only in the households of the wealthiest or status-conscious or when there was a difficulty with a birth that the midwife could not handle. For most people in eighteenth-century North America, however, childbirth remained an event attended and run by women.

Most likely, childbirth was a woman-centered event for Native American women, as well, but present-day scholars do not have a great amount of information about it. Because European men wrote most of the extant sources that mention Native American women and childbirth, their observations are limited and often biased. European men were not likely to have been present during the births of many Native American infants. Among Indian tribes in New England and Canada, women in active labor usually went to a special hut just outside of the village. They might go alone, or one or two women might attend them. The new mother stayed in this hut for several days. Women also separated themselves from the tribe during menstruation. Indians who became Christian were forced to abandon separate menstrual huts, and their childbirth customs probably also changed.[4]

Some women summoned the midwife at the first sign of labor, especially when travel conditions seemed uncertain. For example, in early December 1793, Martha Ballard spent five days at the Parker house because the river was "dificult to pass." While waiting for Mrs. Parker to give birth, Martha knitted two pairs of gloves and five and one half pair of mittens.[5] During early labor, most women were active and kept busy with housework. When labor became more intense, it was time to call the other women, who would assist during the birth. In general, these birth attendants were relatives and/or nearby neighbors. Although there was no reason why several women should wait around during the early stages of labor, their help was often crucial during delivery. As one historian has noted, "Most early American women literally gave birth in the arms or on the laps of their neighbors." The women also provided emotional comfort to the new mother. In addition, the presence of other women meant that there were witnesses if the laboring mother was single and asked to name the father of her child, or if there were any irregular circumstances that occurred during the birth.[6] (For more on illegitimate births, see Chapter 1 on Women, Marriage, and the Family and Chapter 2 on Women and the Law.) After the birth, the women who attended the delivery usually stayed to celebrate with food and drink. In Hallowell, Maine, tea, sugar, and rum were commonly purchased and consumed during the lying-in period after the birth. Sometimes the birth attendants spent the night, especially when the birth occurred late at night or in bad traveling weather.

Martha Ballard kept records of deliveries, trade with neighbors, and other transactions within her diary, but many eighteenth-century women did not have their own account books, or their records have been lost. Some women, however, used methods other than account books and ledgers to keep track of debts, credit, and payment. For example, Rhoda Childs, a midwife in Deerfield, Massachusetts, was said to have marked her accounts in chalk on her cellar door. Other women's records are contained within account books attributed to their husbands or other male family members. Reuban Champion, a physician in the Connecticut Valley, kept an account book in the 1760s. Yet, over one-third of the entries are debts owed to his wife, Lydia Duncan Champion, for the clothing she produced or altered. Reuban's notations mentioning "debtor to us" make it clear that he was aware this was income generated by his wife.[7]

Martha Ballard's standard midwifery fee was six shillings, regardless of how long she spent with the laboring woman. Sometimes the fee was paid in food or goods, instead of cash, or the fee was supplemented with other products. Occasionally, she received a larger sum from the wealthier men in the town after safely delivering their wives. Midwifery paid better than most occupations open to women, but a skilled midwife such as Martha Ballard most certainly earned her fee.[8] Loyalist Janet Cumming claimed to have earned four hundred pounds sterling per year as a midwife in Charleston by charging forty pounds for the delivery of a white woman and ten pounds for the delivery of a black woman. Her witnesses for the claims commission after the Revolutionary War supported her statement.[9]

Most midwives did not earn the sums generated by Janet Cumming. In many cases, the fees they earned helped support their families, along with the money made by their husbands, and the goods they and their families produced. Women also earned money by nursing. Women who could afford to do so had nurses attend them after childbirth, and, as discussed in Chapter 1, some women used wet nurses for their infants, but nurses also cared for people who were sick or injured. Although they were not paid as well as midwives, nurses, like servants, were often in demand. For example, in September 1795, after her daughter, Nancy, gave birth, Elizabeth Drinker of Philadelphia noted the problem of finding a nurse to attend her. "Patty Jones, who was to have nursed Nancy, when we sent for her let us know that her Eyes were so sore that she could not attend—We have been all day at times, looking out for a Nurse but have not yet succeeded . . . Sister is out looking for a Nurse . . . Sister came in the afternoon with Nurse Howel, who appears to be agreeable—I left Nancy about nine o'clock to the care of her Nurse—and came home."[10]

Women learned how to be nurses and how to deliver babies by watching other women and by assisting them. Some women then turned these skills into revenue. Margaret Hill Morris had an apothecary shop in Burlington, New Jersey, for a brief period after she was widowed, but most of her medicinal work was performed as unpaid labor and advice given to family members, servants, and friends. She moved to Philadelphia sometime after 1785. Her medical efforts were especially trying during the Philadelphia yellow fever epidemic in 1793. In October of that year, she wrote to Gulielma:

> I had the beds & bedding used in the sickness all buryd & the room whitewashed & well cleaned—so that I hope no infection is left in the house—at the time I stood most in need of help, I coud not get a Creature to wash the Sheets . . . I put them in tubs on the grass plott & pound vinegar on them & after lying all Night, had to wash them myself—Sally bled so much from her mouth, that in half an hour a Coarse double sheet woud be dripping . . . I had floors daily washed with Vinegar & having 2 beds in the front parlor & 2 in the back, my house was like a hospital.[11]

Margaret advised Gulielma to "observe the directions I gave in my late letter about herbs &c." and commented, "I think I never made such free use of Wine. I give it to all my familly 2 or 3 times a day & wash myself all over with Vinegar & sprinkle every room with it & burn Tobacco & tar & rosin in all the rooms from the Garret to the Kitchens."[12] The yellow fever epidemic was a devastating event that took the lives of many. Margaret Hill Morris's son and daughter-in-law died during the epidemic, leaving her with five grandchildren to raise. Most Philadelphians who could afford to do so fled the city. Poor residents who could not flee, and who generally lived in crowded, unsanitary conditions, suffered the highest mortality rates. During one five-day period in October 1793, the death carts traveling through the city picked up five hundred bodies.[13]

Illness was a particular problem for poor, working women. Women who were sick, pregnant, elderly, or injured could not work. If they did not have family members who could help them, they might have to appeal to the local almshouse. For example, the pregnant Catharine Cannon, who had been deserted by her husband, entered the Philadelphia almshouse in 1796. She died ten days later from smallpox and the complications of childbirth.[14]

Women were employed in a variety of occupations, often in addition to household responsibilities. In 1775, approximately 15 percent of Philadelphia women were engaged in retail trade of some sort or involved in the management of property. Others worked as artisans, laborers, and teachers. In Boston and in other cities, women toiled as brewmasters, bakers, soap makers, saddlers, and milliners, among other occupations. Perhaps more unusual was the enslaved Alice of Dunk's Ferry, who collected fees and took charge of the ferry that crossed the Delaware River north of Philadelphia. For about forty years, beginning around 1726, Alice worked at the ferry. She was also a notable fisherwoman, even after she had lost her eyesight as an elderly woman.[15]

Few women were able to support themselves through writing or painting at this time. (See Chapter 7 for more on women writers and artists.) Henrietta Johnston, however, did help support her family by painting portraits. One scholar has called her "America's first professional woman artist."[16] Henrietta was born in France to a French Huguenot family. She moved to England and then to Ireland, with her first husband. After his death, she may have supported herself by painting portraits in Dublin. Her second husband was Gideon Johnston, an Anglican minister who was involved with the Society for the Propagation of the Gospel in Foreign Parts. This organization was a missionary section of the Anglican Church. Gideon received a posting in Charles Town (later Charleston), South Carolina, where the Church of England wanted to establish a strong presence to counteract the Catholic presence in Spain, as well as convert Native Americans and Africans.[17]

On the way to Carolina in 1707, the Johnston's ship stopped in the Madeira Islands. Gideon went ashore but did not return to the ship in time, and it left without him. Henrietta and her four children arrived in Charles Town without him. Gideon arrived later, but only after he was marooned on an offshore island for twelve days without food or water. He never fully recovered from this experience. Henrietta's portrait painting helped the couple and their children survive. Gideon acknowledged this in a letter he wrote to the bishop of Salisbury, England, in 1709. He stated, "Were it not for the Assistance my wife gives me by drawing of Pictures (which can last but a little time in a place so ill peopled) I shou'd not have been able to live."[18]

Little is known of Henrietta's training. She may have received private instruction from artists she knew in England and Ireland. She worked in pastels, which was very unusual for the time, but which gave her work a luminous quality. She painted portraits of the elite of South Carolina, both adults and children, and she was particularly close to the large French Huguenot population living in the Charleston area.[19]

A more common occupation for women was that of shopkeeper. Although some women ran businesses from their homes and may have earned little money, others were quite successful. For example, Elizabeth Murray Smith became an entrepreneur in Boston. As is often true, however, it took a little while for her business to flourish. Thus, in addition to selling a variety of goods in her shop, including muslins, "newest Fashion Caps," needles, pins, and thread, Elizabeth also advertised in the 1750s that she would teach embroidery and provide "young Ladies with Board."[20]

Elizabeth Murray was born in Scotland. Her parents died when she was young. Although as a young woman she could have continued to live with one of her siblings, instead she decided to live independently in Boston, and her older brother, James, helped her acquire a dry-goods store. Elizabeth married Thomas Campbell in 1755. In 1760, when the thirty-four-year-old widow married her second husband, James Smith, a wealthy seventy-year-old sugar merchant, she first insisted on having a prenuptial agreement that gave her control over her own property and permitted her to dispose of it as she wished. When she married for a third time at age forty-five, she was quite a wealthy widow. Her prenuptial agreement with Ralph Inman again guaranteed that she would have control over both her real and personal property, as well as receive two hundred pounds each year for her own use. Elizabeth never had children of her own, but she was a mentor for a number of younger women, and she helped them learn skills and provided financial backing for them to open their own businesses.[21]

The relatively high literacy rate for women in British America and the growing interest in education in the eighteenth century enabled some women to find work as teachers. Informal "Dame Schools" had existed in the seventeenth century, but in the eighteenth century, as education assumed new importance in the young republic, more women became teachers, and teaching began to be seen as a career choice for women. Women taught in both charity schools and in more elite private academies, where young women were schooled in a variety of subjects, including grammar, arithmetic, history, and geography, as well as in needlework and music. (For more on education, see Chapter 7.)

A few women held prominent positions as printers. Elizabeth Timothy, for example, took over the publishing of the *South-Carolina Gazette* after the death of her husband, Lewis, in 1738. She ran the paper so successfully that she was able to pay off the debt her husband had owed to Benjamin Franklin. In 1739, she became "the first woman in the American colonies to own and publish a newspaper." Elizabeth Timothy also took over her husband's position as official printer for South Carolina. When her eldest son Peter reached legal age, she turned the printing business over to him, but she opened a stationery and bookstore next door. Peter and his wife Ann continued to run the family business. When Peter, two of their children, and a grandchild died in a shipwreck, Ann took over the publication of the *Gazette*. She ran the paper until her death in 1792. In addition, she published almanacs and other items. In 1783, South Carolina appointed her printer to the state.[22]

In both urban and rural areas, women often ran taverns (sometimes with their husbands) and inns. In 1734, Cathrine Pattison of Darby, Pennsylvania (outside of Philadelphia), applied for a tavern license "for another year." Her husband had deserted her, and she begged the magistrates to help her, because she was "left almost destitute of relief" and had no other means of supporting herself. In Philadelphia, as elsewhere, women often had experience helping their husbands, fathers, or other men run taverns, but they were granted licenses only if they had been widowed or deserted and were forced to support themselves and their families.[23]

Elizabeth Steele in Rowan County, North Carolina, was the only woman in the county to hold a tavern license in 1764, when she married for the second time. During her first marriage, her husband's business ventures almost forced them into bankruptcy. Elizabeth's *feme covert* status prevented her from participating in legal actions, such as going to court to collect debts. When her first husband died, she settled the estate, bought a tavern in her own name, and frequently went to court. She kept her property in her own name in 1764, after she married William Steele, who owned a neighboring tavern. After William died, Elizabeth was a wealthy woman, and she continued to run the tavern.[24]

Many women, however, sold small amounts of alcohol they brewed at home and did not bother with the formalities of obtaining a license. Some homes became unofficial inns because of their proximity to ferries, markets, or other trading areas. This may have been the situation with Mary Cooper's house, located near the entrance of Oyster Bay Harbor. There seemed to be a constant stream of visitors staying there—visitors whom Mary did not always welcome. Guests, whether welcomed or not, always added to Mary's workload, but these men seemed particularly unpleasant. For example, on August 1, 1769, she wrote, "Ben Hildrith is come here in a littel boate with two men with him. I am up late and much freted them and thier two dogs which they keep att tabel and in the bedroom with them." The next day, she noted that the day began with the sound of the dogs barking in the bedroom. "They did nothing but drink them selves drunk all the day long and sent for more rum." On August 4, Mary wrote, "They set sail to go home to my great joy, and I desier I may never se them here again. I greately dread the cleaning of [ ] hous after this detested gang."[25]

In frontier areas, unlicensed and informal inns and taverns were probably quite common. Often, they were run by women, or, as in the case of Mary Cooper, women bore the burden of providing for travelers and houseguests. By the mid-eighteenth-century, Native American women controlled much of the alcohol trade in frontier fur trading areas. In some instances, Indian women received rum for sex with European men. Then they sold the rum to other Indians. Later, they swapped furs for alcohol. By the 1760s, as one scholar notes, "Indian leaders began denouncing the trade, complaining that traders were sexually abusing respectable married women." European men often had trouble interpreting Native American rituals, and interpreting when Indian women were "available."[26]

Yet European men also categorized white women who ventured out alone at nights as sexually available. Wars, the growth of cities, and poverty forced many women into prostitution. During the Revolutionary War, prostitutes found eager customers among the soldiers of both armies. Despite the demand for their services, however, many viewed prostitutes as symbols of the moral decay of society. (For more on prostitutes during the Revolutionary War, see Chapter 5.)[27]

In contrast, taking in lodgers was something a "genteel" woman could do to earn additional income. In college towns, for instance, families provided temporary homes for students and professors. Esther Edwards Burr sometimes housed students from the College of New Jersey. In New Haven, Connecticut, the widowed Mary Fish boarded young men attending Yale. She also housed some of the elite men of the state. In other cities, too, such as Boston and Philadelphia, elite women provided lodging to respectable men or single women who did not have living parents or family who could give them a home.[28]

Throughout British North America, women of all classes, races, ages, and marital status participated in some aspect of cloth or clothing production. All clothing had to be hand-stitched, as did table and bed linens. Even elite women did some sewing, although servants or slaves did most of the household sewing in the wealthiest households. In the eighteenth century, middle-class women, especially urban women, could afford to purchase most of their clothing, although they might still make repairs and do basic sewing.

Clothes-making involved a variety of skills. As a historian of needlework in New England notes, "occupations within the clothing trades, though related, were not interchangeable. Tailoresses, tailors, gown makers, milliners, and stay makers specialized in different aspects of clothing production and possessed specialized knowledge appropriate to those tasks." Gowns, for example, were garments that had to be cut and sewn in a special way to ensure the proper fit. They were better quality attire, and most women owned only one or two. Many women did not want to risk ruining expensive fabric and called upon the skills of gown-makers when they wanted a gown made. For example, Catherine Parsons, who was an experienced Connecticut River Valley tailor, employed the gown-maker Esther Wright to make silk gowns for herself and her daughters.[29]

On large plantations, slaves would have done most of the sewing and spinning, but plantation mistresses supervised and may have done much of the cutting and the fine sewing. Young gentry women made clothing, stitched stockings, and worked on table linen. Thomas Jefferson considered needlework to be an important and valuable skill for his daughters to learn. He monitored how well his daughters learned to sew and cook and expected them to be as proficient in domestic skills as they were in more intellectual and ornamental ones. He also made certain that Sally Hemings, a slave who was his wife's half-sister and who most probably became his mistress, was trained as a seamstress. Enslaved women with specialized skills were more valuable, and some slaves, both male and female, earned money for doing work in addition to their regular duties. White masters and mistresses viewed the specialized training they provided to some slaves as a mark of favoritism. Moreover, in their quest for gentility, Virginia planters most likely believed that if needlework was a genteel and proper occupation for their wives and daughters, it was also a good skill for their personal maids to learn. The maids could then use their knowledge to care for clothing that became increasingly more elaborate in the eighteenth century.[30]

Enslaved women may have had an entirely different reaction to performing household duties, even if their chores were less onerous than those that field slaves had to do. Female slaves who worked as ladies' maids and in other household positions spent all of their time with their white owners. Such forced

Martha Washington, published by L. Prang, after a painting by Gilbert Stuart. Courtesy Library of Congress.

intimacy was not always pleasant. Oney Judge was a slave at Mt. Vernon, the Washington family's Virginia plantation. Like Sally Hemings, Oney Judge was of mixed race. At about age ten, she was brought to live in the main house, perhaps to be a playmate for Martha Washington's granddaughter, Nelly. Martha Washington was said to be very fond of Oney and taught her to sew and embroider and "for several years they sat working together daily."[31] Along with some other slaves, Oney was brought to live in the president's house in New York City and then to Philadelphia, when it became the capital in 1790. While in Philadelphia, Oney became friendly with some members of the city's large free black population. Pennsylvania had passed a gradual abolition law, and the Washingtons were careful not to have their slaves reside long enough in the state to have the law apply to them.[32]

In 1796, Martha Washington's granddaughter, Elizabeth Custis, married Thomas Law. Oney was to be given to Elizabeth as a wedding present. Oney knew that if she returned to Virginia, she would never be freed. With the help of some free black friends, she escaped and eventually ended up in Portsmith, New Hampshire. The Washingtons tried to have her brought back to them. They were upset at what they considered to be her "unfaithfulness." They believed that they had treated her well. Oney, however, wanted to be free. She did not consider them to be her foster parents—they were her masters. Oney eventually married a sailor, Jack Staines, and had three children with him, but she remained a fugitive. She died in New Hampshire in 1848. In the interviews given to abolitionist newspapers shortly before her death, she indicated that she was still angry and resentful toward the Washingtons. Although Martha Washington had taught Oney to sew and do fine needlework, she had never taught her to read. She had given her a room of her own in which to sleep, but she had not given her freedom. Skills that were taught to elite white women to enhance their roles as wives and mothers were only another form of work to an enslaved woman.[33] (For more on women's education, see Chapter 7.)

Needlework and cloth-making crossed all class boundaries. As noted, it was done by both gentry women and slaves. Charitable organizations and businesses gave poor women sewing and spinning work. A Boston sailcloth factory employed young female spinners and a matron to supervise them. In Philadelphia, some black girls were apprenticed to learn a trade such as spinning.[34] In New York City, the Society for the Promotion of Arts, Agriculture and Economy set up a linen factory in 1764 that used women and children to spin flax "as part of the movement to stop the importation of British goods." Public spinning bees—demonstrations by women in support of boycotts—occurred in many places in the years leading up to the Revolution. Even elite women wore homespun and took part in the events designed to raise public awareness of high taxes and boycotts of English manufactured goods. (For more on women's involvement in Revolutionary War activities, see Chapter 5.) After the war, however, those who could afford to do so returned to purchasing cloth, and elite women generally confined their needlework to more ornamental forms, while spinning and weaving on a regular basis became associated with poorer women.[35]

The prosperity of British North America led to a growth in consumerism. The increase in better quality cloth and fashionable clothing meant that garments required better care and more frequent cleaning. Clean clothing, especially clean white linen, became associated with gentility. Yet, laundry was not done on a daily or even necessarily on a weekly basis because it required so much heavy work—lifting and carrying buckets of water because homes did not have indoor plumbing, building and watching the fires to heat the water, wringing and scrubbing wet clothing, and heating and using heavy irons. In late eighteenth-century New England, as in Philadelphia, laundresses were often free black women. "Old Phillis," a former slave, was hired by a number of women in the Connecticut River Valley area to do their laundry. Peggy Browning, who had been a slave for the Wadsworth family in Connecticut, continued to live on the family's property and worked as a laundress.[36]

In addition to outside occupations, such as midwifery and shopkeeping, and occasional chores, such as laundry, most wives had many daily tasks to perform within their homes. These chores had to be done without running water, refrigeration, and sometimes even without much light. People often moved their work to areas where they had sunlight. Candles were expensive to buy, and in many homes they were used sparingly. In rural households, families produced dipped candles, made most often from beef tallow. Making these candles was a time-consuming process, usually done in the fall. Because it took so long, women tried to make enough candles at one time to last through the winter. The candles then had to be stored carefully to prevent them from melting or from being eaten by mice.[37]

For Jewish women, household work also included keeping a kosher home. Jewish dietary laws meant that certain foods, such as pork and shellfish, could not be eaten at all. They were *treif,* or nonkosher. Kosher meat, however, had to be slaughtered in a particular way by a kosher butcher, and even kosher meat and dairy products could not be mixed or eaten together. The dishes, pots, and utensils used for meat and dairy also had to be kept separated from each other. Jewish wives were in charge of food preparation, and it was up to them to make sure that dietary laws were followed in the household, but, to do so, they needed a community in which kosher foods could be obtained.[38]

This was often difficult to do in areas where there were few Jewish residents. Rebecca Samuel was thrilled with the peace and prosperity she and her husband found in Petersburg, Virginia. As she wrote to her parents, who had remained in Hamburg, Germany, Virginia is "the greatest province in the whole of America. And America is the greatest section of the world." They were treated well by their Christian neighbors, and Hyman's watchmaking business was very successful. Yet Rebecca noted that they had "a *shochet* [ritual slaughterer] here who goes to market and buys *terefa* [unkosher] meat and then brings it home." How could she keep a kosher home under such conditions? Rebecca complained to her parents and said, "You must believe me that in our house we live as Jews as much as we can." The family left Petersburg and moved to Charleston, South Carolina, where there was a much larger Jewish population.[39]

For farmwives, there were a multitude of tasks to be done—both inside the house and outside in the garden, orchards, poultry coops, and dairy. Even within the house, there were seasonal or occasional jobs to be done, such as preserving food, making candles, and spinning. These activities were necessary if the farm was to be successful. Indeed, running a farm without a wife (and additional female help) was difficult. French observer, Brissot de Warville, took note of this fact when he visited the farm of a French bachelor, M. Le Gaux, who farmed along the Schulkill River, just north of Philadelphia. As Brissot de Warville wrote in his *New Travels in the United States of America, 1788*, "As he is without a family he does not have any poultry or pigeons and makes no cheese, nor does he have any spinning done or collect goose feathers. It is a great disadvantage for him not to be able to profit from these domestic farm industries, which can be carried on well only by women." In contrast, when he visited another farm in the region—this one the home of a Quaker family—Brissot de Warville noted and was pleased with the fine bed linens, the spinning that the women of the family did, and their production and sale of vegetables.[40]

Farmwives throughout the North undertook or oversaw many seasonal agricultural tasks. In August, Martha Ballard in Maine spent time "pulling flax," as did the farm daughters and hired help at many Chester County farms. In October, Mary Cooper, a farm housewife in Long Island, "hurred" to dry apples before it rained, and, in early December after killing the hogs, she complained that she was "distressed with harde worke makeing sausages and boile souse, bakeing and cooking." At age seventy-four, Martha Ballard still worked steadily in her garden, seasonal work that provided her family with food for much of the year. As the frozen ground of the Maine farm began to thaw in late April or early May, Martha went to work, setting turnips and cabbage "stumps," the roots of the previous year's crops that had been kept in the cellar over the winter. In 1809, after the turnips and cabbage, she planted cucumber and "three kinds of squash." A few days later, she "dug ground west of the hous" and then planted more squash, cucumbers, musk melons, and watermelons on the east side of the house. In the next week, she planted "long squash by the hogg pen" and began sowing peppergrass and setting sage. In addition, she took advantage of the warm spring weather to wash her husband's and son's "old over Coats" and her gown. Within the next couple of weeks, she planted quince and apple trees, planted strawberries and potatoes, and sowed string beans. On May 22, she proudly noted that she had "squash & Cucumber Come up in the bed East side the hous." She referred to the field that the men plowed as "our field," but the garden was hers, and she was proud of what she accomplished with it.[41]

In contrast, Mary Cooper did not express pride in her accomplishments, at least not in her diary. Gardening was just another chore in the endless round of work she had to do. She seemed perpetually overworked and overwhelmed, even when she had help. Sometimes she found the help less than satisfactory, as she noted in her diary entry for November 18, 1772, "I was mighty angry this morning becaus our peopel [slaves] did not bring in the pumkins and they are all frose and spoiled." On June 13, 1773, with a house full of people and a sick husband, Mary Cooper wrote, "I have not been a bed in many nights. I am so hurred waiteing on this famaly . . . I am forst to stay att home. Dadde is very sik. I am forst to climbe the cherre tree and fetch the bees down in my a pron."[42]

The extant diary of Mary Cooper begins in 1768, when she was fifty-four years old. Of her six children, only one was alive at this point, her daughter Esther. Esther lived with her parents after separating from her husband Simon, who was also her first cousin. Esther was often upset or away from home, and consequently she was not always a help to her mother. For example, on September 25, 1769, Mary wrote, "Ester has freted most grevously all day long about cleaning the house."[43]

The presence or absence of daughters often determined what type of work—or how much—farmwives could complete. Martha Ballard's midwifery practice became practical only after she was finished with childbearing and nursing. A nursing mother could not suddenly leave her baby, nor could she carry him or her through bad weather in the middle of the night while she attended a laboring woman for hours or even days. Although she delivered some babies while she still had young children, Martha Ballard did not build an extensive practice until 1785—when her youngest child was six and the next youngest was twelve. Moreover, Martha Ballard had older daughters who could help with the housework.[44]

Between 1785 and 1796, Martha Ballard's daughters, nieces, and their friends performed most of the daily household chores and contributed as well to a busy and profitable system of home production. These young women were reliable, and they were connected to and lived within the Ballard household. When they married and left the Ballard house, Martha had to hire workers who did not stay as long or work as well. Moreover, without the constant help of daughters, the additional production of textiles and other goods in the Ballard household became nearly impossible.[45]

While the Ballard "girls" were living at home, they did the spinning, learned to weave, produced clothing, and took over much of the routine housework. They also wove for neighbors. A typical 1789 entry in Martha's diary reports: "My girls spun 23 double skeins and wove 27 ½ yds last weak and did the housework besides." With the young women in control of the work at home, Martha could concentrate on her midwifery practice.[46]

Young women often participated in work parties, commonly known as "frolics." In November 1790, the girls at Martha Ballard's house spent a couple of days quilting. On November 10, Martha Ballard reported, "My girls had some neighbours to help them quilt a bed quilt, 15 ladies. They began to quilt at 3 hour pm. Finisht and took it out at 7 evening. There were 12 gentlemen took tea. They danced a little while after supper. Behaved exceedingly cleverly . . . Were all returned home before the 11th hour."[47]

Married women also participated in frolics, although they were not used as occasions for courting, but rather were social events. For example, on March 18, 1755, Esther Burr wrote that she was "making Cake for spinning-frollick to day, which is to be attended tomorrow and several days after I suppose." On April 10, 1756, she reported that she was "Extreamly ingaged—what with preparing for my spinning frolick . . ."[48]

Of course, with or without daughters, many wives relied upon servants or slaves to help with household chores. Most of the Connecticut River Valley gentry women who so actively engaged in regular quilting get-togethers were only able to do so because they owned slaves or had other household help. Married women and their daughters were expected to attend these events that combined work fit for elite women, such as quilting petticoats or doing ornamental needlework, with opportunities to display gentility and make social alliances. On these

The Accident in Lombard Street, designed and engraved by C. W. Peale. Daughters or servants could be sent on errands, giving the mistress of the house more leisure time. Accidents, however, sometimes occurred on city streets. Courtesy Library of Congress.

occasions, the hostess supplied food and hospitality and put on view her best china, furniture, and status symbols. Among the New England elite, these social gatherings were taken very seriously. At the same time, the work of the household—and of the households of all those attending—had to continue. Thus, slaves or other workers had to attend to it.[49]

Women elsewhere also used the presence of hired or bound help to give themselves the time to engage in leisure activities. As discussed in Chapter 1, the well-to-do Philadelphia Quaker Elizabeth Drinker always had at least five or six servants in her household. She usually had both indentured servants, who were generally taken into the household as children, and unbound live-in maids, who did much of the housework and childcare. In addition, she hired nurses, on an occasional basis, and day workers to sew, iron, or paint. Although Elizabeth Drinker knitted, sewed, and performed other household tasks, she still had time for reading and other leisure activities.[50]

On farms in both the north and the south, free white women and black enslaved women frequently worked side by side to complete household duties. For example, the household of Thomas and Elizabeth Porter included Elizabeth's widowed mother Barbara, who turned over management of the Virginia Piedmont farm to Elizabeth and Thomas but continued to live with the couple. Elizabeth's father, Pierre Dutoy, had stated that the farm was to go to Elizabeth after Barbara died. When Elizabeth and Thomas wed, the household included three slaves; the couple added eight children to it.[51]

Two of the slaves, Peg and Joseph, were also a couple, although they could not marry legally. They had two children. Most likely, Peg worked in both the tobacco fields and the house. Because of her, Barbara Dutoy's daughters did not have to help with fieldwork. The women of the household did work in the vegetable garden and tended to the sheep and geese. They milked the cows; carded, spun, and wove wool and flax; and prepared meals. They rendered lard to make candles and soap. The feathers and down of the geese were used to make feather beds—each worth as much as a horse. The women of the household made enough feather beds for each child to inherit one. For Barbara, Elizabeth, and Elizabeth's daughters, there may have been some satisfaction in knowing that their work contributed to the household production that benefited the entire family. For Peg and her daughter Amy, the work was just part of the labor they were forced to do as slaves.[52]

In the eighteenth century, women began to work with livestock more often. They generally milked cows and raised poultry. Raising poultry, butchering it, and collecting the feathers became a job for women. In addition, women probably sold the eggs of hens, ducks, and turkeys, but it is difficult to trace how common this was, because few records were kept. Inventories reveal, however, a great increase in the number of feather beds that existed after the mid-eighteenth century. As noted, members of the Porter family inherited feather beds. Feather beds were valued by their weight. Some inventories record feather beds weighing

50 to 60 pounds. One widow in Chester County, Pennsylvania, had a feather
bed that weighed 76 pounds.[53]

Women also became heavily involved in dairying and butter-making, especially later in the eighteenth century. Although men built barns, produced hay
(often with the help of women), and cleaned the stables, women usually milked
the cows and made butter for their homes and for the market. Often children
and servants helped women with the process of butter-making, which involved
several steps after the initial milking. The separated cream was churned, turned
into blocks of butter, and then preserved and packed for the market.[54]

In the first part of the eighteenth century, women in Pennsylvania and
Delaware probably used cellars for butter-making. By mid-century, however,
springhouses were becoming common. One historian explains that "by 1798
more than seven hundred stone springhouses dotted Chester County, with 52
percent of the farms having them." Springhouses were built over a spring, which
kept the milk cold. They usually had shelves and plenty of space to churn and
store the butter.[55]

Women in the Philadelphia region often took the butter to market—either to
Philadelphia or to Wilmington, Delaware. One account in 1798 mentions
women bringing their farm produce to market in "handsomely woven baskets."
Often they carried the butter and other goods on horseback, but sometimes they
arrived by wagon. Those who lived near rivers might take boats to markets or
have riverboat captains take and sell their produce. At the markets, women
bought goods they needed before returning home. Women also traded their butter locally for services, such as shoemaking.[56]

On small farms without slaves, white women worked in the fields. On northern farms, farm workers might be white, black, or Indian. In Chester County,
Pennsylvania, young women helped the men harvest rye in early July. Later, they
helped the men with haying. It was the women's job to "pull flax." "Flax pulling
was often done cooperatively, with the woman whose field had been pulled providing the an evening of food and entertainment as pay. The other cutting was
usually hired, sometimes with farm daughters joining the hired hands in the
fields." Processing flax involved several steps, including separating the fibers, drying the flax, and "hackling" it, that is separating the fiber from the broken
strands. This processing could take several months and continue into the winter,
when it was time to spin the flax. Ultimately, the yarn was woven, bleached,
dyed, and sewn into clothing.[57]

By age twelve or fourteen, many young women went into households to spin,
sew, or help with the harvest. Of course, this depended upon the economic status of the family. The wealthiest families in the north had year-round servants or
slaves. The wealthiest families in the south increasingly relied upon slave labor,
in both the house and the fields. For the most part, the mistresses of southern
plantations supervised but did not necessarily engage in farm labor. Yet, at least
one wealthy southern woman tended to her hens by candlelight.[58]

Some women took charge of farms and plantations, especially after they became widows. Eliza Lucas Pinckney, however, began managing her father's plantations while she was still in her teens. Eliza was born in the West Indies, schooled in England, and then moved to South Carolina in 1738 when she was fifteen. She first took over the household duties from her mother, who suffered from chronic illness. Then when her father, George Lucas, who was a British Army officer, left to fight in the War of Jenkins's Ear, she took over the management of one of Lucas's three plantations, the 600-acre Wappoo plantation. In addition, she supervised the overseers at the other two plantations.

Colonel Lucas had great confidence in his daughter's abilities. He sent her indigo seeds, with the hopes that indigo could be grown in South Carolina. After several years of setbacks and experimentation, Eliza finally managed to grow and market the crop, which is used to make blue dye, and it became a valuable export for the colony. She was very much involved in the promoting, marketing, and selling of her crops. In 1744, Eliza married forty-five-year-old Charles Pickney, a man she had known for years. When he died, fourteen years later, leaving her with three children, she once again resumed the responsibilities of managing an eighteenth-century estate.[59]

Of course, Eliza Lucas Pinckney did not do all the work on her plantations by herself. Without detracting from her accomplishments as an amateur botanist, entrepreneur, farm and household manager, and mother, it is important to note that it was the efforts of slaves—many of them enslaved women—whose work permitted her to use her keen mind and determined nature to accomplish so much. The black population of South Carolina outnumbered the white population. As one historian has commented: "African Americans were a constant presence in her life, but Eliza Lucas rarely commented on the institution of slavery . . . Yet in all kinds of everyday ways, the institution of slavery made her life what it was. Slave women working in the fields put into practice the agricultural experiments she devised; indeed the familiarity of many West African blacks with the delicate cultivation of rice and indigo provided expertise Anglo-Americans lacked. Slave women cooked Eliza Lucas's dinner and saw to the needs of her visitors. Slave women nursed her children, setting aside the needs of their own offspring in the process."[60]

The production of indigo required a great deal of labor. First, the plants had to be grown and harvested. Then, the indigo plants had to be processed and the dye made from them. This process involved allowing the plants to rot and ferment, producing a disgusting odor as the pigment left the plants. Then slaves beat the plants to release the indigo, which fell in flakes to the bottom of the vats. Finally, slaves took the indigo, which then had a pudding-like consistency, and placed it in cloth bags. After draining overnight, the indigo was pressed and dried into bricks or "cakes." During the peak of South Carolina's indigo boom, cakes of indigo were used as currency.[61]

Agriculture was also important to most of the Indian tribes of eastern North America. Although men sometimes helped prepare fields and might help with hoeing, women usually owned both the fields and the crops that they planted. Among the crops grown were beans, peas, corn, and squash. Women also gathered berries, fruit, nuts, seeds, and processed the sap from maple trees to make maple syrup and sugar. Men generally did the hunting, but women produced leather from the deerskin.[62]

Cherokee women were the main producers of food within their tribes. As in many other tribes, they were in charge of farming, although men sometimes helped. By the beginning of the eighteenth century, the crops grown by Cherokee women included new plants brought by Africans and Europeans, such as peach trees, sweet potatoes, watermelons, and black-eyed peas, as well as corn. When Carolina troops began building forts on Cherokee land, Cherokee women saw this as an opportunity to make a profit on the crops they grew. The commander of the Carolina troops, Raymond Demere, reported that, within a few months of its establishment, Fort Loudon had begun "to have the Appearance of a Market" instead of a fort, because Cherokee women sold corn and other foods.[63]

Cherokee women became major suppliers of corn and other essentials. In fact, they did their best to prevent the soldiers within the garrisons from growing their own corn. "Just as warriors sought trading opportunities for the deerskins they traded, female farmers also sought to keep the farm-produce markets open." In the mid-eighteenth century, the forts in South Carolina and Virginia remained heavily dependent on the Cherokee villages around them for food.[64]

The success of Britain's North American colonies, and later of the new United States, affected Native American tribes in various ways. As European settlers moved westward, creating towns and fencing in farms, many tribes were displaced, and their traditional ways of living were disrupted. Among the Delaware and Mahican, for example, male and female work roles were changing in the eighteenth century. Like the Cherokee and many other tribes, Delaware and Mahican women were the "owners" of the land, and they grew and produced most of the food for their households. In the mission towns of Pennsylvania, however, Moravians actively promoted the idea that men should take charge of agricultural tasks. Indian men who had become Christians became more involved in growing cash crops of flax, corn, wheat, barley, and rye. By the mid-eighteenth century, wage work had become important for both men and women. Indian women worked in the fields of whites, performing such tasks as pulling flax and reaping oats. For this, they received about one shilling per day. In contrast, Indian men could work at many different types of tasks, including working on roads and floating lumber to mills, and they received better pay.[65]

Wage labor had a great impact on both gender roles and the way of life for many Indians. For example, the Pennsylvania government did not acknowledge the right of Indian women to own property. This threatened their role in agricultural production. In addition, women were becoming less important in the fur trade. Those who did wage work earned less for their efforts than men. Thus, many women began selling food and goods that they produced, such as brooms, baskets, and wooden spoons and bowls. It has been noted that "like their seventeenth-century grandmothers, Delaware and Mahican women used the winter season to manufacture items for home use. Unlike past generations, however, in the eighteenth century women increasingly manufactured these items specifically for sale to neighboring white communities." Brooms sold for about three pence each, and bowls sold for about four pence.[66]

Hannah Freeman, considered "the last identified Lenape in Chester County, Pennsylvania," was also a wageworker and lived a life similar to that of the single, poor, white women around her. By 1731, when Hannah was born, the Lenape in southeastern Pennsylvania who still lived in a traditional way were finding it more difficult to do so. Colonial settlements and milldams altered the areas along the Delaware River where they camped during the summer months, fishing and gathering food. Hannah's immediate family, however, most likely already lived among the colonists. For several years, Hannah lived in various households, where she sewed and did other chores. As she got older, she worked only for her board and made baskets, but she no longer received wages. Eventually, she became too old and infirm to work, and she applied to the Overseers of the Poor for assistance.[67]

In British colonial America, the boundaries between work and home were often quite fluid. Many men owned farms *and* ran businesses. Often business was conducted at home, where wives overheard conversations or witnessed transactions, even if they were not directly participating. Similarly, a woman's work roles were often flexible. In one day, she might move between housework and childcare to cloth and butter production, to bartering or trading services with local merchants, to handling business matters on her husband's behalf, and, finally, to entertaining guests.

For some women, however, life was much different. Although the unmarried daughters of families with some means often worked hard in home production, they were also able to attend frolics and other gatherings of young people. In contrast, poor women of all races struggled just to make ends meet.

New opportunities for women arose after the American Revolution. For example, many began to believe that teaching students in real schools was an occupation that was suitable for women. During the Revolution, women ran businesses and farms while men were away. Home manufacturing and production were important, both for sustenance and as a show of patriotism, because trade was interrupted by boycotts and war. In the post-Revolutionary period, however, home and business, public and private, started to become more separated. This was a result of a number of factors, including the growth of cities and expanded markets, larger homes with public and private areas, and a more formal credit system.

Perceptions about women were changing in the eighteenth century, which also affected the type of work they did. By the latter part of the century, women were perceived as being ideally suited to domestic concerns, the home and family. Domesticity could extend beyond one's family to teaching children in schools. Yet many women did not and could not match this idealized image of domesticity. Most black women, Native American women, and poor working women could never hope to achieve the ideal of domestic womanhood.

NOTES

1. Gulielma M. Smith to Margaret Hill Morris, Feb. 22, 1795, in Gulielma M. Howland Collection, Mss 1000, Box 10, Quaker Collection, Haverford College Library, Haverford, PA.

2. Gulielma M. Smith to Margaret Hill Morris, August 1, 1795, in Howland Collection, Box 10. Quaker Collection.

3. Laurel Thatcher Ulrich, "Martha Ballard and Her Girls: Women's Work in Eighteenth-Century Maine," in *Work and Labor in Early America*, Stephen Innes, ed., (Chapel Hill: University of North Carolina Press, 1988), 77–79; Laurel Thatcher Ulrich, *A Midwife's Tale: The Life of Martha Ballard Based on Her Diary, 1785–1812* (New York: Knopf, 1990), 11–12, 170–171.

4. Ann Marie Plane, "Childbirth Practices among Native American Women of New England and Canada, 1600–1800," in *Women and Health in America: Historical Readings*, 2nd ed., edited by Judith Walzer Leavitt (Madison: University of Wisconsin Press, 1999), 39–41, 43.

5. Ulrich, *A Midwife's Tale*, 164.

6. Ulrich, *A Midwife's Tale*, 185–189.

7. Marla R. Miller, *The Needle's Eye: Women and Work in the Age of Revolution* (Amherst: University of Massachusetts Press, 2006), 9–10, 238 (n. 23).

8. Ulrich, *A Midwife's Tale*, 197–199.

9. Mary Beth Norton, *Liberty's Daughters: The Revolutionary Experience of American Women, 1750–1800* (Ithaca, NY: Cornell University Press, 1996), 140.

10. Elaine Forman Crane, ed. *The Diary of Elizabeth Drinker* (Boston: Northeastern University Press, 1991, vol. 1, 728.

11. Margaret Hill Morris to Gulielma M. Smith, October 31, 1793, in Gulielma M. Howland Collection, Box 7, Folder 3, Quaker Collection, Haverford College Library.

12. Margaret Hill Morris to Gulielma M. Smith, October 31, 1793, in Gulielma M. Howland Collection, Box 7, Folder 3, Quaker Collection, Haverford College Library.

13. Before the 1790s, most Philadelphia residents had not been exposed to yellow fever and therefore did not possess any immunity to the disease. It is transmitted through the bite of the *Aedes aegypti* mosquito, which was most likely brought to Philadelphia on ships from the West Indies. The hot, humid Philadelphia summers and swampy areas provided breeding grounds for the insects. The disease usually appeared in August, peaked in September and October, and ended in November as cold weather moved in. Billy G. Smith, *The "Lower Sort": Philadelphia's Laboring People, 1750–1800* (Ithaca, NY: Cornell University Press, 1990), 50–51.

14. Daily Occurrence Docket, 30 November 1796, Guardians of the Poor, Philadelphia City Archives.

15. Joan R. Gunderson, *To Be Useful to the World: Women in Revolutionary America, 1740–1790*, rev. ed., (Chapel Hill: University of North Carolina Press, 2006), 81–82.

16. Elizabeth Louise Roark, *Artists of Colonial America* (Westport, CT: Greenwood Press, 2003), 91.

17. Roark, *Artists of Colonial America*, 91, 96.

18. Quoted in Roark, *Artists of Colonial America*, 91.

19. Roark, *Artists of Colonial America*, 93–98.

20. For a complete biography of Elizabeth Murray, see Patricia Cleary, *Elizabeth Murray: A Woman's Pursuit of Independence in Eighteenth-Century America* (Amherst: University of Massachusetts Press, 2003). *Boston Evening-Post*, March 12, 1753, Elizabeth Murray Project, http://salticid.nmc.csulb.edu/cgi-bin/WebObjects/eMurray.woa/wa/select?page=homepage.

21. Norton, *Liberty's Daughters*, 147–151. For a look at Elizabeth Murray's prenuptial agreements, see the online Elizabeth Murray Project.

22. Martha J. King, "'What Providence Has Brought Them to Be': Widows, Work, and Print Culture in Colonial Charlestown," in *Women and Freedom in Early America*, edited by Larry D. Eldridge (New York: New York University Press, 1997), 153–155, 158–161.

23. Cathrine Pattison, #125, Tavern Papers, vol. 2, 1729–1736, Chester County Archives, West Chester, PA; Peter Thompson, *Rum Punch and Revolution: Taverngoing and Public Life in Eighteenth-Century Philadelphia* (Philadelphia: University of Pennsylvania Press, 1999), 40–41.

24. Johanna Miller Lewis, "Women and Economic Freedom in the North Carolina Backcountry," in Eldridge, *Women and Freedom*, 198–199.

25. Field Horne, ed. *The Diary of Mary Cooper: Life on a Long Island Farm 1768–1773* (Oyster Bay, NY: Oyster Bay Historical Society, 1981), 16–17.

26. Gunderson, *To Be Useful to the World*, 34, 83.

27. Gunderson, *To Be Useful to the World*, 142–143.

28. Gunderson, 82; Joy Day Buel and Richard Buel, Jr. *The Way of Duty: A Woman and Her Family in Revolutionary America* (New York: Norton, 1984), 65.

29. Miller, *The Needle's Eye*, 64–65.

30. Pat Gibbs, "Daily Schedule for a Young Gentry Woman," Colonial Williamsburg Web Site, http://research.history.org/Historical_Research/Research_Themes/ThemeFamily/GentryWoman.cfm; Annette Gordon-Reed, *The Hemingses of Monticello: An American Family* (New York, Norton, 2008), 237, 279.

31. Despite Martha Washington's image as a dowdy matron, she appeared to have been quite fond of fashionable clothing, at least when she was a young woman. She probably needed skilled slaves to take care of her fashionable attire. See Brigid Schulte, "Fresh Look at Martha Washington: Less First Frump, More Foxy Lady," *Washington Post*, Feb. 2, 2009 online http://www.washingtonpost.com/wp-dyn/content/article/2009/02/01/AR2009020102023_pf.html.

Similarly, while in France, Thomas Jefferson and his daughters dressed in the latest fashions. Sally Hemings probably received training there to help with this clothing. See Gordon-Reed, *The Hemingses of Monticello*, 244.

32. Mechal Sobel, *The World They Made Together: Black and White Values in Eighteenth-Century Virginia* (Princeton, NJ: Princeton University Press, 1987), 139; Edward Lawler, Jr. "Oney Judge," The President's House in Philadelphia Web site, http://www.ushistory.org/presidentshouse/slaves/oney.htm.

33. Lawler, "Oney Judge." Also see the two 1840s articles on the President's House in Philadelphia Web site.

34. Jean R. Soderlund, "Black Women in Colonial Pennsylvania," *Pennsylvania Magazine of History and Biography* (January 1983), 61.

35. Christine Stansell, *City of Women: Sex and Class in New York, 1789–1860* (New York, Knopf, 1986), 16; Gunderson, *To Be Useful to the World*, 75–78.

36. Miller, *The Needle's Eye*, 68.

37. Jane C. Nylander, *Our Own Snug Fireside: Images of the New England Home: 1760–1860* (New Haven, CT: Yale University Press, 1994), 106, 109–111.

38. Hasia R. Diner and Beryl Lieff Benderly, *Her Works Praise Her: A History of Jewish Women in America from Colonial Times to the Present* (New York: Basic Books, 2002), 35–36.

39. Diner and Benderly, *Her Works Praise Her*, 15, 23.

40. J. P. Brissot de Warville, *New Travels in the United States of America, 1788*, ed. Durand Echeverria, (Cambridge, MA: Harvard University Press, 1964), 204–208, 162–64, quoted in Joan M. Jensen, *Loosening the Bonds: Mid-Atlantic Farm Women, 1750–1850* (New Haven, CT: Yale University Press, 1986), 53–54.

41. Horne, *The Diary of Mary Cooper*, 1 (October 11, 1768), 24 (December 2, 1769); Jensen, *Loosening the Bonds*, 36–37; Ulrich, *A Midwife's Tale*, see Chapter 10, May 1809, "Workt in my gardin."

42. *The Diary of Mary Cooper*, 44, 60.

43. *The Diary of Mary Cooper*, 19.

44. Ulrich, "Martha Ballard and Her Girls," 88–89.

45. Ulrich, "Martha Ballard and Her Girls," 90–99.

46. Ulrich, "Martha Ballard and Her Girls," 90–93.

47. Ulrich, *A Midwife's Tale*, 146.

48. Carol F. Karlsen and Laurie Crumpacker, eds., *The Journal of Esther Edwards Burr* (New Haven, CT: Yale University Press, 1984), 101, 191.

49. Miller, *The Needle's Eye*, CH3.

50. Elaine F. Crane, "The World of Elizabeth Drinker," *Pennsylvania Magazine of History and Biography* (January 1983), 9–10, 14–15.

51. Gunderson, *To Be Useful to the World*, 2–6.

52. Gunderson, *To Be Useful to the World*, 73.

53. Jensen, *Loosening the Bonds*, 48–49.

54. Jensen, *Loosening the Bonds*, 93.

55. For a discussion of the technology of butter-making, see Jensen, *Loosening the Bonds*, especially Chapter 6.

56. Jensen, *Loosening the Bonds*, 111–112.

57. Jensen, *Loosening the Bonds*, 36–37.

58. Gunderson, *To Be Useful to the World*, 70.

59. Carol Berkin, *First Generations: Women in Colonial America* (New York: Hill and Wang, 1996), 129–136; Elise Pickney, ed, *The Letterbook of Eliza Lucas Pickney, 1739–1762* (Charleston: University of South Carolina Press, 1997), xv–xxv.

60. Nancy F. Cott, *No Small Courage: A History of Women in the United States* (New York: Oxford University Press, 2000), 104.

61. For slavery and indigo, see Jean M. West, "The Devil's Blue Dye: Indigo and Slavery," Slavery in America http://www.slaveryinamerica.org/history/hs_es_indigo.htm.

62. Gunderson, *To Be Useful to the World*, 72, 73.

63. Tom Hatley, *The Dividing Paths: Cherokees and South Carolinians through the Revolutionary Era* (New York: Oxford University Press, 1995), 8–9, 96–97.

64. Hatley, *The Dividing Paths*, 96–98.

65. Jane T. Merritt, *At the Crossroads: Indians and Empires on a Mid-Atlantic Frontier, 1700–1763* (Chapel Hill: University of North Carolina, 2003), 152–153.

66. Merritt, *At the Crossroads*, 153–154.

67. Marshall J. Becker, "Hannah Freeman: An Eighteenth-Century Lenape Living and Working among Colonial Farmers," *Pennsylvania Magazine of History and Biography* CXIV (April 1990): 249–269.

SUGGESTED READING

Berkin, Carol. *First Generations: Women in Colonial America*. New York: Hill and Wang, 1996.

Cleary, Patricia. *Elizabeth Murray: A Woman's Pursuit of Independence in Eighteenth-Century America*. Amherst: University of Massachusetts Press, 2003.

Crane, Elaine Forman, ed. *The Diary of Elizabeth Drinker*. Boston: Northeastern University Press, 1991.

Gunderson, Joan R. *To Be Useful to the World: Women in Revolutionary America, 1740–1790*, Revised ed. Chapel Hill: University of North Carolina Press, 2006.

Horne, Field, ed. *The Diary of Mary Cooper: Life on a Long Island Farm 1768–1773*. Oyster Bay, NY: Oyster Bay Historical Society, 1981.

Jensen, Joan M. *Loosening the Bonds: Mid-Atlantic Farm Women, 1750–1850*. New Haven, CT: Yale University Press, 1986.

Miller, Marla R. *The Needle's Eye: Women and Work in the Age of Revolution*. Amherst: University of Massachusetts Press, 2006.

Norton, Mary Beth. *Liberty's Daughters: The Revolutionary Experience of American Women, 1750–1800*. Ithaca, NY: Cornell University Press, 1996.

Ulrich, Laurel Thatcher. *A Midwife's Tale: The Life of Martha Ballard Based on Her Diary, 1785–1812*. New York: Knopf, 1990.

4

---❀❀❀---

Women and Travel

As one historian has observed, "Late-eighteenth-century America was a society in constant motion."[1] Women, as well as men, moved about for many reasons. They went on short or long visits to see family and friends. They moved because of marriage or widowhood and for other family reasons, such as to make weaning a baby easier. They moved to find work. The women of some Native American tribes moved from place to place to forage or to plant crops, depending on the season. Enslaved African women moved when they were sold to new owners. Other women left their homes in other countries and traveled across the Atlantic Ocean as they sought refuge from persecution or better economic opportunities. Some women were displaced by war and forced to move because their homes were destroyed. Whatever the reason, their gender and status shaped and affected the way in which women experienced travel.

In June 1787, Sarah (Sally) Hemings arrived in London. The fourteen-year-old Sally traveled there as a companion to nine-year-old Polly Jefferson, who was to join her father Thomas in Paris. For Sally, who had never before left Virginia, the voyage across the ocean to London and then to Paris was an adventure that she never forgot. As a young enslaved woman, she was not asked whether she wanted to go, but because she traveled as young Polly's playmate, she was probably treated well. Because she was a child, Polly also had no choice in deciding whether to go on this voyage or not; she had to obey her father.[2]

The journey to Europe changed the lives of both Sally and Polly. In Paris, Polly lived at and attended a Catholic convent school with her sister Patsy. In December 1788, both Polly and Patsy contracted typhus. For several weeks, Polly was deaf and mentally impaired. According to comments made many years later by Patsy, the typhus may even have caused permanent damage to Polly's brain. Sally, however, was sent away from the contagion. While in Paris, she saw and experienced life in a cosmopolitan city that was vastly different from the provincial world of rural Virginia. There, too, she most likely became the mistress of Thomas Jefferson, her master and the future president of the United States.[3]

Sally and Polly's voyage on the ship, the *Robert*, took about five weeks. The length of time it took to cross the Atlantic Ocean depended on several factors, most notably the wind and the weather. Johann Christoph Sauer, who emigrated from Germany in 1724 with his wife and young son, noted this in the description he wrote of their journey: "During this voyage of 6 weeks and 3 days, we lacked only the necessary east wind, and were obliged to sail with nothing but tack and head-winds, and it was wonderful that the sailors knew so exactly in what part of the sea they were."

Even after crossing the ocean, however, dangers existed. As Johann Sauer's ship got close to the Delaware River, the ship repeatedly struck a sandbar.

> The captain cried aloud and grew quite pale. Because, however, all sails were still set, the wind lifted the ship from one hill to the other. Then they wished to cut the mast. The head helmsman wished to have the three boats lowered and the people taken ashore, for we were scarcely half a league away from it. The captain forbade it because he was afraid everybody might desire to be first and therefore they might get drowned sooner than in the ship. When this distress had lasted a quarter of an hour, we were in deep water again. Then we rode at anchor until daybreak and got a favorable wind.

After all this, the ship was still 100 miles "from the boundary of Pennsylvania." Fortunately, "instead of taking 8 to 10 days, as many do getting up the river, we with an extraordinarily good wind, arrived in Philadelphia Sunday noon, October first." Before the anchor was cast, the ship fired a gun salute. A crowd of people rushed to the dock to greet the new arrivals.[4]

Many German-speaking immigrants first settled in the area near Philadelphia and then migrated to the interior. For example, the Lutheran pastor Henry Melchior Muhlenberg noted that within the first five years of his ministry in Providence (Trappe), Pennsylvania, half of his congregation had moved to the frontier. German migrants frequently used the Philadelphia Wagon Road that went west to Lancaster. From there, they took Harris's Ferry over the Susquehanna River to York and then took Williams's Ferry across the Potomac River to the Shenandoah Valley. After that, they followed an Indian Trail, the "Valley Pike." By 1776, "approximately 20,000 to 25,000 German settlers lived among the Valley's approximately 50,000 residents." The rest of the white population was composed mainly of Scots-Irish and English.[5]

Gottlieb Mittleberger was another German immigrant who authored an account of a voyage to Pennsylvania. He was a "music master" who brought an organ from Germany to Pennsylvania in 1750, and he traveled aboard the

Osgood with 500 other German passengers. In his account, he explained that for many immigrants the journey to American soil was often preceded by several months of travel within Europe. According to his narrative, many of the Germans with whom he traveled had begun their journey by first sailing to Holland. This trip often took several weeks because the passengers were forced to stop at numerous customhouses. In the Netherlands, they frequently endured a long wait for a ship leaving from Rotterdam or Amsterdam. After that, there was a journey of anywhere from a week to a month, depending on the wind and the weather, to get to England. Finally, the immigrants sailed for America.[6]

Gottlieb Mittleberger's account highlights the misery and dangers of travel. He discusses the bad and inadequate food; the illnesses that could rage aboard a ship, bad weather, foul conditions, the agony and despair of the passengers, and the deaths of loved ones. For women there were additional risks, because some had to endure pregnancy or childbirth while at sea. Gottlieb mentions that on his journey a woman went into labor during a storm. Unable to give birth, she was pushed through a porthole into the ocean.[7]

Certainly not all sea voyages were as unpleasant or gruesome as the one Gottlieb Mittleberger described. Yet, there was always a threat of danger. Elizabeth Drinker recorded in her diary an event that occurred in December 1797. The *John,* a ship carrying German redemptioners, was caught in the ice in the Delaware River and was wrecked on the shoals. (Redemptioners were people who arrived without a contract. They were given a particular length of time to raise the money they owed for their passage. If they could not raise it, they negotiated the service contracts for themselves or family members.) The captain of the ship had been told to contact Henry Drinker, Elizabeth's husband, in an emergency. Henry Drinker brought others to assist the ship and its passengers, but the rescue took several days, although the captain sent the elderly men, the women, and children off on "the long boat."[8]

Even without bad weather and other disasters, sea voyages were long and uncomfortable, whether the passengers were poor servants or well-to-do travelers. When Abigail Adams traveled to London in 1784 to meet her husband, John, who was at the Hague, she wrote him that all but the captain and "dr [Clark] who had frequently been to sea before, were the only persons who were not sea sick." Then she continued her letter and wrote:

> How often did I reflect during my voyage upon what I once heard you say, that no object in Nature was more dissagreeable than a Lady at sea. It realy reconciled me to the thought of being without you, for heaven be my witness, in no situation would I be willing to appear thus to you. I will add an observation of my own, that I think no inducement less that that of comeing to the tenderest of Friends could ever prevail with me to cross the ocean, nor do I ever wish to try it but once more.[9]

For those who were brought in bondage, the journey across the ocean was much worse than anything Abigail Adams experienced. In the eighteenth century, British ships transported 45,000 African slaves per year.[10] Between 1725 and 1775, more than 58,918 Africans were brought to Virginia. Far more were carried to Britain's profitable island colonies to toil on the sugar plantations, where they experienced what "was literally a killing work regime."[11] In the first half of the eighteenth century, slave traders brought fewer women than men to the British colonies, because women could be sold for a higher price within Africa, whereas men brought higher prices in the transatlantic slave trade.[12]

The first part of the journey to enslavement began with the kidnapping of potential slaves by African traders. Men, women, and children were abducted or taken as prisoners during wars and raids and forced to march in shackles from interior locations to forts along the coast. Most women who crossed the Atlantic as slaves did so from the Bight of Biafra on the west coast of Africa. Then they had to endure the infamous Middle Passage, the transport of slaves across the Atlantic. This trip usually took two to three months, but it could take as long as four months. It has been noted that "the slave trade on average recorded about 60 deaths per month per thousand people shipped. This rate was four times greater than that among German emigrants to Philadelphia in the eighteenth century."[13] On these voyages, men, women, and children, who were often already weak from the forced march to the coast, were usually packed tightly in underground holds, chained together, and often forced to lie in the feces and urine of those next to them. Women were sometimes permitted to remain on an upper deck, and sometimes they were left unchained. However, they were then more at risk of being sexually abused by the ship's crew. This is the type of experience Sally Hemings's African grandmother most likely had on her way to Virginia.[14]

Some English women were forced into involuntary servitude by circumstances, although they were not slaves for life and their slave status was not passed to their children. In 1718, the English Parliament passed the Transportation Act, which made possible the deportation of convicts. If a convict agreed to be transported, his or her death sentence was overturned. Some preferred death to bondage. Transported convicts usually served terms ranging from seven to fourteen years, longer than that of most indentured servants. About one-fifth of the convicts shipped to America were women. They were cheaper than indentured servants, but they were frequently humiliated and treated unkindly. Unlike those women serving "regular" terms of indenture, many convict women felt stigmatized. One female convict servant thought, "many Negroes are better used." Thus, many transported convicts recrossed the Atlantic Ocean and returned to England after they had served their terms in North America.[15]

In contrast, indentured servants deliberately chose to go to the colonies, and they generally arrived with the expectation that their lives would be better than they had been in Ireland, England, or Germany. In the eighteenth century, indentured servants became less important in the southern slaveholding states, but in places such as Philadelphia, where there was a need for laborers, indentured male laborers were in demand. For most of the eighteenth century, the majority of indentured servants were men, but the percentage of female servants began to rise just before the American Revolution. This coincided with a demand for domestic labor, although most domestic servants were from Philadelphia or its environs and were not bound servants. When possible, masters usually preferred to hire servants rather than to purchase the time and be bound by a contract for an indentured servant.[16]

In the mid-eighteenth century, merchants began to instruct ship captains and agents working for them in England to refrain from sending female servants. The merchant Thomas Willing, who was later mayor of Philadelphia, wrote to his agents in 1754 and told them, "the servants should not be above 30 or less than 16 years old and no women." Another Philadelphia merchant, Benjamin Marshal, told his agent in 1764 that "the less women the better as they are very troublesome."[17]

Some indentured women arrived alone, separated from their friends, families, and communities; others came with a husband or other family members. Yet sometimes spouses were sold to different owners, forcing husband and wife to live separately once they reached America. This is what happened when Eleanor Bradley, her husband Roger, and their children arrived in Pennsylvania. Roger and the couple's daughters worked for Randolph Blackshaw, a Bucks County, Pennsylvania, yeoman; a different owner in Maryland had purchased Eleanor and their three sons. Roger probably moved to Maryland to be reunited with his wife and sons, after he served the term of his indenture. A 1765 Pennsylvania statute, however, prohibited the separation of servants who were already married.[18]

Once purchased, a servant became the legal property of an owner until his or her term of indenture had been completed. Servants were not permitted to marry unless their owners had given consent. Although female servants in Philadelphia normally performed household duties, such as cooking, caring for children, and cleaning, they were often given the most disagreeable chores to do, and they were expected to be available at all times. During the cold winter months, for instance, servants usually arose before the family members to get the fires started and breakfast prepared.[19] (For more on work, see Chapter 3.)

Some servants continued to travel—voluntarily and involuntarily—even after they were purchased. For one thing, an owner could sell a bound servant to another person, forcing the servant to change households and sometimes moving a distance. Carolina Bosinger was a thirty-year-old Dutch servant. She decided to run away after a fifth owner purchased her. Some women ran away, however, after being abused by only one master. Other women ran away to join husbands or lovers. Mary Musgrove supposedly ran away because she was "remarkable fond of a sweetheart." Many female servants ran away because they were pregnant. If caught, the court extended a pregnant servant's term of indenture to compensate her owner for expenses incurred during her pregnancy, labor, and nursing. The infant might also be bound to serve the master. Servants who were not pregnant but who ran away also had to make up their time if they were caught. Under Pennsylvania law, a runaway servant had to work five days for every day missed, as well as pay back expenses the master incurred in trying to capture the servant. This compensation was usually paid with additional labor, because servants rarely had money.[20]

Pregnant servants in Virginia sometimes ran away in order to avoid a court appearance. If her case was brought before the court several times but the woman did not appear, the case might be dropped. It might have been easier for women to disappear in the eighteenth century than it was in the seventeenth, because both the settlements and the population were larger in the eighteenth century. Thus, a pregnant servant might hope to blend into the crowd after concocting a plausible story. Yet, in the eighteenth century, there were more incentives for capturing and returning servants to their masters. Based on the examination of hundreds of cases in Virginia, one scholar notes "in most county courts after 1700, claims for rewards for servants returned to masters ten to fifteen miles away bespoke the existence of an increasingly vigilant population eager to receive monetary compensation for policing the laborers of other individuals."[21]

In the decades preceding the American Revolution, thousands of immigrants arrived in the British North American colonies. Most of them came from the British Isles, Germany, and Switzerland, but immigrants also arrived from Italy, France, Greece, and the Caribbean. Unlike African women, who were separated from their families and friends as well as their homes and culture, most white immigrant women arrived in family groups. Traveling with other women made conditions easier for women who were pregnant or nursing or who had young children.

Married couples did not always immigrate together. Yet the distance could pose a problem, because it took time for letters to cross the Atlantic. Sometimes circumstances mentioned in a letter had changed by the time the recipient read and replied to the communication. In July 1740, the wife of Alexander Gilbert arrived in Maryland from Scotland. As she wrote in the advertisement she placed in *The Pennsylvania Gazette,* she believed from "several letters from her said Husband dated 1734, 1736, and 1737, that he lodged at one John Van Beskerk's in Philadelphia County in the Manner of Moreland." She added that her husband had asked her to come, and it was noted that "This is therefore to inform him that she is to be found at Madam Hawkin's in Queen Anne's County Maryland, where she has at her own Disposal, Money and several Chests of Goods, and other things of Value."[22]

Often families and individuals settled near people with similar backgrounds. For example, many Welsh Quakers settled in the fertile area around Philadelphia. Yet Quakers, like other immigrant groups, continued to migrate as land became more difficult to obtain. By the 1750s, Quaker out-migration had already begun. Women as well as men moved to find better opportunities. Quakers moved south first from Pennsylvania, generally to North Carolina, but by the end of the century they were moving west to Ohio.[23]

Immigrants commonly endured a "seasoning" period. This was particularly true in the Chesapeake, where malaria and other diseases often debilitated new arrivals and could prove fatal to pregnant women. Mortality rates were often higher for immigrants than for native-born residents. In addition to potential illnesses, immigrants had to adjust to a new climate and setting, probably learn new customs, eat new or unfamiliar foods, and perhaps learn to communicate in a new language.

Women immigrated for a variety of reasons. As well as arriving as servants, women and their families left their homelands to flee political or religious persecution. For example, French Protestants, known as Huguenots, began to leave France after the Catholic King Louis XIV revoked the Edict of Nantes in 1685. The revocation made Protestantism illegal in France and closed churches and schools. Thousands of Protestants fled France and settled in the American colonies or elsewhere in Europe. Barbara de Bonnett Dutoy, her sister, and parents were Huguenots who narrowly escaped with their lives. Her parents hid Barbara and her sister in saddlebags. As they attempted to cross the French border, a soldier plunged his sword into the bags and wounded one of the girls. Yet the family managed to complete their journey to America. The de Bonnett family was part of an organized French Huguenot expedition to Virginia. The English crown was willing and eager to take in Protestant settlers as a strike against Catholic France, and it granted land to them in the colonies.[24]

Other religious refugees also journeyed to the American colonies in the eighteenth century. In the 1740s, groups of German Pietists, including Moravians and other groups, settled in several communities in British North America. There were large Moravian communities in North Carolina and Pennsylvania. After Moravian men prepared the way, Moravian families and single women immigrated to live in the communities. Many other German religious refugees traveled to the colonies in the first half of the eighteenth century. These groups included Lutherans, Mennonites, and German Baptists (Dunkards), among others. (For more on German religious denominations, see Chapter 6.)

The religious sect known as the Shakers was brought to America with the immigration of one woman. Ann Lee was the illiterate daughter of a blacksmith in Manchester, England. She became a member of a sect known as Shaking Quakers, but she was persecuted for her faith and imprisoned while in England. In 1771, she formed a group called the United Society of Believers in Christ's Second Appearing. The small sect became known as the Shakers because of their ecstatic dancing. In 1774, Ann Lee immigrated to America from England, along with her husband and eight followers. They settled near Albany, New York. Ann Lee believed that Christ had a dual male/female nature and that celibacy was necessary for salvation. Like Quakers and Moravians, Shakers attracted a large percentage of female followers. Although the group was small, it grew in the nineteenth century, and there is still one community remaining in the United States.[25] (For more on the Shakers, see Chapter 6.)

Unlike other churches of the time, Quakers accepted women ministers. Like their male counterparts, they were known as Public Friends. Quakers do not ordain ministers, but Public Friends received certificates and sat in a special area of the meetinghouse on raised chairs. Female ministers became public leaders within their meetings, and they traveled frequently, both long and short distances. Married female Quaker ministers were permitted to travel with men who were not their husbands, as well as with other female ministers. They traveled to England and throughout the colonies, sometime journeying great distances on horseback in order to preach. For example, it was noted that Ann Moore "logged over a thousand miles and ninety-one meetings in 1756."[26]

Economic opportunities and business concerns induced some women to travel. Esther Pinheiro became a merchant after the death of her husband, Isaac. The Pinheiros were Jews who lived on the Caribbean island of Nevis. Between 1720 and 1728, Esther co-owned four ships along with non-Jewish merchants in Boston and Nevis. She frequently visited the ports of Boston and New York, "becoming a well-known figure in both towns."[27]

Elizabeth Murray also traveled to oversee her business concerns. In fact, she crossed the Atlantic several times during her life. When she was twelve and newly orphaned, she left England with her brother to go to America but returned with him to England a few years later. In 1749, she was back in America and decided to remain in Boston and open a shop rather than live as a dependent in her brother's household in North Carolina. She sailed back to England in 1753 to oversee the purchasing of items for her shop in Boston. In 1769, she returned to England for a visit after the death of her second husband.[28]

Despite the seeming ease with which Esther Pinheiro and Elizabeth Murray traveled, many well-to-do women found that there were limits placed on how, where, and when they traveled. Elite women, particularly the wives and daughters of wealthy southern planters, had constraints placed on them because of their class and gender. Although they might have more leisure time available for travel, they needed to arrange trips around domestic concerns, and they needed suitable accommodations. Elite women rarely traveled alone. For a woman of any class to travel without male protection or the clear indication that she was the wife or daughter of a gentleman connoted that she was not respectable or, worse, that she was sexually available. Servants and enslaved women were particularly vulnerable to lewd remarks and sexual attacks when traveling alone.

Lucy Byrd, the wife of the wealthy Virginia planter William Byrd, apparently arranged her travel schedule around her husband's. After he left for a trip to Williamsburg, she felt free to visit friends or relatives, often arranging to meet her husband at some point along the way. When she remained at home, she often entertained friends and relatives. Elite women usually stayed in the homes of other elites when possible rather than risk encountering objectionable strangers in an inn or tavern.[29]

Well-to-do families sometimes had more than one residence, often a city residence and a country house. Elizabeth Murray and her third husband, Ralph Inman, owned two estates outside of Boston, as well as a residence within the city. During the early part of the Revolutionary War, Elizabeth, who supported the American side, tried to protect her properties by spending her days at the Cambridge estate and sleeping at the other one, called Brush Hill. Ralph, who was a British supporter, stayed in Boston with the English.[30] (For more on women and war, see Chapter 5.)

Eliza Lucas also traveled as a young woman. Born in the West Indies and educated in England for a few years, she lived on the island of Antigua until her father moved the family to South Carolina, where he owned three plantations. When she married Charles Pinckney in 1744, he built her a mansion in Charleston that overlooked the harbor. She spent a great deal of time there and at their Belmont plantation. They owned several other properties as well. The couple and their children also traveled to England and spent nearly five years there. Their two sons remained in school there after Eliza, Charles, and their daughter Harriott returned to South Carolina. When Charles died of malaria in 1758, shortly after their return from England, Eliza was left in charge of three properties in Charleston and six plantations scattered throughout South Carolina.[31]

The Quaker Elizabeth Drinker and her family also owned more than one house. They, like many other wealthy Philadelphians, attempted to escape the steamy Philadelphia summers. They had a summer house just outside the city in Frankford, and, in the 1790s, they also owned a farm called Clearfield. Moreover, the family used four conveyances for their travels—a cart, a wagon, a chaise, and a carriage. While in the city, however, they often went by foot on visits to family members and friends.[32]

The wives of less wealthy and prominent men did not have the same social constraints placed upon them, but they had less money and time to spend upon travel. Nevertheless, they did visit family and friends, although in general they did not travel as far as elite woman did on visits. During visits to neighbors, women traded both gossip and items they had produced in their own households. At night, women sometimes gathered together to socialize in homes or informal taverns. In at least one instance this nighttime socializing led to playing pranks. In 1722, a group of Virginia women came before the court for scaring unsuspecting people as they passed by in the darkness. As a one scholar has observed, this prank inverted the more typical situation of women being terrorized at night.[33]

The lives of the laboring poor in both urban and rural areas often involved a great deal of travel in order to find work. Hannah Freeman, "the last identified Lenape in Chester County, Pennsylvania," moved throughout her lifetime. As a young child, she and her family followed traditional practices and moved from their cabin, built on the land of William Webb in Kennett, Pennsylvania, to

Newlin each summer to plant corn. Then "the Indian were not allowed to Plant Corn any longer." Hannah's father moved west to live with other Indians. Later, Hannah lived with Indians in New Jersey, but she returned to Pennsylvania a few years later. After her grandmother and mother died, Hannah lived in various households. According to her poorhouse examination, she

> lived a little while at Swithin Chandler's (may be two months) then went to White Thos Chandler's in N. Castle County where she lived about two years worked at Sewing &c. and received 3/6 per week wages. From there to Black Thos Chandler's where she staid about three Years Sewing &c. and recd wages or Sheets for her work. She then went again to Swithin Chandler's for a few weeks & recd 3/6 per week wages she worked a few weeks in some other places . . . then went to her Aunt Nanny at Concord but having almost forgot to talk Indian and not liking their manner of living so well as white peoples She came to Wm. Webbs worked for her board and sometimes but got no money except for baskets, besoms &c.[34]

After that, she lived in various places, but never for long, and, by then, her age and declining health meant she was unable to support herself. Friends and neighbors supported her until the new Chester County Poorhouse was completed in 1800. Her examination by authorities was to assure them that she was a legal resident of the county and entitled to its services. Hannah Freeman died in the poorhouse in 1802.[35]

The settlements of white farmers in what had been Lenape territory disrupted the tribe's traditional way of life. Yet, despite her background, Hannah Freeman's experience was not much different from that of poor white women in Chester County, Pennsylvania. In the eighteenth century, as the number of slaves and indentured servants decreased in Pennsylvania, young native-born white women took their place. It has been noted that "they were probably a very mobile group, moving from farm to farm and township to township, never settling permanently because they owned no land." Alice Clark came to the attention of the trustees of the poor because she had given birth to two illegitimate children and her family could not care for them. Her father, Joseph Clark, revealed to the trustees that he had worked on various farms for his entire life. Sometimes he paid rent, and sometimes he worked for shares. Alice and her mother would have followed him to the farms and worked as well. Many such families took to the road on April 1 in search of better opportunities. One Chester County man observed that April 1, 1793 "was remarkably favorable for Flitting families" and remarked on the number of wagons that passed through West Chester.[36]

How people traveled depended on their wealth and position. For wealthy Virginia planters, the method of travel was a reflection of their status and demonstrated their gentility to those around them. Elite planters, for example, kept fine horses and bought expensive coaches. Although young men from gentry families often traveled by horseback, the women of these families rode sidesaddle for short distances but used a carriage to travel farther. Wealthy planters ordered elaborate coaches from England or refurbished older ones in order to present themselves as English gentlemen.[37]

New Englanders also owned and used carriages and other vehicles to display their wealth and status. For example, when the well-to-do women of the eighteenth-century Connecticut River Valley got together for quilting parties, those who could do so chose to arrive in a conveyance of some sort. Although traveling by carriage permitted women to journey farther away from their homes and kept them from arriving dusty, dirty, or wet, using a carriage was also a conspicuous display of wealth. When Elizabeth Porter was a child, her family was one of the few in Hadley, Massachusetts, that owned a carriage. Toward the end of the century, however, most of the families in her social circle owned carriages, chaises, or riding chairs. When she and Charles Phelps became engaged, he bought a new carriage in Boston. By 1795, the couple owned several vehicles and housed them in a shelter built for that purpose. Looking back decades later, William Shipman bemoaned the new standards of gentility that arose toward the latter part of the eighteenth century, as he remembered the women of childhood who "mounted and dismounted" horses without assistance "every hour of the day."[38]

Visiting was an important duty for women of Elizabeth Porter Phelps's social circle. She sometimes entertained 200 people in a single year. Social calls, however, were reciprocal. Women kept track and noticed those who were remiss in making calls and in extending hospitality to others. One August, Elizabeth admitted in a letter to her daughter that there had "not been any women to see her" recently. She reported, with some embarrassment, that her husband, Charles, understood why. It was because "I owe visits to all." Although such visits were sometimes "drudgery," they "carried an exchange value less tangible than that of goods or labor but no less significant," because women shared gossip, tea, and cakes but also displayed fine china, tea tables, and other elements that defined their class and status. These visits were "fundamentally public encounters that occurred in traditionally private spaces."[39]

Less formal visits also took place between neighbors. Women frequently brought sewing or knitting with them on such casual visits. Usually, these were small projects that could be completed within a few hours. For those who lived in rural areas, there was less time to drop in on neighbors in the summer and fall, when farm work and harvests required so much time. Nevertheless, they did get together in various planned frolics, or work parties. As discussed in previous chapters, such parties included corn husking, quilting, spinning, and barn raisings and were occasions when young men and women could be together and court.[40]

Women with babies and young children often found it difficult to go out and about, especially if the weather was especially bad. It appears that pregnant women did not necessarily refrain from traveling, except during the last two months of pregnancy. For example, when she was five months pregnant with her tenth child, Elizabeth Patten of Bedford, New Hampshire, journeyed more than eighty miles to Boston. She went by herself on horseback to sell cloth and thread. Usually, her husband, Matthew, made the trip, but he was busy taking care of the harvest.[41]

Breastfeeding, however, did restrict women's travel. Women who were nursing infants could not travel without them, but, unless necessary, they also did not want to subject their babies to adverse conditions. Infants who were older than a few months made traveling even more difficult, because they were more active. Yet, when their babies became about one year old, many women began to travel. It is possible that this was done in many cases in order to wean or assist in weaning their babies from their breasts. The Reverend Joseph Green of Salem Village, Massachusetts (now Danvers), recorded such an event in his diary on April 12, 1702. He took his wife, Elizabeth, to her parents' home, and then he "came home to wean John," their seventeen-month-old son.[42]

Childcare and household responsibilities limited the amount of traveling that female Quaker ministers could do. In 1790, Elizabeth Collins wrote, "It was no small trial to leave home at this time, having several children, but was favoured to get where I could leave them to the care of Him, who is the great care-taker of his people." Those who did leave their young children to travel and preach often had mothers or other female relatives who cared for them while the mother was away. Delays and problems with communication added to the distress of those who were parted from their families.[43]

As well as nursing, health, money, and family responsibilities, weather placed restrictions on women's travel. Yet people often had more time for visiting during the winter months, when farm duties were lighter. In the north, snow-covered roads were ideal for sleigh rides. Sometimes people traveled by sleigh on visits to friends five to ten miles away, returning the same night. Occasionally, couples bundled up their children in a sleigh and ventured out as a family. There were also large sleighing parties, in which young people of both sexes went out, often stopping at a tavern for drinking and sometimes dancing.[44]

Within the cities of British North America, it was not simply inclement weather that caused problems for those traveling by foot or by carriage. Filthy streets were a major problem. In New York City, the council passed numerous laws over a period of time in the eighteenth century prohibiting people from dumping garbage and waste onto the streets. The laws, however, had little effect on keeping the streets clean. The streets of Philadelphia were just as bad as those of New York. When he traveled through Philadelphia in 1744, the Maryland physician Alexander Hamilton reported that the streets were "unpaved, and therefor full of rubbish and mire." Benjamin Franklin managed to convince the Assembly to pave the streets of the city, but they continued to be noticeably dirty and filled with filth. Elizabeth Drinker, for example, noted in her diary on January 20, 1760 that she did not attend meeting because it was very dark and "the Streets dirty." On a cold, dark winter night, it would be particularly unpleasant to step into some unseen filth in the street. In 1783, *The Pennsylvania Gazette* was still commenting on the state of the city's streets when it joked, "dead dogs, cats, fowls, and the offals of the market, are among the cleanest articles" found in the streets. Elizabeth Drinker and other residents were probably used to seeing animals roam in the street. In 1805, she did not comment on the fact that pigs or other animals wandered about, but she did note the horrific torture that had been done to a pig her grandson saw as he walked to his aunt's house.[45]

Broken wagons or balking horses could also hinder travel. Elizabeth Drinker reported that, on June 13, 1772, she had "set of in the Waggon for Frankford, but could not get the Horses' cross Race Street corner, they run back and behav'd so ill that we were oblig'd to get out and stay at home." Presumably the horse cooperated later in the month, when Elizabeth and various family members set off on a five-day journey in their chaise. The trip had many stops, including a visit to taste some mineral waters where a bath had been constructed. They continued on, taking a ferry to New Jersey. Once back in Pennsylvania, they stopped at their lodging, but "our Chaise being left at the Door without securing the Horse, he set off with one of SHs. Sons in the Chaise, and soon after was over set on the side of a Hill, without hurt to the Boy, and no great damage to the Carrage."[46]

Despite the discomfort and occasional unpleasantness, some travel was necessary. For example, after marrying, most couples moved to a new home. In some cases, the couple shared quarters with one set of parents. In other instances, they moved into their own home, sometimes nearby but sometimes some distance away. When Esther Edwards accepted Aaron Burr's sudden marriage proposal, she quickly moved from Massachusetts to Newark, New Jersey, where Aaron was pastor of the Newark Presbyterian church and president of the College of New Jersey. The wedding was held in Newark, and her mother was the only member of her family who attended the ceremony.[47]

Not all marriages were happy, however, and sometimes one spouse chose to run away. In an advertisement he placed in *The Pennsylvania Gazette* in January 1779, Henry Haas reported that his wife Ann Mary "in the night of the 17th of December last did elope from him the ninth time, and has since contracted debts on him." This marriage seemed particularly troubled, and Henry, in a reversal of his wedding vows, stated that Ann Mary was "fond of strong liquor, and he will not take her into his house in sickness or health."[48]

Some women, however, did not run away but chose not to follow their husbands. In 1754, the Christian Mahican Abraham decided political alliances between the Mahican and the Six Nations required him to move his family from the safety of Gnadenhütten, the mission town, to the Wyoming Valley, along the Susquehanna River in Pennsylvania. His son Jonathan decided that he also needed to move. Jonathan's wife Anna did not believe it was safe to leave the security of the mission town. When Jonathan left, she remained behind with their young children. The following year she wrote to the Moravians, telling them that the move to the Wyoming Valley "will go badly for me and my children. We would suffer hunger there. I wouldn't have what I have here; that distresses me."[49]

The demand for land pushed white settlers into frontier areas. The constant westward movement forced Native Americans to move, too, or to adjust their lifestyles to changes in their environment as colonists built homes and towns. Throughout much of the eighteenth century, there was conflict between Native Americans and white settlers in frontier areas. The conflict was compounded by often-fragile alliances made between various tribes and the English or the French. Thus, Indians, settlers, soldiers, missionaries, and traders were all moving about in frontier areas as situations and alliances changed. In what is now New England, New York, Pennsylvania, and Canada, war was almost a constant condition, from the Pequot War in 1636–1637 until the Seven Years War/French and Indian War of 1756–1763. Wars continued well into the nineteenth century, however, as English, French, Spanish, and Indians competed for territories in the Ohio and Mississippi Valleys and later in Texas and the western United States. (For more on women and war, see Chapter 5.)

During raids on English villages, Native Americans often took captives. (Whites took Native Americans as captives, too.) One such episode occurred in Deerfield, Massachusetts, on February 29, 1704, when a group of Native Americans, consisting of Wôbanakiak, Kanienkehaka (Mohawk), Wendat (Huron), plus French soldiers and canadiens (men of French ancestry born in Canada), attacked the settlement shortly before dawn. During the attack, the Native Americans took captives and afterward began marching them to Canada. Although the route was familiar to the Native Americans, it was totally unknown to their prisoners. As the Reverend John Williams later wrote, they were "carried away from God's sanctuary" on a journey of "at least three hundred miles," and "we never inured to such hardships and fatigues."[50]

As minister of Deerfield, John Williams was probably the town's most prominent citizen. His background was impressive, but his wife's was even more so. Eunice Mather Williams was the daughter of Eleazar Mather, pastor of Northampton, Massachusetts, niece of Increase Mather, and stepdaughter of Solomon Stoddard, who became the minister in Northampton after her father's death. John Williams may have been singled out as a captive during the raid. It is possible that the French wanted to exchange him for an important prisoner held by the English.[51] Eventually, the Reverend Williams was ransomed and returned to his pulpit in Deerfield.

Several members of the Williams's family were also captured in the early morning raid. His wife, Eunice Mather Williams, was one of them. She had given birth to their daughter Jerusha only six weeks before the raid, and she had not yet regained her strength. During the attack, the Indians killed Jerusha, the Williams's six-year-old son John, and their slave Parthena. Parthena's body was found in the doorway of the home. It is not known if she was killed because of her color or because she resisted capture. The other children, Samuel, Esther, Stephen, Warham, and Eunice, were taken prisoner.

As they marched through snow and ice in frigid temperatures, the captives were weak, hungry, and cold. During the long march, Indians carried Warham and Eunice. Mrs. Williams, however, struggled to keep up. On the second day of the march, Mrs. Williams fell into a river. She pulled herself to the riverbank, but she was unable to continue the journey. An Indian killed her when it became clear that she could not walk. Although it seems cruel, the Native Americans were being practical. They were unable to carry her, their own wounded, and some of the captive children. Therefore, they could either leave her to die slowly and painfully, or they could kill her quickly.[52]

Of the 112 Deerfield captives, "twenty die along the way, ninety-two reach Canada; the rate of survival for the group as a whole is a little better than four in five." Yet survival was also linked to gender and age. Infants generally were killed. Children between ages three and twelve mostly survived because they could be carried if they could not keep up on the march. All twenty-one teenagers survived. Adult women fared the worst: ten died on the route and six-teen survived. Of the adult men, four died and twenty-two survived. As one his-torian has stated, "If you are living at Deerfield in 1704, and if capture is your fate, it's better by far to be a grown man than a woman, and best of all to be a teenager."[53]

A party from Deerfield discovered Eunice Mather Williams's body and buried her in Deerfield. Over 100 years later, a group of Wôbanakiak stopped at her grave site. They were her descendants from her daughter Eunice, who had remained with the Indians, married a Kanienkehaka man, and had three children with him.[54] (For more on captivity, see Chapter 5.)

Deerfield endured other raids. In 1746, the French-allied Abenaki attacked the town and killed five people. Lucy Terry Prince, an enslaved woman owned by Ebenezer Wells, wrote a poem describing the event. The Abenaki warriors did not capture Lucy during this raid, but she knew what it was like to be taken cap-tive. She had been captured in Africa by slavers when she was an infant or young child. She was taken to Bristol, Rhode Island, and, eventually, Ebenezer Wells purchased her when she was about four years old. Thus, by the time of the raid on Deerfield, she had already traveled great distances. In 1756, she married Abijah Prince, a free black man. He was a prosperous man who may have bought her freedom, or Ebenezer Wells may have freed her. A few years later, the couple and their children moved to Guilford, Vermont. (For more on Lucy Terry Prince and her poem, "Bars Fight," see Chapter 7.)

Wars, particularly the French and Indian War and the Revolutionary War, dis-rupted the lives of many women. Eighteenth-century war and its impact on women are discussed in greater detail in the next chapter, but it should be noted here how war caused or motivated women to travel. For example, Ann Eliza Bleecker, whose writings were published after her death, lived in Tomhanick,

New York, about eighteen miles north of Albany. Ann was born and grew up in New York City, the daughter of a prosperous merchant. She moved to the isolated rural estate in Tomhanick after she married John J. Bleecker when she was seventeen. Life in Tomhanick was quite different from the life she had led in the city. In the summer of 1777, Ann and her family had to flee from the approaching British troops under the command of General John Burgoyne. During their flight to safety, her infant daughter Abella died of dysentery. Ann's mother, who had joined them on the journey, also died. As they traveled back to Tomhanick, Ann's sister, Caty Swits, traveled with them, but she died, too. Ann never recovered from the trauma of 1777, and she suffered bouts of depression. She died in 1783. Her surviving daughter, Margaretta, later published her writings, including a novel, called *Maria Kittle,* about a woman held captive by Indians.[55]

In contrast to Ann Eliza Bleecker and others who ran from the British troops, many slaves fled *to* the British during the Revolutionary War because the British commanders offered them freedom, excluding those belonging to Loyalists. Many of those slaves who ran to the British were women with children. Fifty-three slaves ran away from the South Carolina plantations of John Ball in 1780. Eighteen of them were women, and eight had children with them. One fifteen-member group, referred to by John Ball as "Pino's gang," escaped on Ball's flatboat. The group consisted of Pino and his wife, along with members of their extended family, including daughters, their spouses, and grandchildren. The British commander in New York City, Sir Guy Carleton, ordered a record made of each slave who sought freedom with them as the British troops evacuated. Because the preliminary peace terms agreed upon in November 1782 required the British to return slaves, only those who sought freedom before that time were permitted to leave with the British. These records, however, reveal that large numbers of women with children were able to escape to join the British.[56]

The continuous wars and conflicts of the eighteenth century affected women of all races and class. Both Loyalist women and patriot women became refugees when their homes were destroyed or occupied by soldiers. Native American women were caught in the middle of these wars. During the French and Indian War, the number of Native American casualties devastated a number of tribes. This led to new forms of diplomacy that limited the role of women. During the American Revolution, the Iroquois were involved in a civil war, as well as caught in the contest between England, the newly formed United States, and other European powers. In Kentucky and Ohio, as settlers encroached on the land of the Shawnee and Creek, the fighting was particularly brutal. In all of these conflicts, Native American women, white women, and even some enslaved black women were killed or taken captive. Although movement to the West brought some white families cheaper and more "available" land, it displaced Native American women, and it split and uprooted the families of African American women, as slaves were bought, sold, and brought to Western venues.[57]

NOTES

1. Joan R. Gunderson, *To Be Useful to the World: Women in Revolutionary America, 1740–1790*, rev. ed., (Chapel Hill: University of North Carolina Press, 2006), 17.

2. Annette Gordon-Reed, *The Hemingses of Monticello: An American Family* (New York: Norton, 2008), 49, 50, 193–194.

3. Gordon-Reed, *The Hemingses of Monticello*, 245–248, 264.

4. R. W. Kelsey, "Letter of Christopher Sower, Written in 1724, Describing Conditions in Philadelphia and Vicinity, and the Sea Voyage from Europe," *Pennsylvania Magazine of History and Biography* 45 (1921), 243–254.

5. John B. Franze, "The Religious Development of the Early German Settlers in 'Greater Pennsylvania': The Shenandoah Valley of Virginia," *Pennsylvania History* 68 (Winter 2001): 73–75.

6. "Gottlieb Mittelberger's Journey to Pennsylvania, 1754," Exploring Diversity in Pennsylvania History, Historical Society of Pennsylvania, www.hsp.org.

7. Mittleberger, "Journey to Pennsylvania," 4.

8. December 25, 1797, December 28, 1797, December 29, 1797, December 30, 1797, Elaine Forman Crane, ed. *The Diary of Elizabeth Drinker* (Boston: Northeastern University Press, 1991), 988–990.

9. Abigail Adams to John Adams, July 23, 1784, in Margaret A. Hogan and C. James Taylor, eds., *My Dearest Friend: Letters of Abigail and John Adams* (Cambridge, MA: Belknap Press, 2007), 305–307.

10. "Africans in America," www.pbs.org/wgbh/aia/part1/map1.html.

11. Philip D. Morgan, "Slaves and Poverty," in *Down and Out in Early America*, Billy G. Smith, ed. (University Park: Pennsylvania State University Press, 2004), 104.

12. Gunderson, *To Be Useful to the World*, 24; G. Ugo Nwokeji, "African Conceptions of Gender and the Slave Traffic," *William and Mary Quarterly*, LVIII (January 2001), 48–49.

13. Morgan, "Slaves and Poverty," 103.

14. Nwokeji, "Gender and the Slave Trade," 49; The African Slave Trade and the Middle Passage, Africans in America, http://www.pbs.org/wgbh/aia/part1/1narr4.html; Gunderson, *To Be Useful to the World*, 24; Gordon-Reed, *The Hemingses of Monticello*, 49, 50.

15. Morgan, "Slaves and Poverty," 102; Dorothy A. Mays, *Women in Early America: Struggle, Survival, and Freedom in a New World* (Santa Barbara, CA: ABC-CLIO, 2004), 198.

16. Sharon V. Salinger, "'Send No More Women': Female Servants in Eighteenth-Century Philadelphia," *Pennsylvania Magazine of History and Biography* CVII (January 1983), 30, 31, 32.

17. Quoted in Salinger, "Send No More Women," 32–33.

18. Salinger, "Send No More Women," 33–34, 38.

19. Salinger, "Send No More Women," 36–37.

20. Salinger, "Send No More Women," 38–40.

21. Kathleen M. Brown, *Good Wives, Nasty Wenches, and Anxious Patriarchs: Gender, Race, and Power in Colonial Virginia* (Chapel Hill: University of North Carolina Press, 1996), 203.

22. *The Pennsylvania Gazette*, July 31, 1740.

23. Joan M. Jensen, *Loosening the Bonds: Mid-Atlantic Farm Women, 1750–1850* (New Haven, CT: Yale University Press, 1986), 15.

24. For an online version of this document, see http://history.hanover.edu/texts/nonantes.html; Gunderson, *To Be Useful to the World*, 18.

25. Gunderson, *To Be Useful to the World*, 127–128; "About the Community, Sabbathday Lake Shaker Village," http://www.shaker.lib.me.us/about.html.

26. Jensen, *Loosening the Bonds*, 150, 151.

27. Eli Farber, *Jews, Slaves, and the Slave Trade: Setting the Record Straight* (New York: New York University Press, 1998), 102; Hasia R. Diner and Beryl Lieff Benderly, *Her Works Praise Her: A History of Jewish Women in America from Colonial Times to the Present* (New York: Basic Books, 2002), 49.

28. Elizabeth Murray Project, http://salticid.nmc.csulb.edu/cgi-bin/WebObjects/eMurray .woa/wa/select?page=homepage; Mary Beth Norton, *Liberty's Daughters: The Revolutionary Experience of American Women, 1750–1800*, with a new preface (Ithaca, NY: Cornell University Press, 1996), 147–151.

29. Brown, *Good Wives, Nasty Wenches*, 275.

30. Gunderson, *To Be Useful to the World*, 186.

31. Elise Pinckney, ed. *The Letterbook of Eliza Lucas Pinckney, 1739–1762* (Columbia: University of South Carolina Press, 1997), xxi–xxiii.

32. Crane, *Diary of Elizabeth Drinker*, xiii.

33. Brown, *Good Wives, Nasty Wenches*, 276.

34. "The Examination of Indian Hannah, alias Hannah Freeman (July 28, 1797)," edited and reproduced in Marshall J. Becker, "Hannah Freeman: An Eighteenth-Century Lenape Living and Working Among Colonial Farmers," *The Pennsylvania Magazine of History and Biography* (April 1990), 251–252.

35. Becker, "Hannah Freeman," 266–268.

36. Jensen, *Loosening the Bonds*, 42–43.

37. Brown, *Good Wives, Nasty Wenches*, 275.

38. Marla R. Miller, *The Needle's Eye: Women and Work in the Age of Revolution* (Amherst: University of Massachusetts Press, 2006), 105–106.

39. Miller, *The Needle's Eye*, 108, 109–110.

40. Jane C. Nylander, *Our Own Snug Fireside: Images of the New England Home, 1760–1860* (New Haven, CT: Yale University Press, 1994), 222–224; 225–227.

41. Laurel Thatcher Ulrich, *Good Wives: Image and Reality in the Lives of Women in Northern New England, 1650–1750* (New York: Oxford University Press, 1982), 140.

42. Ulrich, *Good Wives*, 141–142.

43. Quoted in Jensen, *Loosening the Bonds*, 158.

44. Nylander, *Our Own Snug Fireside*, 237.

45. Kathleen M. Brown, *Foul Bodies: Cleanliness in Early America* (New Haven, CT: Yale University Press, 2009), 124–125; Crane, *The Diary of Elizabeth Drinker*, vol. 1, 44, vol. 3, 1884.

46. Crane, *The Diary of Elizabeth Drinker*, vol. 1, 176–177.

47. Carol F. Karlsen and Laurie Crumpacker, eds., *The Journal of Esther Edwards Burr, 1754–1757* (New Haven, CT: Yale University Press, 1984), 13.

48. *The Pennsylvania Gazette*, January 1779.

49. Jane T. Merritt, "Cultural Encounters along a Gender Frontier: Mahican, Delaware, and German Women in Eighteenth-Century Pennsylvania," *Pennsylvania History* vol. 76, no. 4 (Autumn 2000): 528–529.

50. Quoted in John Demos, *The Unredeemed Captive: A Family Story from Early America* (New York: Vintage Books, 1994), 27. Information on the raid and the people involved can also be found on the Web site, "Raid on Deerfield: The Many Stories of 1704," http://1704.deerfield.history.museum/home.do.

51. Demos, *The Unredeemed Captive*, 16.

52. Demos, *The Unredeemed Captive*, 28–29. Also see the narrative on Eunice Mather Williams on the "Raid on Deerfield" Web site.

53. Demos, *The Unredeemed Captive*, 38–39.

54. Narrative on Eunice Mather Williams on the "Raid on Deerfield" Web site.

55. Alison Giffen, Frank Shuffelton, and Wendy Martin, "Ann Eliza Bleecker," The Textbook Site for *The Heath Anthology of American Literature*, 5th ed., http://college.cengage.com/english/lauter/heath/4e/students/author_pages/eighteenth/bleecker_an.html; Norton, *Liberty's Daughters*, 199.

56. Norton, *Liberty's Daughters*, 209–211.

57. Gunderson, *To Be Useful to the World*, 38, 39–40, 43.

SUGGESTED READING

Crane, Elaine Forman, ed. *The Diary of Elizabeth Drinker*. 3 vols. Boston: Northeastern University Press, 1991.

Demos, John. *The Unredeemed Captive: A Family Story from Early America*. New York: Vintage Books, 1994.

Gordon-Reed, Annette. *The Hemingses of Monticello: An American Family*. New York: Norton, 2008.

Gunderson, Joan R. *To Be Useful to the World: Women in Revolutionary America, 1740–1790*, rev. ed. Chapel Hill: University of North Carolina Press, 2006.

Karlsen, Carol F. and Laurie Crumpacker, eds. *The Journal of Esther Edwards Burr, 1754–1757*. New Haven, CT: Yale University Press. 1984

Miller, Marla R. *The Needle's Eye: Women and Work in the Age of Revolution*. Amherst: University of Massachusetts Press, 2006.

Smith, Billy G., ed. *Down and Out in Early America*. University Park: Pennsylvania State University Press, 2004.

Ulrich, Laurel Thatcher. *Good Wives: Image and Reality in the Lives of Women in Northern New England, 1650–1750*. New York: Oxford University Press, 1982.

5

⟨⟨⟨⟩⟩⟩

Women and War

For eighteenth-century American women, war was an all-too-common occurrence. Women of all races, classes, and backgrounds became caught up in both the small skirmishes along the frontier and the larger global wars. How often and to what extent each individual woman experienced war depended on many factors. There were women who were taken captive or raped; there were others who fought attackers, and there were even some who took part in attacks. There were women who actively protested and participated in boycotts, and there were women who ignored political events. Many women became refugees as a result of war; others learned that they were capable of managing homes, farms, and businesses while their husbands or fathers were away fighting.

Frontier regions were volatile areas that required little fuel in order to ignite. For white settlers, the threat of Indian attacks was a constant during much of the eighteenth century. The threat alone could disrupt the routine travel plans of people. In a letter to her closest friend, Sarah Prince of Massachusetts, Esther Edwards Burr wrote from New Jersey on July 17, 1755, about a planned visit to her family, "I am not so sertain about going to Stockbridge for the Indians have made thier appearrance near Stockbridge, and I dont like to be killed by the *barbarous* retches." The next day she wrote, "I think you may determine that I sha'n't go to Stockbridge this fall. The Indians are so thick about in the Woods there."[1] Although the decision not to make a trip to visit family or friends in frontier regions might appear to be a relatively minor manner, the risk of danger was real. Throughout much of the eighteenth century, people living in the borderlands in both the north and south frequently faced violent encounters with Indians and other Europeans.

For example, Eunice Mathers Williams, discussed in Chapter 4, was captured during the 1704 raid on Deerfield, Massachusetts. The raiders were Native Americans and their French allies. Eunice, who was still weak from having recently given birth, died during the march to Canada, but she had lived through previous Indian attacks. When she was eleven years old, Metacom's Rebellion (King Philip's War) began. In March 1676, Native American warriors got through the palisade that had been erected around the town of Northampton, Massachusetts, the frontier town in which she lived. They killed four men and one young girl. As a consequence of this war and subsequent unrest in the region, the threat of Indian attacks was always present during her teenage years.[2] Yet Eunice Mathers Williams's experience was not unusual. For those living in the New England borderlands— the areas being fought over by the English, French, and Native Americans—the threat of war was constant between 1676 and 1763. Warfare continued after this time, too, but the action moved further to the south and west.

Throughout the eighteenth century, various conflicts between European nations carried over to their colonies in America. The dispute over who should rule Spain began one such war. On November 1, 1700, King Charles II of Spain died. He had no heirs but had named Philippe of Anjou, grandson of Louis XIV of France, as his successor. Thus, the French Philippe became King Philip V of Spain. Because they were alarmed about the uniting of Spain and France, two powerful countries, King William III of England and the Holy Roman Emperor Leopold I formed a "Grand Alliance" to fight them. The ensuing war became known as the War of the Spanish Succession, and it lasted for ten years. When William died in 1702, his successor, Queen Anne, continued it.[3]

As a consequence, in 1703, while this war was still going on in Europe, French soldiers and "French Indian" warriors in Canada began attacks against English settlements in Maine. The English struck back. By the end of 1703, the French began planning an unusual winter attack on British settlements in Massachusetts. Their expedition included an assortment of Native American warriors from among tribes that were allied with the French. Many of the Indians allied with the French had been baptized by the Jesuit priests who came as missionaries to New France. The expedition that the French were planning became the raid on Deerfield, Massachusetts, in February 1704, during which Eunice Mathers Williams was taken captive and died. During this raid, her daughter Eunice and other family members were also captured. The younger Eunice, however, remained with the Indians; married a Native American man, and declined to return to her English family.[4]

That some captives chose to remain with their Native American captors or with the French in Canada was unsettling and fearful to the colonists of British North America, who believed that rejecting "civilized" society or even embracing Catholicism doomed these captives to a life of immorality and endangered their souls. When John Gyles and his mother were taken captive in Maine, he recalled her last words to him: "Oh! My dear Child! If it were God's will, I had rather follow you to your Grave! Or never see you more in this World, than you should be sold to a Jesuit."[5]

For Puritans in New England, settling the frontier was part of a divine mission to bring godliness and order to wild and savage regions. Every captive lost to the French or Indians was a lost soul, and the loss advanced the forces of British America's evil enemies. Thus, when Eunice Williams, the daughter of a prominent New England minister, was baptized a Catholic and elected to remain

The Indians Delivering up the English Captives to Colonel Bouquet. As part of the peace settlement during the French and Indian War, Native American tribes were forced to relinquish their captives. Some of the captives had lived with their Indian families for many years and did not want to leave them. Courtesy Library of Congress.

with the Indians, it was a particular blow to her family and New England society. Yet many captives, particularly young single women, remained in New
France (Canada). As one historian asserts, this "can be attributed to three factors:
the primacy of marriage, the influence of religion, and the supportive power of
female networks."[6]

It may have been easier for female captives to find husbands and marry in New
France, where many male settlers were looking for wives among the few
European women there. In New France, young women who had been captured
in New England were far away from their parents or guardians, who might have
objected to French or Indian suitors. As more English women assimilated into
the society and faith of New France, it became easier for others to follow.
Catholicism also gave some young women another life choice—that of becoming a nun. Thus, New France provided some young women with more options
than they would have had in their own New England towns. They had an
increased chance of marrying, or they could choose to live with other women of
faith. There were two important religious institutions in Montréal for women,
the Congrégation de Notre-Dame and the L'Hôtel-Dieu, a hospital.[7] (See
Chapter 6 for more on women and religion.)

In contrast to those taken captive, some white women in frontier areas successfully fought Native American warriors alongside or in place of men. In the
late eighteenth century, Jeremy Belknap collected stories of heroines in Oyster
River, New Hampshire. In one such anecdote, he describes the attack on the gar-
rison near John Drew's house in April 1706. There were no men there at the
time, so the women "seeing nothing but death before them, fired an alarm, and
then putting on hats, and loosening their hair that they might appear like men,
they fired so briskly that the enemy, apprehending the people were alarmed, fled
without burning or even plundering the house which they had attacked." He
also described a 1712 incident in which a "woman named Esther Jones mounted
guard and with a commanding voice called so loudly and resolutely as made the
enemy think there was help at hand, and prevented further mischief."[8] In both
of these vignettes, women stepped into the role usually reserved for men and, in
fact, pretended to be men. Nevertheless, they established their bravery and
became celebrated as heroines.

Eighteenth-century America was a violent place, but Euroamericans did not
analyze violence as such. Instead, they viewed each person's behavior within a
particular context and role. Any individual could commit a particular act of
violence without others perceiving him or her as a violent person.[9] Thus, no matter how gory or brutal her acts were, a white woman who fought off Indians was
considered heroic. According to one historian, women, in "their roles as defend-
ers of the home and families against Indian 'savages' never drew anything but
praise at this time." These women were not acting as soldiers, but rather they
were stepping in alongside or in place of absent husbands to defend their
families.[10]

In many Native American tribes, women had war-related roles. For example, many tribes tortured male captives. Indian men proved their bravery and demonstrated their performance as warriors if they could endure torture with bravery and even defiance. In the 1750s, a French observer reported on the torture of a Mohawk warrior by members of the Ottawa. "To show his bravery, the Mohawk began to sing, daring his tormentors to do their worst."[11] Among the Algonquian and Iroquois, as in many other tribes, it was the women who determined the fate of captives. A scholar of war and gender during this period describes the role of Native American women this way, "Parties of women— usually older women—commonly greeted captives upon their arrival at an Indian village or fort, and these women seem to have had a strong role in deciding which captives would live and which would die in ritual torture and sacrifice, which would be tortured or maimed just a little (by comparison), and which would be adopted and by whom, and what their roles in their new families would be." In one example from Queen Anne's War (1702–1713), the widow of a warrior decided on the fate of the English man who killed her husband. The captive became her servant, but it appears that, in sparing his life, she prevailed against the judgment of her tribe.[12]

The stripping of clothing from bodies, alive and dead, was a significant and conspicuous part of Iroquois warfare. The stripping and redressing of both male and female captives was often part of an elaborate ritual designed to adopt captives into their Indian family and the community. Sometimes the adopted captive was even dressed in the clothing of the dead family member he or she was replacing.

Both whites and Indians understood the cultural significance of clothing. When captives were redeemed and returned to white society, they often wanted to change from their Indian clothing to European clothing as quickly as possible. By the end of the seventeenth century, however, cultural cross-dressing was widespread and open to interpretation. An Indian dressed in European clothing might be a successful trader, a Christian Indian, or he or she might be dressed in items taken as trophies from an enemy.[13] By the mid-eighteenth century, the adoption of European clothing by Native Americans was so commonplace that when Robert Eastburn, who had been captured in western Massachusetts, was stripped of his clothing and given new clothing by his new Indian mother in 1750, he reported that she replaced his dirty and ragged shirt with "a new One, with ruffled Sleeves (saying that is good) which I thankfully accepted."[14]

Whites and Native Americans encountered the dangers of the frontier, as well as its lures. William Byrd, the Virginia planter, believed "the true reason of the fatal war which the nations round about made upon Carolina in the year 1713" was as a result of the white Carolina traders treatment toward the Indians, "abusing their women and evil entreating their men."[15] Violence toward women occurred on both sides of Indian/white wars. Toward the late 1750s, as the Seven Years War (1754–1763) engulfed both sides of the Atlantic, the French began to spread rumors that the English officers at forts in South Carolina were taking Indian women from their husbands and giving them to their soldiers to be used sexually. The English assured the Indians that this was not true, although, in fact, they did not appear entirely sure that it was not happening.[16]

During the Cherokee War (1759–1761), however, English soldiers did rape Cherokee women who were being held captive in Charleston. Colonel Grant visited the lieutenant governor in 1761 to tell him "great abuses were daily committed by the soldiers on duty at the main guard upon the Cherokee women, prisoners in part of the said guard house." The colonel asked that the women be moved elsewhere, because he could not control the behavior of the soldiers.[17]

The Cherokee War altered colonial images of Cherokee women. Earlier colonial accounts of Cherokee women portrayed them as strong and sexually uninhibited. Although many white men found them attractive, they also felt threatened by Cherokee women because their strength and independence went against the belief held by most Englishmen—that a woman needed to be controlled by a man, either her father, husband, or a male guardian. Colonial observers considered Cherokee women to be completely free from male control. As one Englishman wrote about the Cherokee, "they have been a considerable while under petticoat government, and allow their women full liberty to plant their brow with horns as oft as they please, without fear of punishment. On this account their marriages are ill-observed, and of short continuance; like the Amazons they divorce their fighting bed-fellows at their pleasure, and fail not to execute their authority, when their fancy directs them to a more agreeable choice."[18]

Such accounts should be read with some skepticism, because European men constantly misunderstood and misrepresented the gender roles of the Native Americans they encountered. Indeed, it appears clear that elder Cherokee women enforced and regulated the social and sexual behavior of younger women. They also held some political authority. As one scholar has noted, "Women were the gatekeepers of Cherokee society and in this role were an important force in sanctioning war and keeping peace." Cherokee battles were often fought to avenge the killing of relatives, and it was the women who decided what was to be done with captives. They could decide if a captive would be tortured and killed or adopted.[19]

During and after the Cherokee War, colonial commentators and participants began to portray Cherokee women not so much as alluring sexual temptresses, but rather as threats to male authority. Colonists spread rumors questioning the political role of Cherokee women and observed that even Cherokee warriors scorned them. For example, Christopher Gasden, a captain in the militia and later a delegate to the Continental Congress, reported, "the Cherokees are known to despise their wenches and disregard all they say." These attempts at reshaping the image of Cherokee women and reinterpreting their relationship with Cherokee men may have eased the anxieties of colonial men, who were trying to maintain power and authority within their own changing society.[20]

In contrast to the suspicious and antagonistic views of women held by some men, the woman-to-woman trading of food and domestic goods reveals a shared bond between white women on the South Carolina frontier and Cherokee women. In her memoirs, Ann Matthews, who had been captured and raised by the Cherokee, wrote of a 1759 incident in which a Cherokee woman warned of a planned attack by Cherokee warriors. The Cherokee woman, "disliked very much to think that the white women who had been so good to her in giving her clothes and bread and butter in trading parties would be killed, she became determined to let them know their danger, she started after night, when all was still." The woman walked for twenty-four hours, "spreading the news as she went." Similarly, in 1761, Cherokee women warned Katherine Steel and her children of an approaching raid on their South Carolina farm.[21]

In Pennsylvania frontier regions, too, friendship between Indians and white settlers sometimes kept the white settlers safe when Indians attacked. For example, when Delaware warriors attacked some nearby settlements, they did not harm George Custar, "whose wife spoke fluent Delaware, lived near Gnadenhütten and had a long-standing trade relationship with both the mission Indians and those living on the Susquehanna."[22] Yet much of the violence that did take place was very personal, as Delaware warriors attacked white settlers who were well-known to them. As a scholar of this frontier area asserts, "Through violence, they sought to sever ties to individuals or families who had ignored the obligations that years of personal and economic alliances entailed. In particular, they attacked white settlements situated on land that they claimed as their own."[23]

The Delaware often used extreme violence on people who were known to them. They marked bodies to symbolize their rejection of common values and to flaunt their own power as warriors. In general, they took women as captives, but they did kill some women and then mutilated their bodies. Most often, they mutilated the breasts and reproductive organs of women to "emphasize their rejection of the 'common humanity' that women's bodies and their role as mothers represented." According to one historian, the goal of such brutal attacks was to demonstrate that they could "strike at the heart of an enemy's territory, to destroy body, family, and community."[24]

Colonists exacted extreme violence on those they knew well, too. David Owens, for example, had lived along the Susquehanna River for a number of years. His wife, Maria, was a Delaware. His father had been a trader, and David spoke both Delaware and Shawnee. In 1764, David murdered his wife, their children, and some kinfolk while they were sleeping. Shortly after this, he "hired out his services as interpreter to Colonel Bouquet [the English commander of Ft. Pitt], reconfirming his English allegiance, while using his acquired skills as go-between."[25]

The warfare in Pennsylvania during the Seven Years War caused both Euroamericans and Indians to view one another differently. Even as cultural boundaries blurred, both sides attempted to recast their differences and reinvent their pasts. Colonists moved westward, unimpeded by the French, but tensions with the Indians continued. As part of the peace settlement of the Seven Years War, the Proclamation of 1763 prohibited white settlers from moving west of the line. Yet the line agreed to on paper was not an effective barrier to westward movement, and tensions continued.

Certainly much of the fighting that took place during the American Revolution (1776–1783) occurred outside of the better-known battles between regular army troops. Furthermore, as one historian of war states, "as had been the case throughout the eighteenth century, Indian warfare formed the background to all other military activity."[26] In 1782, militia members slaughtered Moravian Indians in Gnadenhütten. Because the Indians possessed European goods, the white soldiers believed they had been raiding white settlements. The troops slaughtered ninety-six men, women, and children. Troops in Kentucky destroyed Shawnee villages, even after a treaty was signed in 1785. British troops demolished the Catawba villages, which had helped the American side. When troops on either side burned villages and fields and took livestock, Indian women and their families were often left to starve.[27]

As the fighting in Kentucky intensified, the Shawnee began to slaughter prisoners rather than take them captive. Other tribes throughout the south and north, however, continued to take captives. For example, Anna Oosterhout Meyers, her husband, and their four children were taken captive in 1778. She and three children were released soon after, but her husband was not released until 1779, and their son remained with the Indians until after peace was declared in 1783. Ann Meyer's story is particularly poignant because it was her second experience with captivity—Indians had killed her parents and taken her captive when she was child.[28]

As dissatisfaction with Britain's policies continued to grow in the early 1770s, the loyalty of backcountry white settlers to either Great Britain or the Patriot side could not be taken for granted. Many, however, hesitated to confront the British directly. A historian of the Cherokee and South Carolinians of this time notes how ambivalent many of the backcountry settlers were about the political situation. "'Disaffected' men and women without any real political identity on these terms often made up the majority among the western settlements from North Carolina to Georgia," he states. At the same time, both Loyalists and Patriots attempted to woo the Cherokee to their side. By 1776, however, it became evident that attempts at peace between backcountry settlers and the Cherokee had vanished. Rumors were widespread that the Cherokee were ready to attack along with the British, so much so that slaves were also plotting attempts to attain their freedom.[29]

As Cherokee women saw their fields destroyed, many advocated peace. Some brought gifts to council meetings in attempts to maintain peaceful relations. One historian believes that, as a result of the war, the role of Cherokee women within the tribe may have led them to think differently from the men of the tribe. As he comments, "The relative stability of women's village farming, as opposed to indigenous hunting, may have brought tribal women into subtle opposition with hunters." Thus, they aided leaders in trying to establish buffer zones between white settlements and their own. Yet, as a result of changes in the methods of both warfare and diplomacy, the power of clan matrons decreased in the postwar period. The "War Woman of Chota," Nancy Ward, was an official negotiator in the talks in Hopewell, South Carolina, in 1785, which was the last time a Cherokee woman had such a role. The treaty signed there was supposed to establish a westward boundary for white settlement.[30]

At this conference, Nancy Ward spoke before representatives of her tribe and U.S. commissioners. Although she had participated in battle, she was also aware of the destruction brought about by war and its effects on her society.

> I look on you and the red people as my children. Your having determined on peace is most pleasing to me, for I have seen much trouble during the late war. I am old [about 47], but I hope yet to bear children, who will grow up and people our nation, as we are now to be under the protection of Congress and shall have no more disturbance. The talk I have given is from the young warriors I have raised in my town, as well as myself. They rejoice that we have peace, and we hope the chain of friendship will never more be broken.[31]

In northern areas, too, Indian tribes were caught in the conflict between American forces and those of England. Along the Canadian border, both the Americans and the British tried to get the support of the Iroquois Six Nations. At the beginning of the conflict, many of the tribes tried to maintain neutrality, but that did not last; most of the Seneca and the Oneida then supported the Americans, whereas the Mohawk, Seneca, and the Cayuga sided mainly with the British.

White, black, and Native American women faced conflicting loyalties during the American Revolution. At some point, almost all women felt the effects of the war, as they experienced food shortages, had contact with soldiers, or felt the absence of husbands, brothers, fathers, and male suitors. Friends, neighbors, and family members opposed each other, as those loyal to England and its rule opposed those who believed British policies had become horribly repressive. Although there were limits on white women's involvement in political activities, they can and did participate in economic boycotts of British goods that were being taxed. Some Boston women organized a boycott of tea in 1770. They proclaimed, "We the Daughters of those Patriots who have and now do appear for the public Interest . . . do with Pleasure engage with them in denying ourselves the drinking of Foreign Tea."[32] Women in other cities also became involved in boycotts of tea and other British goods. Women of Edenton, North Carolina, who wanted to "follow the laudable example of their husbands," signed a petition in support of the North Carolina resolves against drinking tea and wearing British clothing. After their petition was

Die Americaner wiedersetzen sich der Stempel-Acte, und ver-brennen das aus England nach America gesandte Stempel-Papier zu Boston, im August 1764/D. Chodowiecki del. et sculp. This German print depicts Americans burning Stamp Act proclamations in Boston. Women are part of the crowd. Courtesy Library of Congress.

printed in a London newspaper, the women of Edenton were satirized in a famous British cartoon.[33]

Despite the male mockery, women of all ages participated in boycotts of tea. For example, when nine-year-old Susan Boudinot visited the home of New Jersey governor William Franklin, she politely took the cup of tea offered to her—and then threw the tea out the window. Abigail Dwight of Massachusetts wrote of not feeling well to her daughter Pamela in June 1769. All of her friends

A Society of Patriotic Ladies, at Edenton in North Carolina. This English cartoon satirizes the Edenton women's boycott. Courtesy Library of Congress.

had given up tea drinking, she reported, and she believed her illness was a result of her new practice of "Drinking strong Coffee in the Afternoon."[34]

Some women were less enthusiastic about boycotts and the patriot cause. When Boston patriots decided to boycott the British goods that were taxed under the Townshend Act in 1760, many merchants in Boston took part.

Merchants in Philadelphia, New York, and other port cities soon followed their example. Yet, there were storekeepers who chose to keep shops open and sell British goods. In some cases, they supported the British openly, but, in other cases, they simply could not afford to lose the income generated by their businesses. This was particularly true of single women and widows who did not have other options open to them.

During this period, the Boston shopkeeper Elizabeth Murray was in London, but some of her female friends and protégées became involved in the disputes over selling British imports. Betsy and Anne Cuming were sisters whom Elizabeth Murray had helped when they wanted to go into business. They needed the income they received from their store and believed it was too small to attract any attention. As Betsy explained to Elizabeth Murray, "I told them we have never antred into eney agreement not to import for it was verry trifling owr Business." Nevertheless, they discovered their names published in the newspaper. This worked to the sisters' advantage, however, because the publicity "spirits up our Friends to Purchess from us." Yet the Cuming sisters found the situation uncomfortable enough that they moved to Nova Scotia after the British army left Boston in 1776. Another female shopkeeper in Boston, Jane Eustis, signed the agreement in 1768, but she did not do so in 1769. She decided to close her shop and went back to England, after having her name published in the *Boston Gazette* and being pestered by those who supported the nonimportation agreements.[35]

As a consequence of British taxes and the boycotting of British goods, spinning acquired a new importance. Spinning was a common and often tedious task, but now it became a patriotic duty. Men realized that for boycotts to work, the cooperation of women was necessary. Women had to forego buying tea and other goods, but they also had to increase home production of homespun. Men, therefore, began to recognize the contributions of women publicly. Newspaper coverage of women's activities increased greatly. As one historian notes, "The *Boston Evening Post*, which carried only one previous account of female domestic industry, printed twenty-eight articles on the subject between May and December 1769, and devoted most of its front page on May 29 to an enumeration of these examples of female patriotism." Reporting on a spinning bee in Long Island, for example, *The Boston Evening Post* stated, "the ladies, while they vie with each other in skill and industry in the profitable employment, may vie with the men in contributing to the preservation and prosperity of their country and equally share in the honor of it."[36]

Large public spinning bees, in which respectable young women dressed in homespun, usually took place at the home of a local minister. They ate American-produced food and drank herbal teas. In general, twenty to forty women took part, but sometimes there were more. The events brought spectators, who encouraged the spinners, and sometimes provided entertainment. At some spinning bees, women competed against one another, which probably added to the excitement, as well as increasing production. Between 1768 and 1770, New England women attended at least forty-six spinning bees; thirty were held in 1769. These spinning bees were largely symbolic, because the work produced by the women usually went to the minister. Yet these events encouraged women to spin at home. As one newspaper editor reported, "it was no longer a disgrace for one of our fair sex to be catched at a spinning wheel." Women believed that their spinning and other domestic tasks were now significant, and they "felt Nationly," as well.[37]

Spinning had long been associated with the "good housewife," a woman distinguished by her industriousness, piety, and modesty. Benjamin Franklin, for example, decided to send his sister Jane a spinning wheel instead of a tea table as a wedding gift in 1727. He believed it was a good choice, because he did not wish his sister to be only "a pretty gentlewoman."[38] It should be noted that, in the years leading up to the American Revolution, politics, economics, and morality had merged. Many viewed English fashions as corrupt, whereas American homespun exemplified virtue. The "Daughters of Liberty" responded "to a moral imperative as well as a practical need."[39]

Yet, in contrast, the early 1770s was also a period of conspicuous consumption. After the British repealed taxes on many items (except for tea) in 1770, nonimportation agreements fell apart. Philadelphia, one historian has declared, became the center of "fashion and culture wars."[40] The spending and purchases of the extremely wealthy Philadelphia merchant John Cadwalader and his family during this period exemplifies this sort of conspicuous consumption. A portrait of the family painted by Charles Wilson Peale in 1772 shows John, his wife Elizabeth, and young daughter Anne in fashionable, genteel clothing. Elizabeth's hair is styled in the elaborate "high hair" fashion. As a scholar has noted, "the high style of the late 1760s and early 1770s suggests a certain disregard for, or even outright defiance of, Whig insistence on sacrifice and asceticism, demonstrated by the level of consumption and appetites for fashion."[41]

As Philadelphia became the political capital, tensions increased between those who sported the latest fashions and those who advocated homespun. The occupation of the city by the British led to further strains in the city, because many of the elite women of the city were suspected of having Tory leanings. Many suspected those with high hair rolls. Josiah Bartlett, a delegate to the Continental Congress from New Hampshire, wrote to his wife and reported that, when Congress returned to Philadelphia in the summer of 1778, "they found the Tory Ladies who tarried with the Regulars wearing the most Enormous High Head Dresses after the manner of the Mistresses & Wh[ores] of the British officers." Yet it seems that Whig women also enjoyed the fashion.[42]

Nevertheless, plain, simple fashions and homespun became associated with virtuous women of the Republic. Moreover, spinning and virtue had been conflated and connected to the American Revolution in a number of ways. For example, according to legend, Ann Cooper Whitall, a Quaker matron, sat spinning while the Battle of Red Bank went on around her. Fort Mercer was constructed on part of the Whitall's farm overlooking the Delaware River, now located in the borough of National Park, New Jersey. It was one of the forts designed to protect Philadelphia that were constructed on both sides of the river. An account written early in the twentieth century reports that Ann Whitall disapproved of the fighting and sat "calmly spinning, in the midst of the cannon balls . . . And it was only at last, when a shell burst through the walls and partitions behind her back that she reluctantly and leisurely took up her wheel and went down to continue her spinning in the cellar."[43] After the battle was over, Ann Whitall nursed both the wounded American soldiers and the wounded Hessians. Ann Whitall may or may not have spent the battle calmly sitting at her spinning wheel, but her response after the battle was notable. She took the wounded American and Hessian soldiers into her home and nursed them—first scolding the Hessians, we are told, for coming to her country as mercenaries. Like many other women of her time, she was quite knowledgeable about herbs and healing. The domestic acts of nursing and caring for wounded soldiers redeemed Ann Whitall, whose Quaker pacifism had made her loyalty suspect. She was brave and well versed in domestic arts, the epitome of a virtuous wife and mother.

In the southern states, wealthy women did not spin, but female slaves were put to work spinning and weaving. Before 1775, only limited quantities of linen had been made in Virginia, but the shift to home production was productive and successful. The other southern colonies also began to produce cloth. One historian speculates that positions as spinners and weavers may have become desirable to some enslaved women. For one thing, the job was not as physically onerous as fieldwork. Moreover, planters valued those who could spin or weave well. The jobs required special skills, just as carpentry and other artisan work did. Enslaved women may have gained some feeling of self-worth and confidence in learning to spin and weave.[44]

Boycotts, spinning, and political talk inspired some young women who came of age during this period. A few were fired with a revolutionary fervor. A New York City teenager, Charity Clarke, zealously knitted stockings from the homespun she obtained from a friend. In letters to her English cousin, she wrote, "Heroines may not distinguish themselves at the head of an Army," but women could still defend the nation. She envisioned "a fighting army of amazones . . . armed with spinning wheels." In another letter, she declared, "[Y]ou cannot deprive us [of our property], the arms that supports my family shall defend it, though this body is not clad with silken garments, these limbs are armed with strength, the Soul is fortified by Virtue, and the Love of Liberty is cherished within this bosom."[45]

Other young women were more concerned with meeting young men. Sixteen-year-old Sally Wister was bored living outside of Philadelphia until officers from Maryland, Virginia, and elsewhere came to stay with her family. Her journal is filled with descriptions of her encounters with these officers and their flirtations, what she wore (not homespun), and what they said to her. She found it all utterly exciting, and when the soldiers departed, she was dismayed by the silence in the house.

Rebecca Franks, the daughter of Philadelphia loyalist David Franks, had an exciting time flirting and dancing with British officers. Despite her attraction to the British, she kept her friendship with her patriot friends. In Philadelphia, the Franks entertained British officers in their home, and Rebecca constantly went to dances and concerts. "I've been but three evenings alone since we mov'd to town. I begin now to be almost tired," she reported in a letter to her friend Nancy (Anne "Nancy" Harrison, wife of William Paca, Maryland patriot and delegate to Congress). When her father was exiled from Philadelphia in 1780, Rebecca went with him to New York, where she continued to flirt and dance with British officers. She eventually married a British officer, Henry Johnson, in 1782, and went with him to England to live.[46]

It was difficult to ignore the war, however. Young women could flirt with soldiers, but those soldiers then had to fight, and sometimes they did not return. A woman might *choose* to give up drinking tea, but she had no choice in deciding whether or not to purchase food or supplies when the products were unavailable. Women throughout the country made do with what they had. For example, some women in rural South Carolina substituted thorns for pins. Those suspected of hoarding supplies were often subjected to mob violence. In 1778, Abigail Adams reported how a group of women attacked a merchant who was rumored to be hoarding coffee and selling it at a high price.

> A number of Females, some say a hundred, some say more, assembled with a cart and trunks, marched down to the Whare House and demanded the keys which he refused to deliver. Upon which one of them seizd him by his Neck and tossed him into the cart. Upon his finding no quarter, he delivered the keys when they tipped up the cart and discharged him; then opened the Warehouse, hoisted out the Coffee themselves, put it into the trunks and drove off . . . A large concourse of men stood amazed silent Spectators.[47]

Even when items were available, inflation made them unattainable for many. The pay a common soldier received was not enough to purchase basic supplies. The wife of one soldier wrote, "I am without bread. The Committee will not supply me, my children will starve, or if they do not, they must freeze, we have no wood, neither can we get any—Pray Come Home."[48]

Soldiers on both sides emptied storerooms, took livestock, damaged fences, and plundered homes. South Carolina widow Eliza Wilkinson wrote of her home being looted by British and loyalist troops. A soldier even demanded the buckles from her shoes. Even worse, looters came a second time and this time took everything. "We have been humbled to the dust! Our very doors and window shutters were taken from the house, and carried aboard the vessels which lay in the river opposite our habitation; the sashes beaten out; furniture demolished;

goods carried off; the beds ripped up; stock of every kind driven away; in short, distresses of every nature attended us."[49]

Troops attacked women, as well as their property. British soldiers raped thirteen-year-old Abigail Palmer after they entered her home in Hunterdon County, New Jersey, in 1777. She was there with her grandfather. In her deposition, she recounted the horrific incident. "A great number of soldiers Belonging to the British Army came there, when one of them said to the Deponent, I want to speak with you in the next Room & she told him she woud not go with him when he seizd hold of her &dragd her into a back Room and she screamd & begd of him to let her alone . . . her Grandfather also & Aunt Intreated . . . telling how Cruel & what a shame it was to Use a Girl of that Age after that manner, but . . . finally three of Said Soldiers Ravished her." After that, the soldiers took her and another girl, Elizabeth Cain, to their camp, where they were raped by other soldiers "until an officer came" and took the girls back to their homes. Other women and girls in Hunterdon County also reported rapes, but the widow Rebekah Christopher reported that she had fought off her attacker and narrowly prevented her ten-year-old daughter from being raped.[50]

As one historian notes, mistreatment by soldiers was made "more frightening because the threat of rape was always present." In Cambridge, Massachusetts, British soldiers burst in upon Hannah Adams, the wife of Deacon Joseph Adams, while she was lying-in after childbirth. The soldiers threatened her, forced her outside, and then burned her house, with her five children still inside; however, the fire was quickly extinguished. American troops mistreated a loyalist woman

The British in Wilmington [N.C.]. Reproduction of drawing by Howard Pyle. When soldiers occupied an area, they often harassed the women. Courtesy Library of Congress.

who was also in bed after childbirth. They "stripd her & her Children of all their Linnen & Cloths."[51]

Even when soldiers did not engage in violent acts against civilians or rob them of their belongings, their presence disrupted their lives. Armies had to be housed, clothed, and fed, and their garbage and waste had to be disposed of. While the British occupied Philadelphia, the officers took over the homes of people or quartered themselves with families, as well as in taverns. A British officer, Major Crammon, asked the Quaker Elizabeth Drinker if she would take him in. He promised to keep early hours and have few visitors, and he assured her that his presence would help keep rowdier officers away. During this time, Elizabeth's husband, Henry, was being held prisoner by the American side because, along with other Quakers, he had refused to take a loyalty oath. On December 29, 1777, she finally agreed that the major could come and live with them. "I hope it will be no great inconvenience, tho I have many fears." On December 31, she wrote in her diary: "J. Crammon who is now become one of our Family, appears to be a thoughtful sober young man, his Servant also sober and orderly; which is a great favour to us." The major, however, was not true to his word. He took over much of the house, kept late hours, and had visitors. Elizabeth Drinker was not upset to see him leave when the British troops departed in May 1778.[52]

Women traveled with all of the armies. Some were women who had no other means of supporting themselves and their families while their husbands were away in the army. These women cooked and washed for the troops and received food and money for their services. A directive given to officers in West Point in 1780 ordered them to "make the Strictest inspection into the Carractor of the women who Draw [rations] in their Corps and Report on the honour the Names of Such as are Maryed to non Commsd officers, privates and Artificers." They were ordered to send the single women away but to give married women certificates. Women who did stay, however, were expected to wash clothing.[53]

In fact, as one scholar has recently asserted, "Laundry created an important flash point in the conflict between officers and soldiers, one that provoked the Continental Army's concerns about the moral virtue of the men and women on its payroll." Cleanliness became a sign of gentility in the eighteenth century. The elite could afford to have servants and slaves wash their clothing and bring them clean water to wash their hands and faces. By the mid-eighteenth century, cleanliness had also become associated with virtue. A historian has noted that "in addition to improving health and discipline, maintaining well-regulated, neatly dressed troops would have a positive impact on morale and win divine support for the American cause." Officers generally had the desire and the means to keep themselves clean and well groomed. This was not necessarily true for the common soldiers.[54]

As a consequence, laundry became a complicated and contested issue. Washing and ironing clothing was considered to be women's work, and many men did not want to cross the gender line to wash their own clothes. Because soldiers were separated from their families, they had to pay "camp women" to do their washing, or they had to take care of it themselves. Women who worked and traveled with the army were often suspected of being immoral and sexually promiscuous. Yet the army needed their domestic skills. Consequently, "when women did perform vital services for the army as payrolled employees, they ameliorated the sanitary problems to some degree but made it more difficult for the troops to appear virtuous."[55]

Women who were suspected of being prostitutes were "drummed out" of camps. Although the fears concerning the availability of "lewd" women may appear overblown, it is also true that this was the first time that some young men were exposed to casual or commercial sex. Consequently, the role of women within army camps was ambiguous to many soldiers. Women could help prove their virtue, however, by agreeing to wash the soldiers' clothes. In return, they received rations. Even so, the existence of "camp women" embarrassed some officers, including General Washington. He attempted to keep women and children hidden from public view.

The availability of washerwomen varied from company to company. In the early years of the war, washerwomen were rarely mentioned in accounts. In the winter of 1777–1778 at Valley Forge, the number of women caring for the soldiers reached its nadir—one woman for every forty-four men. After Washington appointed Baron Frederick Von Steuben to be inspector general of the United States in 1778, army conditions improved. Washerwomen begin to appear more often in official records and in the private diaries of soldiers. In April 1782, Private Elijah Fisher noted that he brought buckets of water to "the young women to wash with." Nevertheless, American troops continued to face severe shortages of clothing.[56]

Many of the women who traveled with the armies were lower-class women who desperately needed money and rations. They were looked down upon, even by many enlisted men, and considered to be hardened, masculine, and sluttish. Yet, they were needed as nurses, cooks, and seamstresses, as well as laundresses. Many of these women were desperate, and even the low wages and rations were more than they might otherwise have. For bathing sick and wounded soldiers, emptying their bedpans, and cleaning the hospital wards, they received "one ration and twenty-four cents per day—about ten percent of what surgeons and male attendants made."[57]

In contrast to the laboring camp women, who received rations and payment, were the wives and mistresses of generals. Catherine Greene, the wife of Nathanael Greene, Lucy Knox, the wife of Henry Knox, and Martha Washington, the wife of George Washington, all spent time with their husbands at their encampments. Unlike the common camp women, however, these wives did not sleep in tents or draw rations. At Valley Forge, General Greene had his "Caty" "escorted to a residence far more elegant than that of the commander in chief himself."[58] While the wives of generals were in residence, they often organized dances and dinner parties for the officers. Their presence in camp did not aid the common soldiers in any physical sense; however, they did visit the soldiers and helped boost morale.

The wives of British officers seldom traveled across the ocean to accompany their husbands. Many British officers thus acquired temporary "camp wives." Baroness von Riedesel, the wife of the Hessian commander, however, did make the voyage to be with her husband in Québec, where she was distressed to find that the "cousins" of the British officers she met were not really cousins. As she wrote later, "I learned afterwards, that every one of these gentlemen had the same kind of cousins residing with them . . . who in order to avoid scandal, were forced almost every year to absent themselves for a little while, on account of a certain cause."[59]

The baroness followed her husband on the New York campaign. At the final battle at Saratoga, she moved all who had taken refuge in a house—women, children, and the sick and wounded—into a cellar to escape the bombardment by the American troops. There she acted "the part of an angel of comfort." After the loss at that battle, she, her husband, and their children became prisoners of war, along with many others. This condition lasted for nearly four years, as they were moved from New York, to Boston, to Virginia, and then back to New York City. During their captivity, the baron had an apparent heart attack, from which he recovered, and Frederika gave birth to their fourth daughter, whom they named America. In July 1781, the Riedesels left for Canada, where Frederika gave birth to the couple's fifth daughter, Canada, who died soon afterward. The family departed Canada for England in 1783.[60]

The American Revolution was a civil war. Consequently, families and communities were often divided, and, as one historian asserts, each individual "had to assume a political identity and maintain it with sufficient clarity to satisfy the local authorities."[61] In the town of Pepperell, Massachusetts, the women held a town meeting after the men marched away in April 1775. Moreover, they organized a militia and named Prudence Cummings Wright as the captain. Prudence Wright was the wife of a town leader and the mother of seven children. Although her brothers were loyalists, she and her husband were patriots who named their newborn son Liberty. Liberty did not live long; his death came only nine months after that of her daughter Mary. Despite her grief, however, Prudence took charge of the company named "Mrs. David Wright's Guard." The women of the company dressed in their husbands' clothing and patrolled the roads of the town, armed with guns and pitchforks.[62]

One night the women stopped and arrested a Tory officer, Captain Leonard Whiting. Prudence Wright threatened to kill him if he did not listen to them. The women held him overnight at a tavern before sending him to Groton. The Pepperell town meeting (the official one) reimbursed the women for their duty that night, although they did so somewhat condescendingly, noting, "that Leonard Whiting's guard (so called) be paid seven pounds seventeen shillings and six pence by order of the Treasurer."[63]

Despite examples such as these, women were often considered too innocent or unimportant to worry about. At the same time, Prudence Wright and her company carefully and consciously took over the roles of their husbands, fathers, and brothers because the men were unavailable. The women even dressed in their husbands' attire. This move most likely made patrolling the roads safer and easier, but it was also a symbolic display. It was brave and laudable for women to help defend their town—but only because the men could not do so.

Other women carried important information and messages to both armies. They usually did so because men were unavailable or because women were not scrutinized as carefully as men. For example, after Colonel Henry Champion had received important military information from an exhausted rider, his daughter, twenty-two-year-old Deborah Champion, rode for a full day to deliver the news to General Washington. Accompanied by a servant, Aristarchus, Deborah left her home in Connecticut early in the morning. She and Aristarchus rode all day, changed horses at her uncle's farm, and continued riding through the night. At dawn, they encountered a young British sentry. Deborah convinced him that it was too early to wake his commanding officer. Deborah was wearing a hood, and the officer believed he was talking to an old woman who was on her way to visit a sick friend. He let her and Aristarchus continue on their journey. Deborah was able to deliver to General Washington in Boston the papers that she had hidden in her saddlebags.[64]

Similarly, sixteen-year-old Sybil Ludington rode through the night in April 1777. Her job was to alert the militiamen of Putnam County, New York, that they were needed to defend Danbury, Connecticut. Sybil's father, Colonel Henry Ludington, had received word that Danbury was going to be attacked. Sybil knocked on doors, and the militia troops helped force the British army away from Danbury.[65]

Philadelphia matron Lydia Darragh listened at a keyhole as British officers, who had commandeered a room in her house, planned an attack on Washington's camp outside of Philadelphia. Lydia pretended to have been sound asleep in her room while the meeting was taking place. The next day, she asked for a pass to go outside of the city to buy flour to feed her family. She walked through the winter snow on foot, and she brought the information she had overheard to Washington, preventing a surprise attack by the British.[66]

Because some men regarded women as dimwitted, timid, and unconcerned with politics, women, such as Deborah Champion and Lydia Darragh, who had the opposite qualities, were able to trick them. Margaret Hill Morris, a Quaker widow, wrote an account in her diary in which she seems to revel in her deception of a group of men who were searching for a prominent Tory. The refugee, Dr. Jonathan Odell, was hiding in her house in a secret chamber. "I put on a very simple look, & cryd out, bless me, I hope you are not Hessians—say, good Men are you the Hessians? do we look like Hessians? askd one of them rudely— indeed I don't know; Did you never see a Hessian? No never in my life but they

Mrs. Murray's Strategy. According to legend, Mary Lindley Murray, the wife of Quaker merchant Robert Murray of New York, invited the British troops up to her house for refreshment. She and her daughters charmed General Howe and his men long enough for the American troops to leave the area. Courtesy Library of Congress.

are Men, & you are Men & may be Hessians for any thing I know." She let them into the house to search, "but we coud not find the tory—strange where he could be—we returnd; they greatly disapointed, I pleasd, to think my house was not Suspected."[67]

In another example, an enslaved woman, known as Mammy Kate, decided to free her master, Stephen Heard, who was being held captive by the British at Fort Cornwallis, Georgia. Mammy Kate was a large, imposing black woman. She rode fifty miles on horseback, and, when she got to the fort, she asked for employment as a washerwoman. The British officers were pleased with her skills, and, after some time, Mammy Kate asked to do Stephen Heard's laundry, too. Mammy Kate had a large laundry basket that she carried on top of her head. One evening, she left Heard's cell with him curled up inside her basket. She walked right past the guards, left the camp, and they rode away on horses that Mammy Kate had hidden. Stephen Heard eventually became governor of Georgia. He granted Mammy Kate her freedom and gave her some land and a house. She continued to work for his family, however, until her death.[68]

Other women spied for and aided the British and loyalists. Philadelphia milliner Margaret Hutchinson carried letters to and from British spies in the American troops during the British occupation of Philadelphia. Elizabeth Thompson, a shopkeeper in Charleston, traveled through the American camp to bring letters to the British troops. She also conveyed a disguised British officer in her chaise so that he could see and report back on the American forces. Lorenda Holmes of New York carried messengers back and forth from the invading British troops. She was caught, stripped, and humiliated before a mob, but then she was released. A few months after that, however, she aided some loyalists in their escape from New York City. As punishment, American soldiers held her right foot against hot coals until it burned.[69]

There are some women who are known to have fought in battles, sometimes disguised as male soldiers. There are probably more that were never discovered and that we will never know about. As with Prudence Wright's militia company, or the women who suddenly defended forts or homes, those women who engaged in a "spontaneous crossing of gender lines" were usually more readily accepted than women who dressed as soldiers for money or adventure. Margaret

THE HEROINE OF MONMOUTH.

MOLLY PITCHER., The wife of a Gunner in the American Army, who when her husband was killed, took his place at the gun, and served throughout the battle. (June 28, 1778.)

Heroine of Monmouth, Molly Pitcher. Most historians agree that Molly Pitcher was not a real woman. Most likely, she was a nineteenth-century invention. Her portrayal in this nineteenth-century print idealizes her and the battle scene. Nevertheless, there were real women who fought in Revolutionary War battles. Courtesy Library of Congress.

Corbin, for example, dressed as a man and took her husband's place when he was wounded during a battle. She was wounded and captured, but the new American government provided her with a pension. In contrast, Ann Bailey dressed as a man and enlisted as Samuel Gray. She collected a bounty, but she was then discovered to be a woman, whereupon she was discharged, fined, and jailed. Sally St. Clair, a woman of French and African background, successfully posed as a man until she was killed in battle at the siege of Savannah in 1782.[70]

Native American women sometimes participated in battles, as well. Among the Cherokee, women such as Nancy Ward were honored with the title "War Woman." As one scholar has noted, "The Cherokees probably honored women who excelled in battle because these women challenged the usual categorization of the sexes." Nancy Ward, like Margaret Corbin, took her husband's place in battle when he was struck by a bullet and killed. The Cherokee believed strongly in gender roles. Men were warriors, not women. Men prepared carefully for battle by undergoing rituals of purification and fasting. As one historian has asked, "How the could the Cherokees explain a woman who behaved like a man without bringing disaster, a woman who killed enemy warriors and led Cherokee men to victory? Such a woman was obviously an anomaly, and like certain other anomalies, had exceptional power." Thus, they titled such women "War Women" and permitted them to join male warriors in war dances, and, during particular ceremonies, they sat apart from the other women and ate special foods.[71]

Women of all races and on both sides of the American Revolution were displaced by war. As battles raged nearby, women and their families were sometimes forced to leave their homes and farms. Some women fled because the political leanings of their husbands brought about real or anticipated danger from mobs. Others had their homes confiscated by the government. As *feme coverts,* married women were believed to have no political identity separate from their husbands. (See Chapter 2 on women's legal status.) In order to retain property, some wives remained in their homes while their husbands fled with the British forces. Others found themselves capable of adjusting to changed circumstances.

Elizabeth Murray Smith Inman's husband, Ralph, was trapped in Boston when the war began. Ralph was a loyalist, as was Elizabeth's brother James, but Elizabeth supported the American side. Having supported herself in the past, Elizabeth coped with the problem by managing the farms and taking care of business without Ralph—including the selling of a sizeable crop of hay. Hay was in great demand by the army, and Elizabeth expected to make a good profit. Ralph, however, panicked and planned to leave for London without her. Although Ralph changed his mind, Elizabeth never forgave him for his weakness. One of her friends noted that Elizabeth was "above the little fears and weaknesses which are the inseparable companions of our sex." During the war, the couple's Cambridge residence was taken over by American forces for General Putnam, because they claimed that the property belonged to Ralph. Elizabeth retained another property called Brush Hill, and, after the war, she was able to

THE "MINUTE-MEN" OF THE REVOLUTION.

The Minutemen of the Revolution. In contrast to the fighting heroine, this nineteenth-century image depicts a more typical scene of men going to war while their wives and families remain at home. Courtesy Library of Congress.

reclaim the Cambridge property. Elizabeth's wealth was protected by a prenuptial agreement, and she left Ralph only a pittance in her will.[72]

Grace Growden Galloway's life ended differently. Grace came from a wealthy, important family, and her husband, Joseph Galloway, was speaker of the Pennsylvania assembly. Joseph was a Tory, and he helped the British during the occupation of Philadelphia in 1777. When the British forces left the city, he went with them, taking their daughter Betsy. Grace remained behind to try to maintain her claim to the property that she was supposed to inherit from her father and intended to leave to Betsy, her only child. Instead, she was forced out of her house in August 1778, saying "pray take Notice I do not leave my house of My own accord or with my own inclination but by force." The following April, she recorded her scorn for the patriots and those in control in Philadelphia, "[I] Laughed at ye whole wig party. I told them I was ye happyest woman in town for I had been stripped & Turned out of Doors yet I was still ye same & must be Joseph Galloways Wife & Lawrence Growdons daughter & that it was Not in their power to humble Me for shou'd be Grace Growdon Galloway to ye last."[73] Grace died without ever having regained her property, but her daughter Betsy did manage to recover it.

In many colonies, the wives of loyalists who had joined the British were also forced to leave their homes. In 1777, for example, the New Jersey legislature permitted the New Jersey Council of Safety to send loyalist wives into enemy territory if their husbands had joined the British. Sally Medlis pleaded to remain in her home, saying she would "never hold any correspondence whatsoever with her Husband or in any Manner or Way injure the State," but she was sent away with the wives of other loyalists.[74] (For examples of how political loyalties affected married women's legal status, see Chapter 2.)

In Wilmington, North Carolina, patriot women pleaded for officials not to expel the wives of loyalists, even though they themselves had been exiled when the British occupied the town. Indeed, the women suspected that the expulsion of the loyalists' wives was done partly in retaliation for their expulsion, but they believed the policy was unfair and "must affect the helpless and innocent." The loyalists' wives had aided the wives of patriots when needed, and they "strove to mitigate our sufferings." The patriots' wives now asked for mercy for those "whose husbands, though estranged from us in political opinions, have left wives and children much endeared to us."[75]

Other women, however, did not fare so well. Many loyalist women had their homes ransacked and their possessions taken. Elizabeth Bownman's mother would not even give shelter to her and her children after Elizabeth's home was looted and her husband and oldest son were taken prisoner. Elizabeth and the children walked to the Mohawk River and joined some other women and children there. The British commander at Niagara discovered the women, who were trying to survive on a small crop of corn and potatoes. The group of five women and thirty-one children possessed only one pair of shoes. The British officer took them back to the fort.[76]

Mary (Molly) Brant was another woman who was displaced by the Revolution. She was the daughter of Margaret Brant, a Christian Mohawk woman who was an important clan leader. Molly became the mistress of the much older William Johnson, a British Indian agent in western New York. William Johnson was a very successful man. He was appointed Superintendent of Indian Affairs for the province of New York, and he was knighted for his work during the Seven Years War. Sir William built a large, elegant home called Johnson Hall, and the couple and their children lived there from 1763 until Sir William's death in 1774. During the Revolutionary War, she aided loyalists, and she helped win the Mohawk over to the British side. Eventually, she was forced to flee, leaving behind her jewelry, silver, furniture, and other valuables. After the war, she settled in Cataraqui (Kingston), Ontario. She received a pension from the British government for her service during the war.[77]

In fact, many loyalist women ended up in Canada. Many of them suffered enormous hardship just getting there. Some had to travel through winter snow and difficult conditions, often while carrying young children. They had to be brave and resourceful. Yet, when they reached their destination, they often appeared modest, frail, and dependent rather than heroic. As one scholar makes clear, this was a necessary tactic, because the women were applying for charity from male officers and government officials who expected them to be grateful and submissive.[78]

Living in exile was difficult, particularly for women of limited means. Many families in these Canadian settlements lived in tents at first, even in the cold winter months. Even wealthier women, who had nicer homes, gardens, and food, still missed their old homes and their active social lives. Some black women also went to Canada. The British had freed some slaves, but others remained the property of loyalists who took them to Canada. The British recorded the names of both freed and enslaved, along with a brief description of each individual, the ship on which he or she had sailed, the ship captain's name, and the destination. This log was called *The Book of Negroes,* and it was meant to prevent ship captains from enslaving freed men and women and selling them in the West Indies. Unfortunately, once in Canada, the former slaves lived in racially segregated areas. They were not given the allotments of food or the grants of land that had been promised to them. Many lived in poverty and were unable to improve their condition.[79]

One historian has stated, "The war was so disruptive to family life that one begins to wonder whether the cult of domesticity—the ideological celebration of women's domestic roles—was not in large measure a response to the wartime disruption and threat of separation of families." And yet, not all women were dismayed to be parted from their spouses. Mary Morris watched women being exiled from Philadelphia. She felt it was cruel to force these women to leave, no matter what their own political beliefs. Then she slyly noted, "There are others [who are] . . . renderd happyer by the banishment of a worthless Husband and who by honest industry gains a Subsistence for themselves and Children."[80] Although disruptive, the Revolution did give some women a chance to create new lives for themselves, free from abusive or "worthless" husbands.

In many cases, wives who were parted from their husbands discovered their ability to cope in difficult situations. Frances Sheftall's husband, Mordecai, and their son Sheftall Sheftall were captured and held prisoner by the British in 1778. Mordecai was a prominent merchant and a "leading Georgia Whig." In June, Mordecai and Sheftall were freed and sent to Philadelphia. Frances (Fanny) and the couple's other children had to remain in Charleston, which was then held by the British. During Moredcai's absence, Frances was forced to support the family. She rented a house in Charleston, but, as she wrote to Mordecai, "whear the money is to come from God only knows." She told him, "I am obliged to take in needle worke to make a living for my family, so I leave you to judge what a livinge that must be." She reported that their slaves had all been sick with yellow fever, but only "poor little Billey" had died. Their own children had had small pox but were now well. Still she wondered, "How I shall be able to the pay the doctor's bill and house rent, God only knowes."[81]

Tories kidnapped Gold Selleck Silliman, Mary Fish Sillman's second husband, from their Connecticut home. They also took Mary's oldest son, Billy. The Tories rowed the Sillimans across the sound to Oyster Bay, New York. Mary, pregnant with her last child at age forty-four, had to take charge of the Silliman's home, farm, and their family. She helped arrange a prisoner exchange to get her husband back. Selleck was a colonel in the county militia, and a suitable person had to be offered in exchange. Finally, it was agreed upon that a Tory judge in New York would be kidnapped. The judge was kidnapped, and the exchange took place. Mary had her husband back. In his absence, she had given birth, endured a raid on the nearby town of Fairfield, and learned to cope without him.[82]

After the war, women petitioned Congress and the individual states for help. Congress granted "half-pay pensions" to the widows and orphans of continental army officers, but not to those of enlisted men or those serving in militias or the navy. Some states granted pensions to individual women. Veterans and their spouses had to wait until the nineteenth century, when Congress finally passed a bill granting them pensions.[83]

As tension between England and the American colonies increased and politics became "the prevailing topic of Conversation," women on both sides engaged in political discussion. Although, at first, many did so apologetically, before too long, some women, such as North Carolinian Elizabeth Steele, described themselves as "great politician[s]." Similarly, Eliza Wilkinson recalled that, after the British invaded her home state of South Carolina in 1780, "none were greater politicians than the several knots of ladies, who met together. All trifling discourse of fashions, and such low chat was thrown by, and we commenced perfect statesmen."[84]

On May 12, 1780, after the British forces took Charleston, South Carolina, morale was low, and, in Pennsylvania, women sought to adopt "public spirited measures." They founded "the first large-scale women's association in American history." On June 10, 1780, Esther DeBerdt Reed's broadside, *The Sentiments of an American Woman,* was published. Esther was a recent immigrant, but she was devoted to the patriot cause.[85]

Esther began the broadside with a review of ancient women heroines. She then discussed the notion that men disapprove of women getting involved in political matters, but she countered that argument with the assertion that those who did so would not be good citizens. She then made her appeal—that women give up their "vain ornaments" and donate the money instead to the patriot troops.

Thirty-six Philadelphia women immediately set to work. They noted that women's monetary donations of any amount would be accepted, and each county would have its own "treasuress." The city of Philadelphia was divided into sections, and women went in pairs, door-to-door, soliciting funds. Some women were honored to give; others felt they were being coerced into donating money. Yet the venture was believed to be a great success, and it inspired similar action by women in other states.

The Philadelphia women helped publicize the cause by writing circular letters to women in other counties and towns. New Jersey women undertook their own campaign at the end of June, and Maryland women began one in early July. General Washington insisted that the money that the women had raised be spent on shirts for the soldiers, because he feared the soldiers would spend extra money on drink. Although some then devalued the women's contribution as "General Washington's Sewing Circle," many women believed that the association had proved patriotic, that virtuous women existed.

Degrees of political consciousness among women varied, of course. Sarah Livingston Jay and Catharine (Kitty) Livingston, the daughters of the wartime governor of New Jersey, were interested in politics and discussed political issues in their letters to each other, as well as to other family members and friends. Kitty sent Sarah a copy of *The Sentiments of an American Woman* when Sarah was in Spain with her husband, John Jay, who was serving as minister there. Mercy Otis Warren and Abigail Adams frequently wrote letters that discussed political matters to each other and to others. Mercy Warren also began to articulate a position that saw a woman's interest in politics as essential to the well-being of her family.[86] In the 1770s, Mercy published three satirical plays, and she later wrote a history of the American Revolution. (For more on the writing of Mercy Otis Warren, see Chapter 7.)

Yet most women confined their political thoughts to their own diaries or to family members and trusted friends. As one historian notes, "their culture had pointedly established that politics was not a female province. The daily lives of women in a preindustrial society were largely spent in a domestic circle, a confinement impossible to ignore. But politics did intrude into the women's world during the trauma of the war and the Confederation . . . To ask what the might have done had they lived instead in a world that allowed political concerns to be women's concerns is to ask an unanswerable question."[87]

NOTES

1. Carol F. Karlsen and Laurie Crumpacker, eds. *The Journal of Esther Edwards Burr, 1754–1757,* (New Haven: Yale University Press, 1984), 135.

2. "Eunice Mathers Williams, "Raid on Deerfield: The Many Stories of 1704," http://1704.deerfield.history.museum/home.do.

3. John Demos, *The Unredeemed Captive: A Family Story from Early America* (New York: Vintage Books, 1995), 9.

4. Demos, *Unredeemed Captive*, 15–16.

5. John Gyles, *Memoirs of Odd Adventures* (Boston, 1736), 4, quoted in Laurel Thatcher Ulrich, *Good Wives: Image and Reality in the Lives of Women in Northern New England, 1650–1750* (New York: Oxford University Press, 1983), 181.

6. Ulrich, *Good Wives*, 208.

7. Ulrich, *Good Wives*, 210.

8. Jeremy Belknap, *The History of New-Hampshire* (Philadelphia, 1784), I, 338–339, 357, quoted in Ulrich, *Good Wives*, 178.

9. Similarly, in the seventeenth and eighteenth centuries, people were not labeled homosexual or heterosexual. Those who engaged in same-sex sexual activity were perceived as choosing to engage in behavior that was sinful, immoral, and illegal. It was commonly believed that such acts threatened society by weakening marital and family bonds and upsetting gender roles.

10. Ulrich, *Good Wives*, 185; Linda Grant De Pauw, *Battle Cries and Lullabies: Women in War from Prehistory to the Present* (Norman: University of Oklahoma Press, 2000), 117.

11. *Travels in New France by J. C. B.*, ed. By William N. Fenton and Elizabeth L. Moore (Harrisburg: Pennsylvania Historical Commission, 1941), 2:155–162, quoted in Ann M. Little, *Abraham in Arms: War and Gender in Colonial New England* (Philadelphia: University of Pennsylvania Press, 2007), 35–36.

12. Little, *Abraham in Arms*, 101–102.

13. Little, *Abraham in Arms*, 70–80.

14. Robert Eastburn, *A Faithful Narrative* (Boston, 1760), 24, quoted in Little, *Abraham in Arms*, 80.

15. Quoted in Richard Godbeer, *Sexual Revolution in Early America* (Baltimore: Johns Hopkins University Press, 2002), 180.

16. Godbeer, *Sexual Revolution*, 181.

17. Godbeer, *Sexual Revolution*, 181.

18. Samuel Cole Williams, *Adair's History of the American Indian* (London: 1775; reprint ed. New York: Promontory Press, 1973), 152–153, quoted in Tom Hatley, *The Dividing Paths: Cherokees and South Carolinians through the Revolutionary Era* (New York: Oxford University Press, 1995), 54.

19. Hatley, *The Dividing Paths*, 56–57.

20. Hatley, *The Dividing Paths*, 148–150.

21. Anne Matthews, "Memoirs," typescript in South Carolina Library, Columbia, 5, quoted in Hatley, *The Dividing Paths*, 89–90.

22. Jane T. Merritt, *At the Crossroads: Indians and Empires on a Mid-Atlantic Frontier, 1700–1763*, (Chapel Hill: University of North Carolina Press, 2003), 181.

23. Merritt, *At the Crossroads*, 177.

24. Merritt, *At the Crossroads*, 178, 179, 180.

25. Merritt, *At the Crossroads*, 299.

26. De Pauw, *Battle Cries and Lullabies*, 116.

27. Joan R. Gunderson, *To Be Useful to the World: Women in Revolutionary America, 1740–1790,* rev. ed., (Chapel Hill: University of North Carolina Press, 2006), 183, 184.

28. Gunderson, *To Be Useful to the World*, 183–184.

29. Hatley, *The Dividing Paths*, 188–189, 191.

30. Hatley, *The Dividing Paths*, 220–221; Gunderson, *To Be Useful to the World*, 214.

31. American State Papers, Class 2: Indian Affairs (Washington, D.C., 1832),1:41.Theda Perdue, "Nancy Ward," in *Portraits of American Women: From Settlement to the Present*, ed. G. J. Barker-Benfield and Catherine Clinton (New York: St. Martin's Press, 1991), 85.

32. T. H. Breen, "Narrative of Commercial Life: Consumption, Ideology, and Community on the Eve of the American Revolution," *William and Mary Quarterly* 50 (July 1993), 490.

33. "The Edenton 'Tea Party,'" North Carolina Digital History, http://www.learnnc.org/lp/editions/nchist-revolution/4234.

The letter was printed in the *Morning Chronicle and London Advertiser*, January 31, 1775, and reprinted by the Edenton Woman's Club in *Historic Edenton and Countryside* (The

Chowan Herald, 1959), 3–4, available online at Eastern North Carolina Digital Library, East Carolina University http://digital.lib.ecu.edu/historyfiction.

34. Abigail Dwight to Pamela Dwight, June 14, 1769, in Sedgwick Papers III, Massachusetts Historical Society, quoted in Norton, *Liberty's Daughters*, 160.

35. Gunderson, *To Be Useful to the World*, 174; "Boycotts," Elizabeth Murray Project. Quotes are from Betsy Cuming to Elizabeth Murray Smith, Nov. 29, 1769, and from Anne Cuming to Elizabeth Murray Smith, Dec. 27, 1769, in James M. Robbins Papers, II, Massachusetts Historical Society, Boston, quoted in Mary Beth Norton, *Liberty's Daughters: The Revolutionary Experience of American Women, 1750–1800* (Ithaca, NY: Cornell University Press, 1996), 157.

36. *Boston Evening Post*, May 29, 1769, and June 19, 1769, quoted in Norton, *Liberty's Daughters*, 166, 167.

37. Norton, *Liberty's Daughters*, 168–169; Gunderson, *To Be Useful to the World*, 77.

38. Quoted in Ulrich, *Good Wives*, 68.

39. Ulrich, *Good Wives*, 82.

40. Kate Haulman, "Fashion and the Culture Wars of Revolutionary Philadelphia," *William and Mary Quarterly* LXII (October 2005): 625

41. Haulman, "Fashion and the Culture Wars," 629–631.

42. Josiah Bartlett to Mary Bartlett, August 24, 1778, quoted in Haulman, "Fashion in the Culture Wars," 653.

43. Logan Pearsall Smith, "Two Generations of Quakers—An Old Diary," *The Atlantic Monthly* 88 (1901): 99. Elizabeth Drinker mentions the battle in her diary; see Crane, *The Diary of Elizabeth Drinker*, 248.

44. Norton, *Liberty's Daughters*, 164–165.

45. Charity Clarke to Joseph Jekyll, Nov. 6, 1768, June 16, 1769, September 10, 1774, in Moore Family Papers, Rare Book and Manuscript Library, Columbia University, New York, quoted in Norton, *Liberty's Daughters*, 169. Also see, George DeWan, "A Woman Ready to Fight," http://www.newsday.com/community/guide/lihistory/ny-history-hs344a,O6698945.story.

46. Jacob R. Marcus, ed. *The American Jewish Woman: A Documentary History* (Cincinnati: American Jewish Archives, 1981), 14–15, 16.

47. Quoted in Carol Berkin, *Revolutionary Mothers: Women in the Struggle for America's Independence* (New York: Knopf, 2006), 32.

48. Quoted in Berkin, *Revolutionary Mothers*, 33.

49. Jean Munn Bracken, ed., *Women in the American Revolution* (Carlisle, MA: Discovery Enterprises Ltd., 1997), 12, quoted in Berkin, *Revolutionary Mothers*, 36.

50. Papers of the Continental Congress (m-247), Roll 66, Item 53:31, 39, in Linda K. Kerber, *Women of the Republic: Intellect and Ideology in Revolutionary America* (Chapel Hill: University of North Carolina Press, 1980), 46 and note 17.

51. Kerber, *Women of the Republic*, 46, 47.

52. Elaine Forman Crane, ed., *The Diary of Elizabeth Drinker* (Boston: Northeastern University Press, 1991), vol. 1, 266, 271, 276, 310.

53. Quoted in Kerber, *Women of the Republic*, 56.

54. Kathleen M. Brown, *Foul Bodies: Cleanliness in Early America* (New Haven, CT: Yale University Press, 2009), 162–169.

55. Brown, *Foul Bodies*, 169.

56. Brown, *Foul Bodies*, 170,171, 175, 182–183.

57. Berkin, *Revolutionary Mothers*, 58.

58. Berkin, *Revolutionary Mothers*, 64.

59. Quoted in Berkin, *Revolutionary Mothers*, 65.

60. Berkin, *Revolutionary Mothers*, 80–91.

61. Kerber, *Women of the Republic*, 48.

62. David Hackett Fischer, *Paul Revere's Ride* (New York: Oxford University Press, 1994), 170.

63. Fischer, *Paul Revere's Ride*, 170–171.

64. Berkin, *Revolutionary Mothers*, 136–137.

65. Berkin, *Revolutionary Mothers*, 139.

66. Berkin, *Revolutionary Mothers*, 141.

67. John W. Jackson, ed. *Margaret Morris, Her Journal with Biographical Sketch and Notes* (Philadelphia: George S. MacManus Co., 1949), 48–49.

68. Berkin, *Revolutionary Mothers*, 142.

69. Norton, *Liberty's Daughters*, 175–176.

70. Berkin, *Revolutionary Mothers*, 60–61.

71. Quotes from Purdue, "Nancy Ward," 89–90. Purdue explains that the title "War Woman" comes from the translation of naturalist William Bartram. It may not be entirely accurate.

72. Norton, *Liberty's Daughters*, 217; Gunderson, *To Be Useful to the World*, 186.

73. Nancy Woloch, *Early American Women: A Documentary History, 1600–1900* (Belmont, CA: Wadsworth Publishing Company, 1992), 174.

74. Quoted in Kerber, *Women of the Republic*, 50.

75. Quoted in Kerber, *Women of the Republic*, 52.

76. Berkin, *Revolutionary Mothers*, 98.

77. Gunderson, *To Be Useful to the World*, 31, 181, 214; Susan M. Bazely, "Who Was Molly Brant?," text of a presentation to the Kingston Historical Society, April 17, 1996, The Cataraqui Archaeological Research Foundation, http://www.carf.info/kingstonpast/mollybrant.php.

78. Berkin, *Revolutionary Mothers*, 103–104.

79. Berkin, *Revolutionary Mothers*, 128.

80. Mary Morris to Catherine Livingston, June 10, 1780, quoted in Kerber, *Women of the Republic*, 53.

81. Marcus, ed. *The American Jewish Woman*, 28, 30.

82. This part of Mary Silliman's life is described in Chapter 6 of Joy Day Buel and Richard Buel, Jr., *The Way of Duty: A Woman and Her Family in Revolutionary America* (New York: Norton, 1984). It is also the subject of the movie *Mary Silliman's War* (Heritage Films, 1993).

83. Gunderson, *To Be Useful to the World*, 187.

84. Quotes are from Norton, *Liberty's Daughters*, 170, 171–172.

85. Norton, *Liberty's Daughters*, 178.

86. The campaign is discussed in Norton, *Liberty's Daughters*, 178–188.

87. Kerber, *Women of the Republic*, 85.

SUGGESTED READING

Berkin, Carol. *Revolutionary Mothers: Women in the Struggle for America's Independence.* New York: Knopf, 2006.

Brown, Kathleen M. *Foul Bodies: Cleanliness in Early America.* New Haven, CT: Yale University Press, 2009.

Crane, Elaine Forman, ed. *The Diary of Elizabeth Drinker.* Boston: Northeastern University Press, 1991.

Demos, John. *The Unredeemed Captive: A Family Story from Early America.* New York: Vintage Books, 1995.

Gunderson, Joan R. *To Be Useful to the World: Women in Revolutionary America, 1740–1790*, rev. ed. Chapel Hill: University of North Carolina Press, 2006.

Hatley, Tom. *The Dividing Paths: Cherokees and South Carolinians through the Revolutionary Era*. New York: Oxford University Press, 1995.

Karlsen, Carol F. and Laurie Crumpacker, eds. *The Journal of Esther Edwards Burr, 1754–1757*. New Haven, CT: Yale University Press, 1984.

Kerber, Linda K. *Women of the Republic: Intellect and Ideology in Revolutionary America*. Chapel Hill: University of North Carolina Press, 1980.

Little, Ann M. *Abraham in Arms: War and Gender in Colonial New England*. Philadelphia: University of Pennsylvania Press, 2007.

Merritt, Jane T. *At the Crossroads: Indians and Empires on a Mid-Atlantic Frontier, 1700–1763*. Chapel Hill: University of North Carolina Press, 2003.

Norton, Mary Beth. *Liberty's Daughters: The Revolutionary Experience of American Women, 1750–1800*. Ithaca, NY: Cornell University Press, 1996.

Ulrich, Laurel Thatcher. *Good Wives: Image and Reality in the Lives of Women in Northern New England, 1650–1750*. New York: Oxford University Press, 1983.

6

———∞∞∞———

Women and Religion

Many woman in eighteenth-century America attended church regularly or practiced daily religious rituals. Moreover, religion was a major element of their society and imbued the culture and politics of Anglo-America. Church-going
Anglican Virginians considered theater performances and dances to be perfectly
acceptable, but Pennsylvania Quakers and Massachusetts Congregationalists did
not. Many households held family worship sessions and provided religious
instruction for their children, servants, and slaves.

When Puritans settled a town in seventeenth-century New England, they
established a meetinghouse in the center of it. People gathered at the meetinghouse for both religious and civil matters, because the two were intertwined during much of the seventeenth century. Courthouses and churches of other
denominations were built in the eighteenth century. As towns grew, people
moved farther away from the center, or they established new towns. In either
case, people asked that new churches be formed. In both the seventeenth and
eighteenth centuries, however, women were often behind the push to form new
congregations. Women who were pregnant, or mothers with nursing infants or
rambunctious toddlers, found it difficult to walk several miles to get to the
church. It was even more difficult if they had to carry their small children.
Although their husbands may have signed the petitions and paid the taxes, it was
often the women who pushed for the new churches.[1]

The Puritans who settled New England brought with them a strong sense of
mission that encompassed their entire way of life. They believed their society
would be a model for the world, a "city on a hill." Consequently, everything that
individuals did and said reflected upon their society and affected their covenant

with God. They were not interested in merely reforming the church, they wanted to reform society as well. Still, despite their disagreement with the Church of England and English society, New England Puritans considered themselves English citizens. Like other English Protestants, they considered France to be their major enemy and rival for control of North American colonies. This fear and distrust of France was intertwined with an extreme loathing for Catholicism.

Many early modern Protestants believed that the mass and other rituals of Catholicism were sensual and seductive and, therefore, especially attractive to women. Because women were thought to be weak and easily tempted, there was a constant need to keep them in check through the supervision of devout Protestant men—fathers, husbands, and clergymen. New Englanders were especially fearful of the numbers of female captives who converted to Catholicism and remained in Canada, away from the influence of their families and communities. They suffered great anxiety, because the loss of these young women affected not only their families, but also New England itself. A historian of this period believes that the "apparent danger to female captives jibed with long-standing puritan fears of women's greater vulnerability to spiritual corruption, as well as their specific susceptibility to the seductions of Catholicism."[2]

Children were even more susceptible to the lures of Catholicism than women. Sometimes they were too young and vulnerable to protest. The fear and loathing of Catholicism and the vulnerability of the young comes through in Elizabeth Hanson's captivity narrative. She was a Quaker who had been captured by Abenakis in Dover, New Hampshire, in 1724. The French purchased her from the Indians—and she was grateful for that. Nevertheless, she noted with horror, "the next Day after I was redeemed, the Romish Priests took my Babe from me, and according to their custom, they baptized it." They explained to her that, if her baby died without being baptized, "it would be damned, like some of our modern pretended reform Priests."[3]

Mary Storer was a captive who decided to remain in Canada. Twenty-two years after she was captured, she began a correspondence with her family in New England. Their letters reveal the attempts her family made to convince her to return to them and to Protestantism. Mary and her cousins, Rachael and Priscilla Storer, were captured in an Abenaki raid in Wells, Maine, in 1703. Mary was eighteen when she was captured; her cousins were also in their late teens. All three young women remained in Canada and married French men. In 1725, Mary visited Boston and saw her family, and shortly after that visit, the correspondence began. Mary's letters make it clear that, even though she loved and missed her family, she did not want to return to them.[4]

Mary's father, however, was not content to leave matters at that. He informed Mary that if she did not return, she would not receive her fifty-pound inheritance. Mary replied that she knew her family's advice for her to return to them and their Protestant community was "for the goode of my soule and bodey," but she had a husband and children in Montréal, and they were her family now. Mary and her brother Ebenezer, who appears to have written for the family, continued to exchange notes about every year or two. When Ebenezer informed Mary of their father's death, she wrote of her love and grief. True to his word, however, Mary's father left her only ten shillings in his will. Ebenezer, their mother, and other siblings could have granted her some of the money they received, but they refused. Mary became estranged from her family, writing only one letter to them several years later. Eight years after that letter, Mary's husband wrote to her New England family to inform them of her death. "You know well my dear brother," he said, "that her death is a great affliction to me, but I must submit to the will of our Creator, as it was he who gave me one of the best women in the world."[5]

Catholicism was appealing to some New England women. Within most churches of this time, women had an ambiguous role. Clearly, women's souls were important, and pious women were respected, but most churches did not permit women to have leadership roles. Catholicism did, however, give women an alternative to the role of wife and mother. Catholic women could choose to be nuns. Young female captives in New France were normally baptized and cared for by French nuns; their involvement with the religious sisters exposed them to new beliefs and experiences that some found very attractive. After some English captives became nuns, they further influenced other female captives. Esther Wheelwright, who, like Mary Storer, was captured in Wells, Maine, took her final vows in 1714. She eventually became the superior at the Ursuline convent in Québec. In 1747, she wrote to her mother, "God himself assures us [that] he who leaves for his sake, Father, Mother, Brothers and Sisters, shall have an hundred fold in this life, and Life eternal in the next."[6]

New England in the first few decades of the eighteenth century was filled with religious women. In most cases, congregations contained more women than men. Congregationalism remained the dominant religion in New England, although other religions were tolerated in the eighteenth century. Women were not permitted to be ministers or vote on church matters in the congregational churches; however, church membership itself was noteworthy. Each congregation was composed of men and women who had demonstrated publicly about their personal relationship with God. A woman could become a church member despite her social or economic status, and she could be a church member even if her husband was not.

In the eighteenth century, women filled the churches throughout British North America. Some historians suggest that this "feminization" of religion was in part a result of the institutionalization of the churches. As the churches became more established, the power of lay people decreased. Men tended to look for power elsewhere, leaving the churches to women. A male pastor, however, supervised the women. Often, women joined a church just before or after they married, even when their husbands were members of other churches or not

Colonial Days. In the eighteenth century, many established religious groups built larger and more elaborate churches. Going to church was often viewed as an opportunity to socialize with friends and neighbors. Courtesy Library of Congress.

church members at all. Mary Fish, the daughter of the Reverend Joseph Fish and his wife, Rebecca, of Stonington, Connecticut, joined her father's church in 1758, after making her formal profession of faith. This was just days before her wedding to John Noyes. Mary's sister Becca joined the church a few months after her marriage to Benjamin Douglas. She had been seriously ill just prior to her wedding. Her conversion experience arose out of the "sudden sense of grace she had experienced as she recovered."[7] During the Great Awakening, the name given to the series of religious revivals that swept through the American colonies in the eighteenth century, women had more choice; churches multiplied and there were more options open to them.[8]

Mary Cooper, a Long Island farmwife, was born into an Anglican family. As an adult, she attended several different churches. In February 1769, she joined the New Light Baptist church. Her sister was a leader and occasional preacher at the meeting. Mary became a member shortly after her nephew, her sister's son, became the minister. Still, she sometimes attended other meetings and heard others preach. For example, on June 1, 1769, she wrote in her diary, "We all went to the Quaker meeten where a multitude were geathered to here a woman preach that lately came from England, and a most amebel woman she is."[9]

The Great Awakening began around 1730, but periodic waves of religious revivalism occurred into the next century. Almost every existing church was affected, and new sects were formed as well. It started in the middle colonies, brought by new immigrants, especially the Scots-Irish, and spread by itinerant preachers. It then spread north and south. Each region experienced revivals at different times. In the South, the Great Awakening brought a religious resurgence to Presbyterians and then to Methodists and Baptists. In the North, many church congregations were split into New Light and Old Light factions, but some members left to join the Baptists and other groups. For example, the Reverend Joseph Fish's church in Stonington was one that split into New Light and Old Light factions. Eventually, the New Light group separated and formed a new church. When Joseph and Rebecca first arrived in Stonington, there were three established churches in the town. That was the case, however, because of the population growing and moving away from the coastal areas, not because of religious beliefs. In doctrine and practice, the three churches were essentially the same.[10]

Even as the Great Awakening split apart some congregations, it also drew people to churches. Jonathan Edwards, the pastor in Northampton, Massachusetts, began a series of revivals in 1734. He was trying to rouse and direct the youth of Northampton toward spiritual matters—the salvation of their souls. He believed that society was going through a moral decline, and it was particularly evident in the young people's licentious behavior. After several months of preaching, he reported that he had saved 300 people in Northampton.[11]

Itinerant preachers spread the message of the Great Awakening. George Whitefield was one of the most famous of these itinerant preachers. He arrived from England and preached throughout the American colonies in 1740. He drew enormous crowds and spoke outdoors to accommodate them. George Whitefield criticized educated ministers, and, according to one historian of religion, "he questioned the sincerity of religionists who privileged reason over faith, status over morality, and eloquence over clarity and truth." The evangelical preachers of the Great Awakening preached rousing sermons, alerting people to their sins and to the need to seek God's grace. Converts did not have to read or to memorize creeds; they did need to repent and accept the Lord sincerely. Revival services were highly emotional and experiential. Thus, conversion was possible for women and men of any race and social status.[12]

The fire of the Great Awakening even affected Jonathan Edwards's wife, Sarah. She had been converted when she was young, but she was "awakened" by the revivals of the 1730s and 1740s. In 1742, she had an "ecstatic religious experience." During this time, Sarah's life was busy and stressful. She was in charge of all the household and business matters, whereas Jonathan "chose to have no care of any worldly business . . . [and] commonly spent thirteen hours every day in his study . . . [and] gave himself wholly to the work of the ministry."[13] The couple had seven children in 1742. The youngest was eighteen months old, and the oldest was thirteen years old. As a good Puritan wife, Sarah was expected to take care of her duties as a wife and mother without complaint. More important,

Parrawankaw [and] Dr. Squintum. George Whitefield was frequently satirized. A disorder in his eyes earned him the title of Dr. Squintum. Parrawankaw was the niece of an Indian chief. Whitefield was rumored to have had a sexual relationship with her. Courtesy Library of Congress.

Sarah believed that this was her proper role. In trying to cope with her situation, she became depressed and even physically ill. As Sarah's biographers note, both Sarah and John "perceived her depression and illness as spiritual failings—attributed to her being 'low in grace'—a consequence of a stubborn reluctance to submit her will completely to God's."[14]

This reluctance disappeared after her religious experience in 1742. A marital spat motivated the experience—Jonathan accused Sarah of being indiscreet when talking to a relative of his. Sarah became upset and burst into tears. She then turned to God. For over two weeks, she experienced an extreme spiritual ecstasy. When she returned to her normal life, she was at peace. She had found God and resigned herself to his will. Her mental and physical pains disappeared, and she could perform all her duties "with a continual, uninterrupted cheerfulness . . . as part of the service to God."[15]

Critics of revivalists were horrified by the disorder and unrestrained passion of their meetings. Many years after he permitted the Reverend James Davenport to use his pulpit, Joseph Fish recalled with great dismay the way that the Reverend Davenport had performed: "He not only gave an unrestrained liberty to *noise* and *outcry*, both of *distress* and *joy*, but promoted *both* with all his might." According to Reverend Fish, Reverend Davenport raised his voice in a high pitch and distorted his face "as if he had aimed, rather at frightening people out of their senses, than by solid argument, nervous reasoning and solemn addresses, to enlighten the mind, and perswade them as reasonable men, to make their escape unto Christ."[16]

The language of both preachers and converts was often erotic. This erotic language and the swooning and moaning that often occurred at meetings led some to accuse the revivals and revivalists of being indecent and immoral. The language that both male and female converts used to describe their sinful state and subsequent finding of God was similar to that used by seventeenth-century Puritans. Sarah Osborn, a Rhode Island schoolteacher, "could utter no other language but, 'Come in Lord Jesus, take full possession; I will come to thee, thou art mine, and I am thine.' . . . surely my heart reached forth in burning desires after the blessed Jesus. O, how was I ravished with his love!" In the eighteenth century, however, the conversion experiences of men and women tended to be more intense and immediate than those experienced by their seventeenth-century counterparts.[17]

In addition, those who converted in the eighteenth century frequently experienced a physical awareness of God or Satan. Some recorded accounts of wrestling with Satan or of being assaulted by him. In the seventeenth century, the converted felt that they received God's grace or felt a presence in their hearts, but, in the eighteenth century, the awakened saw visions.[18]

The pastor of Durham, New Hampshire, Nicholas Gilman, found the visions of Mary Reed so compelling that he listened to her and accepted her as a sort of prophet. During a service in March 1742, he noted, "Mary Reed declared in Publick the close of Her last Vision." After that, the minister "added a word of Exhortation to the People." Nicholas Reed fervently believed that Mary Reed's visions were sent by God, and he was happy to permit her to share them with the community.[19]

The Great Awakening gave some women influence and the belief that they should be heard, although most women probably did not view themselves as religious leaders. Like Mary Reed, they were vessels of God, and, when they preached, they considered themselves to be doing God's will. Some women gathered the courage to speak in public, but they only did so once or twice. Others, even though they did not usually seek to be leaders, were recognized as preachers by both men and women. This led to a backlash in some congregations, however, and efforts were made to reduce women's participation later in the century. In northern Baptists meetings, women continued to preach until the end of the eighteenth century.[20]

In Virginia, white women and black women spoke at meetings. Separate Baptists in Virginia selected women to be deaconesses, who helped take care of the poor and the sick, and eldresses, who counseled women in the congregation. Women who held these positions, however, were not expected to speak in meetings before men and women, although, in some congregations, they were could vote on church matters.[21]

After the Revolution, many congregations sought to limit women's role. The amount and type of participation that women had in church governance depended on each congregation. Some historians suggest that limits were placed on women because "a redefinition of church governance as a public act [was] unsuited to women's new private roles. Churches may also have sought order and 'respectability' by controlling women and conforming to traditional patriarchy."[22]

Yet women did preach and exhort in both small and large groups, and even those who led small household prayer groups could have a wider influence. Devereux Jarratt was one who was so inspired. He was born into an Anglican family in Virginia, but his family was not particularly religious. While he was a young schoolmaster, he boarded at the house of Mrs. Cannon. She read sermons to her family every night, and she asked Devereux to attend these meetings. At first, he thought the sermons were "too experimental and evangelical for one, so ignorant of divine things, as I was, to comprehend." After attending these family meetings for several weeks, he realized that he was "yet in a dark and dangerous place," but this awareness brought about a change in behavior that "soon became visible to my benefactress, which was a matter of great joy." Devereux became a notable Presbyterian minister and preacher during the Great Awakening.[23]

In contrast, Sarah Osborn's spiritual guidance extended directly to her community. Sarah was born in London and immigrated with her mother to Boston when she was a child. Her family later moved to Rhode Island, and that is where she spent most of her life. As a young widow with a child to support, she began teaching school. She married a second time, but her second husband, Henry Osborn, was often sick and unable to work. Thus, Sarah had to support their family, and she returned to school teaching. Her school became quite large; at times, it included up to seventy students. While teaching Mary and Becca Fish, she began a correspondence with the Reverend Fish that lasted well beyond the time of his daughters' schooling.[24]

In the 1740s, Sarah became the leader of a women's prayer group. The group continued to meet for over fifty years, and at its peak there were about sixty members. In 1767, "the high point" of Sarah's "evangelical leadership," she hosted several groups throughout the week. In addition to private meetings of school groups and women's groups, Sarah also hosted groups of African Americans and white men.[25]

Reverend Fish was concerned about her meeting with African Americans and white men, although he was "much pleasd & edifyd with your acct of the Female Religious Society." Sarah replied in a letter to Reverend Fish that she was not teaching men: "I have no thing to do with them, only Have the pleasure of Seting my candlestick and Stool." She insisted that she did not give them instruction, but rather that "They come indeed for Mutual Edification and Sometimes condescend to direct part of conversation to me and so far I bear a part as to answer etc., but no otherway."[26]

Sarah Osborne was equally adamant that she was not teaching African Americans. Because no male religious leader would take over the duty of instructing them, she noted, "I only read to them talk to them and sing a Psalm or Hymn with them." She said they called it a school, rather than a meeting, which pleased her, as did their devotion to attending the sessions. She was also gratified to note that the black attendees had adopted a more moral lifestyle.[27]

Finally, Sarah addressed Reverend Fish's question, "Have you Strength ability and Time consistent with other Duties to fill a Larger sphere by attending the various Exercise of other Meetings in close succession too?" She told him, "it is Evident I gain by Spending; God will no wise suffer me to be a Looser by His Service." She further noted, "I always feel stronger when my companies break up then when they come in." Her family and household did not suffer, because, she said, "I Educate the children of poor Neighbours who Gladly pay me in washing Ironing Mending and Making. I Imagine it is the Same thing as if I did it with my own Hands."[28]

Sarah Osborn was able to transcend the boundaries often placed upon women because she believed she was only doing God's will. Moreover, she insisted she did not aspire to be a religious leader. She considered that to be the role of male ministers, whom she respected. She was merely filling a need to help anyone who desired additional spiritual comfort and prayer.

In contrast to women in most churches of the seventeenth and eighteenth centuries, Quaker women had a great deal of authority and influence. As one scholar notes, however, they would not have "separated their role in the Society from their responsibilities as wives, mothers, and sisters, nor could they have drawn a clear line between their duties as religious leaders and those of their husbands and brothers." Men and women worked together within the Quaker community—they did not compete. Women were particularly important in keeping Quaker families together by transmitting Quaker values and supervising behavior. As this scholar has explained, "Quaker women held no power independent of the men, just as the men claimed no authority separate from the women."[29]

In the seventeenth century, Quakers in the American colonies set up the same multi-tiered system of meetings in the colonies that British Friends had established in Great Britain. Local meetings for worship could be attended by anyone. During these meetings, men and women sat on opposite sides of the meetinghouse. The monthly meetings were the business meetings. During these meetings, attended by "Friends in good standing from several meetings for worship," Friends examined couples who planned to marry, disciplined members, and took care of other business. Representatives from the monthly meetings attended the quarterly meetings and the yearly meeting.[30]

There were separate monthly, quarterly, and yearly meetings for men and women. This division was intended to prevent either sex from being overburdened. Instead, they shared the workload. In addition, the separation permitted some modesty, because each sex could talk separately. Together, the men and women's meetings oversaw the congregation. Quaker belief emphasized the importance of family, and the Quaker community became an extension of the family. The women's meetings and the men's meetings each had their own officers, who were "weighty" Friends. The clerk took minutes and presided over the meeting, but ministers and elders had authority beyond the actual meeting. Ministers were called by God to preach; elders encouraged, supervised, and monitored the ministers. Quaker ministers (male or female) were known as Public Friends, and they were not ordained.[31]

Female Quaker leaders in colonial America usually did not become active in their meeting until they reached their mid-thirties. By this time, they had already raised children and usually had older children at home who could help care for younger siblings. Female leaders were generally married, and their husbands were often, but not always, members in good standing. Frequently, their husbands were officers in the men's meeting. Most of the active women came from wealthy households, and they had slaves or servants who could relieve them of some household duties. This permitted them to take care of business for the meeting. Female leaders paid visits to women who needed investigation, either because of rumors of untoward behavior or to examine them before a wedding could take place. The age and social status of the female leaders also aided them and gave them authority when they had to discipline or disown other women.[32]

Although many preaching women came from wealthy Quaker families, not all of them did. In a few cases, the spiritual accomplishments of a female preacher led to her marriage with a prominent man. For example, Elizabeth Sampson eloped from her home in Cheshire, England, when she was fourteen. Her husband died a few months later, and Elizabeth went to live with relatives in Ireland, because her father would not permit her to return home. These relatives were Quakers, but Elizabeth found their way of living too strict. She indentured herself and went to America, where her master sexually assaulted her. Despite her situation, Elizabeth managed to save money and bought out the last year of her indenture. She worked as a seamstress and then married a schoolteacher. Elizabeth was searching for spiritual awareness among the Quakers. Her husband opposed her search for religion, but ultimately he accepted Quakerism. He joined the army but was beaten because of his pacifist views. He died in 1741.

It took Elizabeth five years to pay her husband's debts, but she did. She then married the wealthy and prominent Chester County Quaker Aaron Ashbridge. After that, Elizabeth felt a call to preach in Great Britain. Although Aaron was not anxious to see his wife leave, he did not try to stop her. Instead he honored her calling. She left Pennsylvania in 1753 and died in Ireland in 1755.[33]

Some Quaker husbands were not so willing to have their wives become Public Friends. In 1700, Jane Biles went before the Philadelphia Yearling Meeting of Ministering Friends. She felt a calling to travel as a minister to England, but her husband objected. The Friends at the meeting sided with Jane, believing that her "divine leanings" were more important than her duty to her husband.[34]

Quakers do not have a church hierarchy or sacraments. They believe everyone has the inner light within them and that those who feel the calling to minister should do so. Nevertheless, making the decision to become a Public Friend was not easy. For many women, the decision to travel and preach was very difficult. Philadelphia Quaker Elizabeth Hudson wrestled with the decision. She felt "unfitness for Such an aufule undertaking and fear of my being Misstaken respecting my being call'd theirto & the Ill Consequence attending Such mis-stakes was Continually before my Eye." Elizabeth Collins recalled a time in 1778 when "her mind became exercised under an aprehension, that she was called to bear public testimony."[35]

Friends experienced "awakenings," just as the members of other churches did. One historian notes that there were "moments of intense collective spirituality that swept through the meetings, leaving an increased number of women who felt the obligation to become Public Friends." In 1732–1734, for example, "one hundred ministers came forth in the Philadelphia Meeting."[36]

The Biblical Deborah became a symbol of female ministry. Deborah was a prophet. She was also a leader who heard God's voice and led an army of men against the Canaanite captain Sisera. Ann Cooper Whitall, a New Jersey Quaker, remembered the male minister who had visited their meeting and declared that a Deborah would arise from among them. In her journal, Ann wrote of her desire for that to happen: "I hope thay ar on there way." A year later, she wrote, "Shall we be brought out of bondage by a Debrow as the Children of Iesral was. o who is Debrow."[37]

Some women did emerge as leaders, and some even founded new sects. Jemima Wilkinson, for example, created a new religion after being seriously ill. Jemima was born a Quaker in Rhode Island, but became a Baptist during a revival in 1774. She believed that she had died during her illness and that she had been reborn as Christ. As she reported the episode, two angels who descended to Earth from Heaven visited her: "And the Angels said, the Spirit of Life from God had descended to earth, to warn a lost and guilty, perishing, dying world, to flee from the wrath which is to come . . . And then taking her leave of the family between the hour of nine and ten in the morning, dropped the dying flesh & yielded up the Ghost. And according to the declaration of the Angels, the Spirit took full possession of the Body it now Animates." Jemima then took a new name, Publick Universal Friend, and she refused to answer to Jemima. According to one scholar, she took on an "ambiguously gendered persona" and wore a long black robe, similar to a clerical robe.[38]

Jemima Wilkinson advocated celibacy, and that, along with her ambiguous gender orientation, upset many people more than her theology. She did, however, attract followers. Some of her disciples even looked upon her as a mes-siah. Nevertheless, she scandalized many, and a mob threw stones at her in Pennsylvania. She retreated to western New York and founded a utopian com-munity there in 1790. Within a decade, it had 260 inhabitants. Nevertheless, she was unable to sustain the movement, and it disintegrated after her death in 1819.[39]

Ann Lee was also a Quaker who created a new sect that became known as the Shakers. She left England and immigrated to the American colonies in 1774. Within a couple of years, she was preaching that she was Christ's female successor or bride, and she became known to her followers as "Mother Ann." Unlike Jemima Wilkinson, Ann Lee dressed as a woman and conducted herself as a woman, but she, too, practiced celibacy, and, in fact, she believed that it was necessary to remain celibate in order to achieve salvation.

Shakers referred to one another as brother and sister, and men and women lived apart, even those who joined as married couples. Because Shaker women did not give birth, Shakers adopted children, who, when they reached the age of twenty-one, could decide if they wanted to remain in the community. Shakers believed in the equality of the sexes, and they lived communally in agricultural communities. Although Mother Ann died in 1784, the Shakers continued to form communities in the Northeast, Ohio, and Kentucky.[40]

Before her spiritual awakening, Ann Lee had given birth to four children, all of whom died in childhood. It is not surprising then that she may have found a celibate life desirable. Similarly, a fear of childbirth, combined with a growing belief and internalization that women were passionless, may have made celibacy attractive to many women. Other sects, such as the Ephrata Cloister in Pennsylvania, also believed in celibacy and an androgynous God.[41]

The Moravians were another religious group that many women found appealing. Arriving in the 1740s, they began recruiting from the German Reformed and Lutheran communities. They built a settlement in Bethlehem, Pennsylvania, and then others in North Carolina and elsewhere. Like the Shakers and other groups, the Moravians lived communally at first. They organized "choirs" by age, gender, and marital status. Thus, there were separate choirs for single men and women, married men and women, and widowed men and women. Women led the women's choirs. Men held the top leadership positions as priests and bishops, but women could be deacons and acolytes. There was a nursery for children over eighteen months old, permitting married women to participate fully in the community. In addition, there was a separate choir for single women, which gave unmarried women a chance to have a significant role without having to marry.[42]

Within the Moravian Indian Missions, women were in charge of services, as well as outreach services to women. In the mission congregations, women served as elders. Female missionaries converted Indians to Christianity. Between 1742 and 1764, Moravians baptized 276 Delaware and Mahican women and girls and 229 men and boys. As a result of Moravian missionary activity among Native Americans, female networks developed. As a scholar of the Moravians and Indians explains, "Between 1746 and 1755, a continual stream of women from Bethlehem and other white communities at the Forks of the Delaware visited native communities, conducted religious services, taught schools, prepared meals, brought gifts, and dressed and buried the dead for Indian women and their families at Gnadenhütten and Meniolagomekah [mission settlements].

Native women expressed the joy of finding other women with whom they might share their household responsibilities and spiritual lives."[43]

In the mission towns, Moravians introduced the custom of godparenting. When they baptized a Native American child, both missionaries and Indians became his or her godparents. A child might have several godparents. For example, the Delaware Maria's daughter Christina was baptized in 1756. She had two German women and three Mahican women as godparents. The custom of godparenting was easily adapted to Native American beliefs, because, as one scholar notes, "Indians, who recognized the responsibility of the entire community in raising children, could understand godparenting as another way to create and use kinship connections."[44]

One historian suggests that "Indian women found Christianity and Moravian religious practices in particular a source of power that could enhance their spiritual authority rather than diminish it." They placed Christian religious practices within the context of their own familiar practices. Furthermore, the female imagery and theology of the Moravian Church may have been attractive to some Indian women. The single sisters lived and worked together, and they "celebrated femaleness" within their religious discussions of the Virgin Mary and themselves as brides of Christ. "Perhaps most important to this female piety, the Moravians portrayed the Holy Spirit as Mother."[45]

Women's roles in many tribes involved both planting and healing. Algonquian women, for example, often served as the religious centers within their households, and they passed their knowledge and traditions on to their daughters. Among the Delaware and Mahican, women performed healing ceremonies and also helped the shaman. Women's power was linked to fertility and reproduction. Women were very powerful, and the seclusion of women during menstruation was seen as a way of keeping their spirits from interfering with the men's hunting. On the other hand, tribes recognized and attempted to harness the power of women and their connection to fertility by putting them in charge of planting and distributing food.[46]

The Great Awakening and evangelizing also converted free and enslaved black men and women. It was difficult to maintain or practice African religions because slavery had uprooted Africans from their homelands. Yet some traditions, such as birthing customs and magic, did survive. Women were usually in charge of these areas. When evangelizing efforts first converted black men and women, they could not usually combine African and Christian practices because the congregations were mainly white. Later, however, when they formed their own congregations in the period after the Revolution, they were able to do so.[47]

First Baptists and then Methodists were particularly successful in converting Africans because they preached that true repentance and acceptance of Christ were the necessary components, not reciting creeds or catechisms. It was possible to be illiterate, unschooled, and yet saved. African women, like white women and Indian women, were the most likely to be converted. At the end of the eighteenth century, 73 percent of black members who joined the Methodist Church were women.[48]

The Revolution and thoughts of equality made some groups question slavery. Quakers began to discuss the morality of slavery in the middle of the eighteenth century. In the 1770s, many Quakers began freeing their slaves, and, in 1776, the Philadelphia Friends' meeting decided to disown slaveholding members. Methodists decided to expel slaveholders in 1784, and some Baptist congregations also did not permit slaveholding members.[49]

The Revolutionary War affected and changed religion and religious practices in eighteenth-century America in other ways. In some churches, for example, ministers left their pulpits to become soldiers. Congregations were split, too, because some members supported the British side and some the American side. Pacifist groups were also affected. Ann Lee and some of her followers were imprisoned on suspicion of aiding the British, because they refused to sign loyalty oaths. Quakers, such as Elizabeth Drinker's husband Henry, were also imprisoned for not signing loyalty oaths. It was difficult to remain neutral or to maintain pacifist principles in the midst of the Revolution.

In addition, the image of women began to change. Instead of being viewed as lustful and easily swayed by temptation, women began to be seen as virtuous and capable of influencing others by their own example. As business concerns began to move outside of the home, women became the moral centers within the home. Following the Revolution, some white women took on the role of Republican mothers, the educators of future citizens. (For more on education, see Chapter 7.)

NOTES

1. Laurel Thatcher Ulrich, *Good Wives: Image and Reality in the Lives of Women in Northern New England, 1650–1750* (New York: Oxford University Press, 1982), 216–219.

2. Ann M. Little, *Abraham in Arms: War and Gender in Colonial New England* (Philadelphia: University of Pennsylvania Press, 2007), 128.

3. Elizabeth Hanson, *God's Mercy Surmounting Man's Cruelty* (Philadelphia, 1729) quoted in Little, *Abraham in Arms*, 136.

4. Little, *Abraham in Arms*, 159–161.

5. Little, *Abraham in Arms*, 161–164.

6. Emma Coleman, *New England Captives Carried to Canada* (Portland, ME: Southworth Press, 1925), I. 429, quoted in Laurel Thatcher Ulrich, *Good Wives: Image and Reality in the Lives of Women in Northern New England, 1650–1750* (New York: Oxford University Press, 1982), 211.

7. Joy Day Buel and Richard Buel, Jr., *The Way of Duty: A Woman and Her Family in Revolutionary America* (New York: W. W. Norton, 1984), 25, 38.

8. Joan R. Gunderson, *To Be Useful to the World: Women in Revolutionary America, 1740–1790*, rev. ed., (Chapel Hill: University of North Carolina Press, 2006), 118; Marilyn J. Westlake, *Women and Religion in Early America, 1600–1850: The Puritan and Evangelical Traditions* (New York: Routledge, 1999), 79–80, 84.

9. Field Horne, ed. *The Diary of Mary Cooper: Life on a Long Island Farm, 1768–1773* (Oyster Bay, NY: Oyster Bay Historical Society, 1981), ix–xi, 8, 13.

10. Buel and Buel, *The Way of Duty*, 4, 9–17.

11. Carol F. Karlsen and Laurie Crumpacker, eds. *The Journal of Esther Edwards Burr, 1754–1757* (New Haven, CT: Yale University Press, 1984), 8.

12. Westlake, *Women and Religion in Early America*, 88, 93–94.

13. Samuel Hopkins, *The Life and Character of the Late Reverend, Learned and Pious Mr. Jonathan Edwards* (Edinburgh: Alexander Jardine , 1799), 46, 57, 113, quoted in Karlsen and Crumpacker, *The Journal of Esther Edwards Burr*, 10.

14. Karlsen and Crumpacker, *The Journal of Esther Edwards Burr*, 10–11.

15. Hopkins, Edwards, 112, quoted in Karlsen and Crumpacker, *The Journal of Esther Edward Burr*, 12.

16. Joseph Fish, *The Church of CHRIST a firm and durable House. . .* (New London, CT, 1767), 116–117, quoted in Buel and Buel, *The Way of Duty*, 11.

17. Samuel Hopkins, *Memoirs of the Life of Mrs. Sarah Osborn* (Catskill, NY: N. Elliot, 1814), 32, quoted in Westlake, *Women and Religion in Early America*, 89.

18. Westlake, *Women and Religion in Early America*, 90.

19. "The Diary of Nicholas Gilman," ed. William Kidder (Unpublished M.A. thesis, U. of New Hampshire, 1967), 253, 243, quoted in Ulrich, *Good Wives*, 224–225.

20. Gunderson, *To Be Useful to the World*, 113–114.

21. Gunderson, *To Be Useful to the World*, 114.

22. Gunderson, *To Be Useful to the World*, 114.

23. Devereux Jarratt, *The Life of the Reverend Devereux Jarratt* (1806), in Rosemary Radford Ruether and Rosemary Skinner Keller, eds. *Women and Religion in America*, vol. 2, *The Colonial and Revolutionary Periods* (New York: Harper & Row, 1983), 214–215, quoted in Westlake, *Women and Religion in Early America*, 97.

24. Westlake, *Women and Religion in Early America*, 98–99.

25. Westlake, *Women and Religion in Early America*, 99–100.

26. Sarah Osborn to Joseph Fish, 28 February–7 March 1767, in Mary Beth Norton, ed., "'My Resting Reaping Times': Sarah Osborn's Defense of her Unfeminine Activities, 1767," *Signs* 2 (Winter 1976), 525, quoted in Westlake, *Women and Religion in Early America*, 100.

27. Norton, "Sarah Osborn," 522–524, in Westlake, *Women and Religion in Early America*, 100–101.

28. Norton, "Sarah Osborn," 526, quoted in Nancy Woloch. ed. *Early American Women: A Documentary History, 1600–1900* (Belmont, CA: Wadsworth Publishing, 1992), 157–158.

29. Jean R. Soderlund, "Women's Authority in Pennsylvania and New Jersey Quaker Meetings, 1680–1760," *William and Mary Quarterly*, XLIV (October 1987), 723–724.

30. Soderlund, "Women's Authority," 725.

31. Soderlund, "Women's Authority," 727; Joan M. Jensen, *Loosening the Bonds: Mid-Atlantic Farm Women, 1750–1850* (New Haven, CT: Yale University Press, 1986), 145.

32. Soderlund, "Women's Authority," 728-736.

33. Westlake, *Women and Religion in Early America*, 82–83.

34. Rebecca Larson, *Daughters of the Light: Quaker Women Preaching and Prophesying in the Colonies and Abroad, 1700–1775* (Chapel Hill: University of North Carolina Press, 2000), 143.

35. Susanna Lightfoot and Elizabeth Daniel, in *A Collection of Memorials Concerning Divers Deceased Ministers and Others of the People Called Quakers* (Philadelphia: Crukshank, 1887), 205, 400, "Memoirs of Elizabeth Collins," 11:472, 452, Friends Library, Swarthmore College, Swarthmore, PA, both in Jensen, *Loosening the Bonds*, 155, 156.

36. Jensen, *Loosening the Bonds*, 155.

37. Ann Cooper Whitall Diary, Quaker Collection, Haverford College, Haverford, PA, quoted in Jensen, *Loosening the Bonds*, 155.

38. "A Memorandum of the Introduction of the Fatal Fever," undated Jemima Wilkinson Papers, 1771–1849, Department of Manuscripts and University Archives, Carl A. Kroch Library, Cornell University Library, in Susan Juster, "'Neither Male nor Female': Jemima Wilkinson and the Politics of Gender in Post-Revolutionary America," in *Possible Pasts: Becoming Colonial in Early America*, Robert Blair St. George, ed. (Ithaca, NY: Cornell University Press, 2000), 361.

39. James Henretta, "'Unruly Women': Jemima Wilkinson and Deborah Sampson, Biographies from Early America," *Early America Review* (Fall 1996), http://www.earlyamerica.com/review/fall96/biography.html; Gunderson, *To Be Useful to the World*, 127.

40. "The Shakers," National Park Service, http://www.nps.gov/history/nr/travel/shaker/shakers.htm.

41. Gunderson, *To Be Useful to the World*, 128.

42. Westlake, *Women and Religion in Early America*, 92; Gunderson, *To Be Useful to the World*, 113.

43. Jane T. Merritt, *At the Crossroads: Indians and Empires on a Mid-Atlantic Frontier, 1700–1763* (Chapel Hill: University of North Carolina Press, 2003), 144.

44. Merritt, *At the Crossroads*, 144.

45. Merritt, *At the Crossroads*, 103, 105.

46. Merritt, *At the Crossroads*, 103–104; Gunderson, *To Be Useful to the World*, 121.

47. Gunderson, *To Be Useful to the World*, 117.

48. Gunderson, *To Be Useful to the World*, 117.

49. Gunderson, *To Be Useful to the World*, 209.

SUGGESTED READING

Buel, Joy Day, and Richard Buel, Jr. *The Way of Duty: A Woman and Her Family in Revolutionary America*. New York: W. W. Norton, 1984.

Gunderson, Joan R. *To Be Useful to the World: Women in Revolutionary America, 1740–1790*, rev. ed. Chapel Hill: University of North Carolina Press, 2006.

Horne, Field, Ed. *The Diary of Mary Cooper: Life on a Long Island Farm, 1768–1773*. Oyster Bay, NY: Oyster Bay Historical Society, 1981.

Jensen, Joan M. *Loosening the Bonds: Mid-Atlantic Farm Women, 1750–1850*. New Haven, CT: Yale University Press, 1986.

Karlsen, Carol F., and Laurie Crumpacker, eds. *The Journal of Esther Edwards Burr, 1754–1757*. New Haven, CT: Yale University Press, 1984.

Merritt, Jane T. *At the Crossroads: Indians and Empires on a Mid-Atlantic Frontier, 1700–1763*. Chapel Hill: University of North Carolina Press, 2003.

Soderlund, Jean R. "Women's Authority in Pennsylvania and New Jersey Quaker Meetings, 1680–1760." *William and Mary Quarterly*, XLIV (October 1987).

Ulrich, Laurel Thatcher. *Good Wives: Image and Reality in the Lives of Women in Northern New England, 1650–1750*. New York: Oxford University Press, 1982.

Westlake, Marilyn J. *Women and Religion in Early America, 1600–1850: The Puritan and Evangelical Traditions*. New York: Routledge, 1999.

7

———∽∞∽———

Women, Education, and the Arts

Before the Revolution, education for most young people was often a random affair. The degree and type of education an individual received depended on class, gender, and race, but it was also affected by location. In 1642, Massachusetts became the first American colony to pass a law requiring that children be taught to read. In 1710, the law was amended to make it clear that boys must be taught to read and write, but girls only had to be taught to read. Changes to the Massachusetts law in 1771 provided new specifications for children apprenticed under the Poor Laws: for "males, reading writing, cyphering; females, reading writing."[1]

The southern colonies did not pass any similar laws requiring apprenticed children to be educated. In fact, there was little provision for any elementary education at all, although there were Latin grammar schools in some larger Virginia towns, and there were individuals, both male and female, who bequeathed land to establish some free schools. Wealthier families employed private tutors—nearly always men—to educate their children. The families provided the tutors with housing and meals, as well as a modest stipend. For extra income, some tutors also taught students who lived outside of the household. In addition to private tutors and a few free schools, colonial Virginia had some private schools, especially in places such as Williamsburg. In 1724, a report from twenty-nine Anglican clergymen noted the existence of several private schools within their parishes.[2]

In contrast to the southern colonies, Pennsylvania passed a law in 1683 requiring parents and masters to make sure that both boys and girls were able to read the scriptures and be able to write by the time they were twelve years old.

Philadelphia Friends Meeting established a school for boys and girls in 1690. Those of means paid a fee, but poor children were educated for free. Although there were not as many schools in rural Pennsylvania, one historian has asserted, "girls of the lowest social class probably had better educational opportunities in Philadelphia than anywhere else in the colonies."[3]

Unlike today, reading and writing were taught separately in the colonial period. Reading was taught orally, using hornbooks and primers, and no writing was required. Colonial Americans considered writing to be a specialized skill, necessary for men to master for business and legal matters, but not so necessary for women to be able to do. For colonial Americans, as one scholar has noted, "Writing was a job-related skill. Because girls were being trained not to hold jobs but to be successful homemakers, penmanship was an irrelevant acquisition for them. The skill that corresponded, for girls, to what writing was for boys was the ability to sew."[4]

Although in the colonies in the seventeenth century women taught reading in numerous informal schools within their homes, known as "dame schools," men almost always taught writing. A late seventeenth-century verse by a Philadelphia judge explained:

Good women, who do very well
Bring little ones to read and spell,
Which fits them for their writing; and then
Here's men to bring them to their pen,
And to instruct and make them quick
In all sorts of arithmetic.[5]

The daughters of the well-to-do learned to write because their parents provided them with private instruction, and not everyone considered it a useless skill for women. For example, Milcah Martha Moore was taught at home. In 1739, her parents, Richard and Deborah Hill, moved to the island of Madeira, where Milcah Martha was born in 1740. Before her birth, six of her siblings had been sent to live with her sister, Hannah Hill, who was sixteen and recently married to her cousin, Samuel Preston Moore. When Deborah died in 1751, Milcah and a brother went to live with Hannah in Philadelphia. Before her death, however, Deborah had written to Hannah, telling her, "I must approve of thy not sending my dear little girls to school, but having them taught at home under thy own eye." Deborah clearly saw no problem with women writing, "[T]he instruction . . . will ground them in a good hand, which they may keep if they write a copy or two a day."[6]

Even at her young age, Milcah Martha apparently wrote well and worked as a copyist at her father's business. As a biographer of Milcah Martha notes, "This emphasis on copying as a means of improving minds and penmanship was a common educational theme." The practice of copying evidently took root in Milcah Martha, who kept a commonplace book for many years.[7]

Yet writing in the eighteenth century presented some technical challenges that modern-day individuals seldom consider. For one thing, in order to write, a person needed pen, ink, and paper. Although more widely available in the eighteenth century than in the seventeenth, these items still needed to be purchased or prepared. Moreover, even if available, these objects were not always ready to use, as the eight-year-old Milcah Martha reported in a letter to her sisters, "I cant mend my pens myself but I will learn that I may have a good pen when I want one."[8]

Opportunities for female education improved during the eighteenth century, because some town schoolmasters taught female students "out of hours."[9] Furthermore, more New England towns began hiring female schoolteachers, thus giving women more prospects to be educated. Penmanship also became easier in the eighteenth century because of a switch from the more ornate secretary hand to the eighteenth-century round hand.[10] The increased availability of secular reading material, the creation of new schools, and the belief that the citizens of the new republic should be educated led to increased literacy for both boys and girls in the period after the Revolution.

Nevertheless, in the eighteenth century, the education of white girls and young women generally involved both practical skills and academics. Even within the same households, most women received a more limited education than their brothers. The granddaughter of Martha Washington, Eliza Custis, received spelling and reading lessons from her mother and cousin in Virginia in the 1780s. Her stepfather then brought in a private tutor to complete her education. Eliza "was an extraordinary child & would if a Boy, make a brilliant figure," her tutor was told, but neither he nor her stepfather would permit her to learn Greek or Latin, because they believed "women ought not to know these things."[11]

The ten-year-old Virginian Elizabeth Pratt understood that her brother William's education was far superior to her own. As she wrote to him:

I find you have got the Start of me in Learning very much, for you write better already than I expect to do as long as I live and you are got as far as the Rule of three in Arethmatick, but I can't cast up a Sum in Adition cleverly, but I am Striving to do better every day, I can perform a great many dances and am now Learning the Sibell but I cannot speak a word of French.[12]

In contrast, Thomas Lee of Stratford Hall in Virginia provided both his sons and his daughters, Alice and Hannah, with a wide-ranging education through private tutors. For example, Hannah read books on a variety of subjects, including law, politics, religion, and literature. More commonly in the households of the gentry, girls were taught basic reading, writing, and arithmetic, while their brothers were also taught Latin and Greek. Both boys and girls received dancing and music lessons.[13]

Many American Jewish families educated both sons and daughters. Because most Jewish families lived in towns, they generally had access to some schooling, in addition to religious education provided by synagogues. Parents also wanted their children to be capable of handling careers in trade, requiring them to be literate (sometimes in several languages). Jewish girls in the American colonies often learned to read both English and Hebrew, although they probably learned only enough Hebrew to follow prayers. Moreover, in New York, and perhaps elsewhere, many Jewish individuals named Jewish women to execute their wills, which may have indicated their confidence in the women being both shrewd and literate.[14]

Wealthy Jewish parents provided their offspring with private tutors, just as wealthy Christian parents did. In New York in the 1730s, Phila Franks "studied with George Brownell, who gave private lesson in reading, writing, arithmetic, accounting, Greek, Latin, embroidery, and dancing." Phila's brother Moses and her sister Richa received comparable educations. Jewish women, especially those born in America, were generally literate. Because their families were often scattered throughout the colonies and Europe, they tended to regard letter writing quite seriously.[15]

In 1797, for example, Jacob Mordecai, a shopkeeper in North Carolina, wrote to his young daughters, Rachel and Ellen, telling them to "mind your reading and writing, that you maybe able to send letters often, for I love you so dearly that I shall always be pleased when you can write to me." Jacob's wife, Judith, had died, and Jacob sent some of his six children to live with relatives.

Mothers often gave both their sons and daughters their first instruction in reading. Many schools expected children to arrive already able to read. Sometimes older children within a family taught the younger ones, or an unmarried aunt or grandmother took over daily instruction. Mary Palmer Tyler was born in Boston shortly before the start of the American Revolution. Her unmarried aunt taught her to read, but her mother listened to her recite her lessons. Mary and her sister Betsy took over the housework when they were teenagers so that their mother could teach their younger siblings. Mary and Betsy, however, taught their youngest sibling, Sophia, but they were not very successful, because, as Mary later reported, they "had not been properly taught ourselves." After Mary married Royall Tyler, the couple moved to Vermont. Mary's younger sister, Amelia, came to stay with the Tylers to teach the couple's eleven children to read.[16]

In most cases, mothers also gave their children their first religious instruction. Rebecca Samuel wrote to her parents from Petersburg, Virginia, around 1792. While bemoaning the lack of Jewish culture, she observed, "My Schoene [my daughter], God bless her, is already three years old; I think it is time that she should learn something, and she has a good head to learn. I have taught her the bedtime prayers and grace after meals in just two lessons. I believe that no one among the Jews here can do as well as she."[17]

Educated men who had the time to do so also took an interest in the education of their sons and daughters. Mary Fish recalled that her parents "early put us to the best schools that Stonington [Connecticut] afforded, but they did not depend on them for our instruction. My father's practice was every day to take us into his study, immediately after family prayers in the morning, and hear us read, and he would give us advice for the day. He would also enjoin it upon us to read our bibles by ourselves every day." In 1751, as discussed in Chapter 6, Mary went to Sarah Osborn's school in Newport.[18]

Barnard Gratz, a member of an influential Jewish family in Philadelphia, was concerned about his daughter Rachel's education. During the Revolution, he sent her away to Lancaster, Pennsylvania, for safety. She was about fifteen years old. Rachel Gratz, who adored her father, wrote to him from Lancaster in 1779, to give him an update on her education: "You mention in your letter about my minding my schooling, which shall do my endeavors to learn as I know it is my dear daddy's desire. I have just begun to cipher and I am very delighted at it. I am in averdepois weight[19] and now can cast up anything."[20]

As the Revolution made them aware that they could be building a new nation, many Americans became more concerned about the state of education. In a letter to her husband John in August 1776, Abigail Adams wrote:

> You remark upon the deficiency of Education in your Countrymen. It never I believe was in a worse state . . . If you complain of neglect of Education in sons, what shall I say with regard to daughters, who every day experience the want of it. With regard to the Education of my own children, I find myself soon out of my debth, and destitute and deficient in every part of Education.
>
> I most sincerely wish that Some more liberal plan might be laid and Excecuted for the Benefit of the rising generation, and that of our New constitution may be distinguished for Learning and virtue. If we mean to have Heroes Statesmen and Philosophers, we should have learned women . . . If much depends as is allowed upon the early Education of youth and the first principals which are instilld take the deepest root, great benifit must arrise from litirary accomplishments in women.[21]

Abigail was evidently concerned about her ability to instruct her own offspring, and, without improvements in education, she feared for future generations. If the new republic was to flourish, its citizens needed to be educated. Clearly, women had to achieve an appropriate level of learning in order to teach their children. In this passage, Abigail Adams articulates an ideology that became popular in the decades following the Revolution. One historian has labeled it "Republican Motherhood."[22]

Many, however, continued to disapprove of female education beyond basic reading and writing. Yet in the new republic, mothers and their role in educating and inculcating moral values in the youth of the nation assumed a new importance. Thus, it was in the best interests of the nation that girls—as future mothers—be educated. Particularly in the North, many schools for girls opened between 1790 and 1830.

Abigail Adams, from an original painting by Gilbert Stuart. Courtesy Library of Congress.

Some of these early educational opportunities were marginal. For example, some New England schools opened their doors to girls and young boys during the summer, when the older boys were working in the fields. The schools did not have to be heated then, and the teachers were young women who did not have

Minerva, the goddess of wisdom, wel-
comes children. In the new republic,
children were to be educated to be virtuous citizens. Classical themes were
popular in the late eighteenth century.
Courtesy Library of Congress.

to be paid as much as men. Yet women also founded and taught girls in a growing number of private schools and academies. In Litchfield, Connecticut, Sarah
Pierce's school grew from a few girls gathered around her dining room table to
one that attracted "students from as far away as the British West Indies."[23]

In the post-Revolutionary period, much attention was given to how girls
should be educated and what they should be taught. Judith Sargent Murray, the
prolific essayist, poet, and playwright from Massachusetts, was an early advocate
for improving women's education. She first developed this theme in an essay, "On
the Equality of the Sexes." She wrote the essay in 1779 but did not publish it until
1790. In this essay, she compares the intellect and training of boys and girls. She
reasons that male and female mental abilities are similar in childhood, but because
the education of girls was so limited, they could not develop their minds fully.[24]

Judith Sargent Murray believed that women should be educated for more than
marriage and that they should be competent and self-reliant. Writing in the

1790s, she declared that, if women were educated properly, "the term, helpless widow, might be rendered as unfrequent and inapplicable as that of helpless widower."[25] Nevertheless, Judith Sargent Murray did realize that most women would marry. Thus, she believed they should be educated so that they could teach their children. She believed women should be able to read and write properly, know French and history, and have some knowledge of geography and astronomy.[26]

The Philadelphia physician, educator, and writer Benjamin Rush also advocated a new curriculum for women. In 1787, he put forth his ideas in a speech made to the Board of Visitors of the Young Ladies' Academy of Philadelphia, later published as "Thoughts Upon Female Education, Accommodated to the Present State of Society, Manners and Government in the United States of America." In addition to reading, writing, and grammar, Rush believed that women should know geography, natural philosophy, and bookkeeping, to enable them to care for their husbands' property and concerns when widowed.[27]

The Young Ladies' Academy did not adopt all of Benjamin Rush's suggestions for its curriculum, but it did include "reading, writing, arithmetic, English grammar, composition, rhetoric, and geography." It did not include natural philosophy, the classics, or advanced mathematics. Neither did it include needlework. The Young Ladies' Academy was a private school. Nearly 100 girls enrolled in the school during its first year. Students and teachers took education seriously at the Young Ladies' Academy. Nevertheless, both the teachers and the young women themselves expected their education would be used to uphold traditional female values, such as modesty and decorum.[28]

Quakers may not have been as influenced by Republican Motherhood as they were by the belief that mothers had to provide a religious education for their children. Some Quaker women were illiterate, and yet, they still needed to be able to educate their offspring. Therefore, even before the Revolution, Quakers were concerned with educating women. After the Revolution, Quakers began to focus on establishing schools for both themselves and for the poor. As Quaker women began to marry at a later age and often had fewer responsibilities at home, teaching became a more an attractive option for them. Consequently, more schools opened, providing both employment for young women and an education for girls. In turn, these newly educated girls became the next generation of teachers.[29]

There were some Quaker female teachers in the schools of pre-Revolutionary Philadelphia, but they usually taught only reading, spelling, and sewing to black children. In general, men taught writing to boys and the more advanced classes given to white boys and girls. In the 1790s, female Quaker ministers encouraged young women to teach Quaker children and the poor. Ruth Walmsley, for example, recommended "a plan for improving the female character, by employing teachers of their own sex to cultivate the minds and improve the manners of female youth," whereas, as Sarah Cresson noted in her diary, the minister Deborah

Darby "encourage[d] Young Women, to undertake the care of not only their own connections, Younger branches of their own families, but also poor children."[30]

As more young women began to teach, their older female relatives became more interested in the schools. Quaker women became active in donating time and money to the building of schools and in overseeing school-related activities. Quaker women also formed and became involved in associations dedicated to teaching the poor.[31]

Toward the end of the eighteenth century, until about 1850, Quakers began building boarding schools. One of the most successful was Westtown, which is still in operation. Westtown was founded in 1799. It was located in rural Chester County, Pennsylvania. Although the school admitted both girls and boys, it became predominantly female by 1824. Girls came from Pennsylvania, New Jersey, and fourteen other states. Along with academic subjects, girls were taught "domestic employments," and the first students were required to bring a "pair of Scissors, Thread-case, Thimble, Work-bag and some plain sewing or knitting to begin with." After the school realized that not all of the female students wanted to sew, Westtown limited the sewing to those "sewing scholars" who did desire to do so.[32]

For much of the eighteenth century, however, girls and young women were instructed in needlework as a matter of course. Some families hired sewing tutors or sent their daughters to sewing schools.[33] Alice Lee Shippen, who had received a more wide-ranging education than many of her peers, encouraged her daughter Nancy to learn other skills she believed to be more important to a woman. These skills included, among others, needlework, holding utensils properly, and learning to curtsey.[34] To Alice Lee Shippen, the daughter of a wealthy planter, it was essential for her daughter to possess the skills needed to run a household smoothly while displaying the outward signs of gentility. Both rich and poor girls in Virginia received gender-specific instruction, but the daughters of the elite received music and dancing lessons, along with learning domestic skills. As apprentices and wives, most young women had to cook, spin, churn butter, sew, take care of children, care for livestock, and perform other household chores. On occasion, they had to help in the fields. In contrast, the wife of a planter supervised staff and, as one historian of women in eighteenth-century Virginia explains, "ran households graciously, cheerfully, and efficiently while maintaining an aura of respectable leisure," as part of "the gentry's culture of hospitality."[35]

Almost all girls learned to sew. At age six or seven, they began to learn some of the basics and were taught to care for their sewing baskets. Completing a sampler was often the first project for a young girl. After that, she might be given simple mending to do or sewing seams. Eventually, she was permitted to cut fabric. The production of clothing took a great deal of time, effort, and resources. Consequently, as a scholar of women and needlework notes, "the ability to prolong the life of a garment, to mend, alter, or remake worn or outdated clothing was among the earliest skills most women acquired."[36]

Eighteenth-century education began early for both boys and girls. In most homes, infants and toddlers remained with their mothers as they did their daily chores. White babies slept in cradles and later scooted about in carts. The infants of enslaved mothers went with their mothers to the fields. Native American mothers placed their infants in cradleboards, although, in the eighteenth century, some Native American mothers had adopted European American customs of childrearing. As children grew older, they imitated adults while they played and did chores, such as grinding corn. At about eight years old, daughters began to help with household work if their families were free. Poor and orphaned children might be apprenticed—usually to learn the skills of housewifery. Sometimes apprenticeship stipulated that the girls would also be taught to read and write or taught a skill, such as spinning. Although they were not formally bound by legal agreements, many young women in the Connecticut Valley apprenticed in the clothing trades. The rural artisans, the girls who were being trained, and the community around them recognized their status as apprentices. Some of these young women came from wealthy families. Patty Smith, the apprentice of gown-maker Rebecca Dickinson, was the daughter of one of the wealthiest men in Hadley, Massachusetts. Of course, other young women served formal apprenticeships in the clothing trades, arranged by either their parents or town selectmen.[37]

For the daughters of enslaved mothers, childhood depended on the wishes of their master. They might be put to work in fields, put in charge of younger children, placed as a companion to a white child, or even sold to another household.[38] Some slaves, however, were taught to read. While managing her father's plantation in South Carolina as a young woman, Eliza Lucas began teaching some of the slaves. In a letter in 1742, she revealed her plans. She first described her typical day, which involved waking at five, reading until seven, overseeing the household, having breakfast, spending time on her music, and practicing other subjects, such as French and shorthand. "After that I devote the rest of the time till I dress for dinner to our little Polly and two black girls who I teach to read, and if I have my paps's approbation (my Mamas I have got) I intend [them] for school mistress's for the rest of the Negroe children." Later in the afternoon, Eliza practiced music again, did needlework "till candle light," and then went to bed to read or write.[39]

The education of slaves was left to the discretion of their owners. Most likely, the slaves on most southern plantations were not taught to read. Some religious groups, however, did establish schools to teach blacks, both slave and free. The Associates of Dr. Bray, who had been an Anglican clergyman, established several schools in the colonies before the Revolution. Deborah Franklin was impressed by the one she visited in Philadelphia and decided to send her family's slave boy there. After receiving the letter that she wrote to him about her decision, Benjamin had it published in England. Benjamin was then asked to become a member of the Associates of Dr. Bray.[40]

Both free and enslaved black children were educated at the Bray School in Williamsburg, Virginia. Ann Wager was the schoolmistress from its opening in 1760 until her death in 1774, at which time the school was closed. After being widowed in 1748, Ann began teaching. She taught students at several plantations and then taught white students in Williamsburg. When the Bray Associates decided to open the Williamsburg School "for the Instruction of Negro Children," they decided that a schoolmistress would be a better choice than a schoolmaster, because the school would educate boys and girls, and "she may teach the Girls to Sew knit, &c. as well as all to read & say their Catechism."[41]

The school was held in Ann Wager's home in Williamsburg. In 1769, the local trustee for the Bray Associates rented a home for her that was large enough to hold all of her students. School began at six in the morning in the summer months and at seven in the morning during the winter. She taught about thirty students, who ranged in age from three to ten years old. In addition to teaching the students reading, writing, and the "Principles of Christian Religion," she was also supposed to teach them how to dress and behave and to impress upon them moral behavior and to be "faithful and obedient to their Masters."[42]

In Philadelphia, Anthony Benezet held evening classes for slaves. He was able to convince the Philadelphia Monthly Meeting to open a school that served black children and adults in 1770. Most schools for slaves taught young children whose labor was not as necessary, but the turnover rate was still high, because masters removed the children to do chores. In most of the schools, boys learned arithmetic, whereas girls were taught knitting, skills that would help them in their future roles.[43]

Religious awakenings and missionary efforts led to the opening of schools for Native Americans. Missionaries believed that it was important to educate girls, because women had so much influence within Indian families; however, they stressed European practices that often dislodged women from the traditional duties. For girls, charity schools generally emphasized the learning of domestic skills over academic ones. In charity schools for Indians, however, there was an even greater emphasis on vocational education. Many of the Indian girls educated in these schools did not learn to write. Furthermore, they usually attended them when they were older, at an age when they would be courting and learning how to be women of their tribe. Thus, they were often caught between two worlds.[44]

Yet, some of the elite women of the Mohawk and other tribes may have been more literate than it appears. Like some white women, they most likely could read, even if they could not write. Moreover, as education assumed increasing importance in the eighteenth century, they may have seen it as necessary in order to cope with and survive in the outside white world.

As literacy levels for women increased after the Revolution, so did their consumption of literature. New methods of printing and publication meant there were more books and magazines available in the latter part of the eighteenth century. As well, women were able to gain access to reading material through circulating libraries—376 were founded between 1730 and 1790.[45]

Much of what Americans read was written in Britain. Two of the most popular novels of the eighteenth century were Samuel Richardson's *Pamela, or Virtue Rewarded* (1740) and *Clarissa, or, the History of a Young Lady* (1747–1748). Both books were read by men and women and involved young women attempting to defend their virtue. Pamela resists Mr. B.'s attempts to seduce her, until he repents. Then she agrees to marry him. *Clarissa* does not end happily. Clarissa's would-be seducer, Lovelace, rapes her. She cannot overcome the shame of losing her chastity, and she eventually dies.

Esther Edwards Burr recorded her reactions to the books in letters to her friend Sarah Prince. On March 10, 1755, she wrote, " I have borrowed *Pamela* and am reading it now. I fancy I shan'nt like it so well as I did *Clarissa*." The next night, she wrote indignantly, "Pray my dear how could Pamela forgive Mr. B. all his Devilish conduct so as to consent to marry him? Sertainly this does not well agree with so much virtue and piety. Nay I think it a very great defect in the performance, and then is'nt it seting up Riches and honnour as the great essentials of happyness in a married state? Perhaps I am two rash in my judgement for I have not read it half out tho' I have enough to see the Devil in the Man." Finally, on March 12, Esther recorded her anger at the author: "He has degraded our sex most horridly, to go and represent such virtue as Pamela, falling in love with Mr. B. in the midst of such foul and abominable actions. I could never pardon him if he had not made it up in Clarissia. I guess he found his mistake, so took care to mend the first opportunity."[46]

The popularity of this literature was wide-ranging. The Maine midwife Martha Ballard mentioned within her diary reading only one book, a religious work. Yet her younger sister Dorothy had named two daughters, Pamela and Clarissa, after Richardson's heroines. Even if Martha did not read the books, she was certainly aware of them. It is unclear what Dorothy thought of these novels chronicling the seduction of women; she was almost five months pregnant when she married.[47]

Although they did little to stop the popularity of seduction novels and other fiction, warnings about the dangers of novel reading were pervasive in the new republic. Many felt that reading these books was a waste of time that could be spent improving oneself, or, worse, that they could put dangerous ideas into the heads of young women. One historian observes that "Even cautionary fiction, like *Charlotte Temple*, could be dangerous because it offered details of seduction in the very act of warning young women to be on their guard against rakes."[48]

Philadelphia Quaker Elizabeth Drinker was a prolific reader. Her diary mentions the many titles she read, which included religious works, as well as histories, poetry, and novels. She read publications such as *The Philadelphia Minerva*, a literary newspaper, too. Yet she always seemed apologetic for spending time reading, especially when she read a novel. Because she did needle-work as her daughter Molly read the novel aloud, she could justify the time she spent hearing Ann Radcliffe's *The Mysteries of Udolpho* in June 1795.[49] Yet, by this time in Elizabeth Drinker's life, she read almost every day. Unlike some women, however, she had the time to sit and read because she had household help. In July 1795, while staying at the family's country house, she noted this fact in her diary: "I have been taking extracts this evening from Brotherss book, being much, since I can up here, in the reading and writing humour, and having little or no work with me, The Servant girl here, is a kind of house-keeper, that I have a time of great leisure."[50]

Women also read a great deal of unpublished work. Poetry was very popular in the eighteenth century, and it was common for women to send their friends small gifts accompanied by a poem. Women also copied poems and essays into commonplace books. Milcah Martha Moore collected and copied both poetry and prose into her commonplace book. Much of the work in her book is by women who were well-known to her and who had some standing within her social circle as being talented writers. The three women who are featured most prominently in Milcah Martha Moore's commonplace book are Hannah Griffits, Susanna Wright, and Elizabeth Graeme Fergusson.[51]

Susanna Wright and Hannah Griffits were Quakers. Neither of them ever married. Susanna, born in 1697, was the oldest of the three women. She spent much of her life in Lancaster County, Pennsylvania. She was considered very pious, but she was also an intellectual, with interests that ranged from local politics to horticulture. She raised silkworms, and Benjamin Franklin presented some of her silk to the royal family. She wrote poetry as well.[52]

Hannah Griffits was born in 1727 and lived in Philadelphia. She exchanged letters and poems with Susanna Wright and used the pseudonym "Fidelia." As one scholar suggests, this was "possibly to indicate her faithfulness to the single life and her commitment to the Quaker faith and community." In contrast, Elizabeth Graeme Fergusson was an Anglican, born in 1737. She was well-known in Philadelphia's literary circles, had work published in the 1780s and 1790s, and held literary salons in her home. She was more cosmopolitan than the other two women; she traveled abroad and wrote about it, and she wrote more secular work than the other two Quaker women.[53]

Collections of poetry and other writing, such as that of Milcah Martha, were sent to family members and friends. Moreover, "this movement of literary material was a regular feature of correspondence."[54] Yet letter writing in itself was a type of art form in the eighteenth century. Epistolary novels, such as *Pamela* and *Clarissa* helped create interest in letter writing as a type of polite communication. Style manuals became popular, and young women in England and the colonies were supposed to practice daily letter writing. The style was supposed to be similar to polite conversation, and it was considered a sign of gentility to be able to write good letters.[55]

People often copied letters into a copybook, and John Adams resolved to begin doing so in 1776. As he made clear in a letter to his wife, Abigail, this would be helpful to him because it would permit him "to write more deliberately," review his work, and keep track of the letters he had written. He then suggested sending Abigail a blank copybook, "as a Present, that you might begin the Practice at the same Time, for I really think that your Letters are much better worth preserving than mine." He further observed, "Your daughter and sons will very soon write so good Hands that they will copy the Letters for you from your Book, which will improve them at the same Time that it relieves you."[56]

Milcah Martha Moore (known as Patsy or Patty to her family and closest friends) was known as an excellent and entertaining writer of letters. In a letter to Milcah Martha from her sister, Margaret Hill Morris, in 1778, Margaret wrote that she did not routinely read Milcah Martha's letters aloud. However, she explained:

When there's a pleasant passage or witty remark in them, I read it for the benefit of our little circle, and then there's a sort of exclamation—oh! children when will you be able to write such a letter, and the daughter gravely replies, if we were to have as much practice as aunt P., we should know how to write letters; yes, but not such as letter as this, and then I display it, as if it was any merit to me (who am such a scribbler), that my sweet Patty writes such a fair hand.[57]

Mercy Otis Warren was also a prolific letter writer. She was born into a political family in Massachusetts and married into one as well. She corresponded with a great number of men and women who were also interested in politics. She kept up a correspondence with Catharine Macaulay, the noted British historian, for two decades. She became friendly with both John and Abigail Adams, and they wrote many letters. Abigail Adams admired and encouraged Mercy to write, telling her, "I love characters drawn by your pen."[58]

Yet, women did publish work in the eighteenth century, especially in the post-Revolutionary period. For example, Judith Sargent Murray wrote plays and poems, as well as essays. Mercy Otis Warren wrote poems, satirical political plays, and a history of the American Revolution. Hannah Adams wrote religious history and a scholarly account of the Revolution. Many more women published works of fiction and nonfiction. Some women's work was published by others after their death. These were often in the form of memoirs, diaries, and meditations. After her death, Ann Eliza Bleeker's daughter published her mother's work in 1790 and 1791, which included a fictionalized Indian captivity novel called *The History of Maria Kittle*.

African American women also wrote. Lucy Terry Prince's poem about an Indian attack on Deerfield in 1746 is credited with being the first poem written by an African American woman. The poem, "Bars Fight," was not published, however, until many years after her death. Lucy married a free man, Abijah Prince, in 1756. He purchased Lucy's freedom. The family moved to Vermont, where Lucy became well-known for her speaking ability.

Phillis Wheatley, who was also a slave, established a reputation as a poet during her lifetime. She became a sort of celebrity when she visited England in 1773, where she secured the patronage of the Countess of Huntingdon. She was considered a "natural genius," that is, a person who was not tutored in the arts but who had emerged with natural gifts and talents. Before she died, Susanna Wheatley, Phillis's mistress, granted her freedom, but with the death of her master, John Wheatley, in 1778, Phillis lost the only home she had ever known. She married John Peters, a free black shopkeeper, and the couple had three children, all of

Phillis Wheatley. Illus. in: Poems on various subjects, religious and moral/ Phillis Wheatley. London: Printed for A. Bell, bookseller, Aldgate, 1773, frontispiece. Courtesy Library of Congress.

whom died young. Phillis's husband left her, and she was forced to work as a servant to support herself. Although she published a poem in 1784 that celebrated the American Revolution, it did not bring her success. She died in poverty that year.

Phillis Wheatley wrote poems on many subjects. For example, she wrote of slaves and Christianity in her poem "On Being Brought from Africa to America." Her poem "To His Excellency George Washington" celebrated Washington's appointment as commander-in-chief of the American Army. It was published in Tom Paine's *Pennsylvania Magazine* in 1776, and, in response, George Washington wrote a letter to Phillis Wheatley, inviting her to visit his headquarters in Cambridge. As one literary scholar has written, "Phillis Wheatley's mastery of poetic technique, such as her ability to shape a persona for rhetorical purposes, shows her to be a more artful poet than we have previously recognized."[59]

Participation in and enjoyment of the fine and performing arts in the eighteenth century varied according to religion, class, and race. As noted, both boys and girls in many well-to-do households were given music and dancing lessons, although this was not usually true of those born to wealthy Quaker parents. Quaker beliefs did not condone activities such as dancing or gambling. For example, in 1716, the Friends yearly meeting advised "against 'going to or being in any way concerned in plays, games, lotteries, music, and dancing.'" Yet, as historians have suggested, if Quakers were being admonished not to engage in such activities, it most likely means that some had already done so.[60]

Yet elsewhere, dancing and dancing instruction were encouraged. Teenage girls of gentry families in eighteenth-century Virginia typically received dancing lessons at about age twelve or thirteen. They also began to attend balls with their parents. It was important that they not begin lessons too late, because, as one scholar has observed, "instruction in dance was deemed important in establishing genteel body carriage, evening social dancing was important preparation for the etiquette of assemblies and because the ability to dance was essential to courtship in Virginia society." After beginning lessons in dance, many girls also learned to play the guitar or harpsichord, but this, it was believed, could wait until they were a bit older.[61]

Both men and women taught dance and music. Eighteenth-century newspapers often advertised their services. The *Virginia Gazette,* for example, printed an advertisement by Monsieur Jean Cadou in November 1779. He planned to open a dancing school. In addition, he offered to teach French, as well as dance, to "Ladies," either in their own homes or at his school. A Mrs. Neill intended to open a boarding school for young ladies in Williamsburg in December 1776. As well as such subjects as reading and needlework, she would teach guitar for an additional fee and would provide "the best masters" to teach dancing and writing. Perhaps a bit more unusual was an advertisement for the return of Sarah Knox, a convict servant in Lancaster County, Virginia, who ran away in July 1752. Her master reported that she sometimes pretended "to be a dancing mistress." Perhaps she really was a skilled dancer. The advertisement asked that she be returned, "or if any person find her qualified to teach Dancing . . . he may purchase between 5–6 years of service of her at fifteen pounds currency."[62]

In mid- and late-eighteenth-century Philadelphia, dance and theater became connected to politics and patriotism, and they were often associated as well with squabbles over the status of the participants. The managers of Philadelphia's Dancing Assembly, a club that met at the City Tavern's long gallery, advised those who were not patriots to stay away. Dances emphasized the partisan politics and were thus given such names as "the success of the campaign" and "Burgoyne's defeat."[63]

By 1790, dances in Philadelphia were often governed by strict rules in order to keep them civil. Hosts also felt the need to regulate dancing at their balls. For example, the Chevalier de la Luzerne intended to avoid conflict at a gala he was hosting by assigning guests to particular sets. (In country and square dances, a particular number of men and women make up a set needed for the dance.) His plan, however, did not quite work out as planned. As one scholar has described the situation, "the presence of 'several Quaker ladies,' presumably members of established Philadelphia families, taxed the chevalier's command of etiquette. These ladies arrived in plain dress, signifying an intention to uphold Quaker values and suggesting that it was unlikely they would take their place in either of the two sets of dancers. To avoid offending either the ladies or the partners they might snub, these guests were accommodated in a private room from which they could view the dancing and be seen by the dancers through 'a gauze curtain.'" To the amazement of some, the strategy worked.[64]

In post-Revolutionary Philadelphia and Boston, the attempt to establish viable theaters was equally contentious. Those promoting theater believed it was a means of educating citizens, whereas those who opposed theater thought it was sinful or that it would lead people to "forget their political duties." Although Quakers and those of some other religions were against theater, opponents also consisted of some with Republican, as opposed to Federalist, views.[65]

During the American Revolution, theatergoing became associated with Britain and British supporters. One historian notes, "By banning the playhouse, with its class-regulated seating and fare of British plays, Americans implemented a cultural boycott to match their embargo on British tea and sugar." In 1789, the law banning theaters was overturned, and plans were put into effect to build a legal theater in Philadelphia. Attempts were made to associate theatergoing with patriotism, and women were on both sides of the issue.[66]

Unlike attending the theater, eighteenth-century Americans did not imbue sitting for portraits or purchasing them with being unpatriotic or corrupt. Indeed, following the Revolution, Americans on all sides of the political spectrum had their portraits painted. In the post-Revolutionary period, many portraits portrayed well-known individuals in classical garb. But strict Quakers, such as Elizabeth Drinker and her husband, Henry, would not even buy portraits. Their sons, however, both sat for portraits.[67]

In contrast, eighteenth-century American Jews were not against having their likenesses preserved. Abigail Bilhah Levy Franks wrote to her son Naphtali and said, "Your pictures Are quite an Acceptable Pres[ent] . . . the whole Family Was in raptures Your father walks abouth the Parlour with Such Pleasure." Naphtali, who was twenty-four when the portrait was painted, had been living in London for almost seven years. Abigail had never seen her son as an adult, and she would never see him in person again. Thus, the portrait was of great value to her.[68]

Portrait paintings were part of Jewish culture in America from its beginning. Although portraits were not a part of Jewish tradition in Europe, Jewish families in America began to imitate the non-Jewish society around them. The subjects in the painting resemble the non-Jewish sitters in portraits painted around the same time. One scholar notes, "Early American portraits were visual declarations that this small band of North American Jews were part of, rather than apart from, the colonial, mercantile society in which they lived."[69] The Levy Franks paintings are extraordinary, however. They consist of a series of seven paintings, and they are "the oldest surviving portraits of colonial American Jews, and the oldest family-series portrait series to survive in all of American painting."[70]

In the eighteenth century, many well-to-do women, as well as men, had their portraits painted. Learning to paint, however, was not a skill in which many of them were trained. Early in the century, Henrietta Johnston helped support her family through painting portraits of the elite families of Charleston. She had probably received some training in Ireland from professional male artists, although the details are not known. (See Chapter 3 for more on Henrietta Johnston.) Patience Lovell Wright was a self-taught sculptor, the nation's first native-born sculptor. She was able to create amazingly lifelike wax models of people; as a widow, she supported her family through shows of these wax creations. She may also have spied for the American side during the Revolution. Yet in the eighteenth century, professional training in art was difficult to come by for men in America as well. Just a few years into the nineteenth century, however, artist Charles Willson Peale, sculptor William Rush, and other Philadelphians founded the Pennsylvania Academy of Fine Arts, the first art museum and school in the nation. The Academy did train women, including the Peale daughters.[71]

Women's education greatly improved in the latter part of the eighteenth century. Many applauded and encouraged women's efforts to improve themselves through reading and study. Yet, once graduated from elite academies, women had few choices open to them. Most of them married, with the approval of society that they would be properly prepared to undertake their roles as "republican mothers." Others decided to teach or write. Only a few succeeded in artistic ventures.

For black women and Native American women, there were fewer choices. As Phillis Wheatley discovered, success was often fleeting for women; for African American women, it was often even more transitory. Furthermore, although they performed domestic tasks and were mothers, most Americans did not consider women of color, enslaved or not, to be proper models of domesticity. For most eighteenth-century women, the home and domestic duties remained the central focus of their lives, but not every woman lived or toiled in a home of her own.

NOTES

1. Robert F. Seybolt, *Apprenticeship and Apprenticeship Education in Colonial New England and New York* (New York, 1917), 46–47, quoted in E. Jennifer Monaghan, "Literacy Instruction and Gender in Colonial New England," in *Reading in America: Literature and Social History*, Cathy N. Davidson, ed. (Baltimore: Johns Hopkins University Press, 1989), 63.

2. E. Jennifer Monaghan, *Learning to Read and Write in Colonial America* (Amherst, MA: University of Massachusetts Press, 2005), 193–194.

3. Monaghan, *Learning to Read and Write*, 194.

4. Monaghan, "Literacy Instruction," 64.

5. Quote from Monica Keifer, "Early American Childhood in the Middle Atlantic," *Pennsylvania Magazine of History and Biography* 68(1944): 17, quoted in Joan M. Jensen, *Loosening the Bonds: Mid-Atlantic Farm Women, 1750–1850* (New Haven, CT: Yale University Press, 1986), 170.

6. Deborah Hill to Hannah Moore, August 23, 1750, in John J. Smith, ed., *Letters of Doctor Richard Hill and His Children* (Philadelphia, 1854), 63, quoted in Catherine La Courreye Blecki and Karin A. Wulf, eds. *Milcah Martha Moore's Book: A Commonplace Book from Revolutionary America* (University Park: Pennsylvania State University Press, 1997), 13.

7. Blecki and Wulf, *Milcah Martha Moore*, 13.

8. Milcah Martha Hill to her sisters, May 17, 1748, in Edward Wanton Smith Collection, Quaker Collection, Haverford College Library, Haverford, PA, quoted in Blecki and Wulf, *Milcah Martha Moore*, xi.

9. Monaghan, "Literacy Instruction," 72.

10. Although the learning of different handwriting styles was simplified in America, boys at Boston's writing schools learned five to eight different hands. Most boys and girls did not, but they were probably aware that many different hands existed. See Tamara Plakins Thorton, *Handwriting in America: A Cultural History* (New Haven, CT: Yale University Press, 1996), 25.

11. Eliza Custis, "Self-Portrait: Eliza Custis 1808," edited by William D. Hoyt, Jr. *Virginia Magazine of History and Biography* 53(1945): 93–94, quoted in Linda Rowe, "Women and Education in Eighteenth-Century Virginia," *Colonial Williamsburg Interpreter*, vol. 23, no. 2 (2002) available at Colonial Williamsburg Research Division Web Site, http://research.history.org/Historical_Research/Research_Themes/ThemeFamily/WomenEducation.cfm.

12. Betty Pratt to William Pratt, Aug. 10, 1732, Roger Jones Family Papers, Library of Congress, in Kathleen M. Brown, *Good Wives, Nasty Wenches, and Anxious Patriarchs: Gender, Race, and Power in Colonial Virginia* (Chapel Hill: University of North Carolina Press, 1996), 297.

13. Rowe, "Women and Education," 5.

14. Hasia R. Diner and Beryl Lieff Benderly, *Her Works Praise Her: A History of Jewish Women in America from Colonial Times to the Present* (New York: Basic Books, 2002), 57.

15. Diner and Benderly, *Her Works Praise Her*, 53, 56.

16. Frederick Tupper and Helen Tyler Brown, eds. *Grandmother Tyler's Book, The Recollections of Mary Palmer Tyler, 1775–1866* (Boston, 1925), 51, 57, 144, 157, quoted in Mary Beth Norton, *Liberty's Daughters: The Revolutionary Experience of American Women, 1750–1800* (Ithaca, NY: Cornell University Press, 1996), 257.

17. Jacob R. Marcus, *The American Jewish Woman: A Documentary History* (New York: Ktav Publishing House, 1981), 45.

18. Joy Day Buel and Richard Buel, Jr. *The Way of Duty: A Woman and Her Family in Revolutionary America* (New York: W.W. Norton, 1984), 7, 18.

19. In both England and its colonies, weight was measured in two ways, troy weight and avoirdupois weight. Troy was used most commonly for measuring gold, silver, and precious stones and bread, wheat, and corn; avoirdupois was used to weigh many things, including groceries, butter, cheese, wool, hemp, flax, and pitch. See "Passages and Quotes Relating to Justices of the Peace in 16th and 17th Century England," online at http://www.commonlaw .com/CoJust.html#CO30.

20. Marcus, *The American Jewish Woman*, 24.

21. Margaret A. Hogan and C. James Taylor, eds. *My Dearest Friend: Letters of Abigail and John Adams* (Cambridge, MA: Harvard University Press, 2007), 140–141.

22. Linda K. Kerber, *Women of the Republic: Intellect and Ideology in Revolutionary America* (Chapel Hill: University of North Carolina Press, 1980), 10–11.

23. Kerber, *Women of the Republic*," 201–202.

24. Norton, *Liberty's Daughters*, 252. An e-text version of "On the Equality of the Sexes" is available at http://digital.library.upenn.edu/women/murray/equality/equality.html.

25. Constantia [Judith Sargent Murray], *The Gleaner, A Miscellaneous Production* (Boston, 1798), III, 219-220, quoted in Norton, *Liberty's Daughters*, 254.

26. Kerber, *Women of the Republic*, 210.

27. Kerber, *Women of the Republic*, 210–211.

28. Kerber, *Women of the Republic*, 212.

29. Jensen, *Loosening the Bonds*, 168–169.

30. "Ruth Walmsley," in *Friends Library*, 6:75–82; Diary of Sarah Cresson, 1789–1892, Quaker Collection, Haverford College, both quoted in Jensen, *Loosening the Bonds*, 170.

31. Jensen, *Loosening the Bonds*, 172.

32. Jensen, *Loosening the Bonds*, 174–175.

33. Joan R. Gunderson, *To Be Useful to the World: Women in Revolutionary America, 1740–1790*, rev. ed., (Chapel Hill: University of North Carolina Press, 2006), 94.

34. Rowe, "Women and Education."

35. Brown, *Good Wives, Nasty Wenches*," 297.

36. Marla R. Miller, *The Needle's Eye: Women and Work in the Age of Revolution* (Amherst, MA: University of Massachusetts Press, 206), 69.

37. Miller, *The Needle's Eye*, 72–74.

38. Gunderson, *To Be Useful to the World*, 90–92.

39. Elise Pinckney, ed. *The Letterbook of Eliza Lucas Pinckney, 1739–1762* (Columbia: University of South Carolina Press, 1997), 34.

40. Gunderson, *To Be Useful to the World*, 96.

41. Emma L. Powers, "A Biographical Sketch of Mrs. Ann Wager," Colonial Williamsburg Research Division Web Site, http://research.history.org/Historical_Research/Research _Themes/ThemeReligion/Wager.cfm.

42. Powers, "Ann Wager."

43. Gunderson, *To Be Useful to the World*, 96, 97.

44. Gunderson, *To Be Useful to the World*, 98–99.

45. Gunderson, *To Be Useful to the World*, 102.

46. Carol F. Karlsen and Laurie Crumpacker, eds. *The Journal of Esther Edwards Burr, 1754–1757* (New Haven, CT: Yale University Press, 1984), 98–99.

47. Laurel Thatcher Ulrich, *The Life of Martha Ballard, Based on Her Diary, 1785–1812* (New York: Knopf, 1990), 10, 157.

48. Kerber, *Women of the Republic*, 241.

49. Kerber, *Women of the Republic*, 238; Elaine Forman Crane, ed., *The Diary of Elizabeth Drinker* (Boston: Northeastern University Press, 1991), 694.

50. She was reading Richard Brothers, *A Revealed Knowledge of the Prophecies and Times, Particularly of the Present Time, the Present War, and the Prophecy Now Fulfilling . . . Book the Second, Containing with Other Great and Remarkable Things, Not Revealed to Any Other Person on Earth, the Sudden and Perpetual Fall of the Turkish, German, and Russian Empires. . .* (London, 1794[Brit. Mus. Cat.]), quoted in Crane, *Diary of Elizabeth Drinker*, 708.

51. Blecki and Wulf, *Milcah Martha Moore's Book*, 27.

52. Blecki and Wulf, *Milcah Martah Moore's Book*, xvi, 27.

53. Blecki and Wulf, *Milcah Martha Moore's Book*, xvii–xviii, 27.

54. Blecki and Wulf, *Milcah Martha Moore's Book*, 28.

55. Edith Belle Gelles, *Portia: The World of Abigail Adams* (Bloomington: Indiana University Press, 1992), 58.

56. John Adams to Abigail Adams, June 2, 1776, Hogan and Taylor, *My Dearest Friend*, 120–121.

57. Margaret Hill Morris to Milcah Martha Moore, March 9, 1778, in J. J. Smith, *Letters of Doctor Richard Hill*, 239 in Blecki and Wulf, *Milcah Martha Moore's Book*, 28.

58. Abigail Adams to Mercy Warren, April 13, 1776, in Lyman Butterfield, ed. *Adams Family Correspondence* (Cambridge, MA: Belknap Press of Harvard University Press, 1963), I:378, quoted in Marianne B. Geiger, "Mercy Otis Warren," in *Portraits of American Women from Settlement to the Present*, edited by G. J. Barker-Benfield and Catherine Clinton (New York: St. Martin's Press, 1991), 125.

59. Charles Scruggs, "Phillis Wheatley," in Barker-Benfield and Clinton, *Portraits of American Women*, 105–107, 113, 114.

60. Oscar Sonneck, *Francis Hopkinson and James Lyon* (Washington, D.C.: 1905), 10–11 quoted in Jo Ann Taricami, "Music in Colonial Philadelphia: Some New Documents," *The Musical Quarterly* 67 (April 1979): 85.

61. Cathleene B. Hellier, "The Adolescence of Gentry Girls in Late Eighteenth-Century Virginia," online Colonial Williamsburg Web site http://research.history.org/Historical _Research/Research_Themes/ThemeFamily/GentryGirls.cfm.

62. *Virginia Gazette*, November 20, 1779, p. 3; December 20, 1776, p. 4; July 3, 1752, p. 3.

63. Peter Thompson, *Rum Punch and Revolution: Taverngoing and Public Life in Eighteenth-Century Philadelphia* (Philadelphia: University of Pennsylvania Press, 1999), 154.

64. Thompson, *Rum Punch and Revolution*, 196–197.

65. Heather S. Nathans, "Forging a Powerful Engine: Building Theaters and Elites in Post-Revolutionary Boston and Philadelphia," *Explorations in Early American Culture, A Supplemental Issue of Pennsylvania History: A Journal of Mid-Atlantic Studies* 66 (1999), 113.

66. Nathans, "Forging a Powerful Engine," 114.

67. Crane, *The Diary of Elizabeth Drinker*, xiv.

68. Abigail Franks to Naphtali Franks, October 17, 1739, in *Letters of the Franks Family (1733–1748)*, ed. Leo Hershowitz and Isidore S. Meyer (Waltham, MA: American Jewish Historical Society, 1968), 66, quoted in Ellen Smith, "Portraits of a Community: The Image and Experience of Early American Jews," in *American Jewish Women's History: A Reader*, edited by Pamela S. Nadell (New York: New York University Press, 2003), 13.

69. Smith "Portraits of a Community," 14.

70. Smith, "Portraits of a Community," 15.

71. Lee L. Schreiber describes the conflicts of the early years of the PAFA in "The Academy: School for Artists or Private Art Club?" *Pennsylvania History* 46 (October 1980), 331–350.

SUGGESTED READING

Blecki, Catherine La Courreye and Karin A. Wulf, eds. *Milcah Martha Moore's Book: A Commonplace Book from Revolutionary America.* University Park: Pennsylvania State University Press, 1997.

Buel, Joy Day and Richard Buel, Jr. *The Way of Duty: A Woman and Her Family in Revolutionary America.* New York: W. W. Norton, 1984.

Crane, Elaine Forman, ed. *The Diary of Elizabeth Drinker.* Boston: Northeastern University Press, 1991.

Gunderson, Joan R. *To Be Useful to the World: Women in Revolutionary America, 1740–1790,* rev. ed., Chapel Hill: University of North Carolina Press, 2006.

Karlsen, Carol F. and Laurie Crumpacker, eds. *The Journal of Esther Edwards Burr, 1754–1757.* New Haven, CT: Yale University Press, 1984.

Kerber, Linda K. *Women of the Republic: Intellect and Ideology in Revolutionary America.* Chapel Hill: University of North Carolina Press, 1980.

Monaghan, E. Jennifer. *Learning to Read and Write in Colonial America.* Amherst, MA: University of Massachusetts Press, 2005.

Selected Bibliography
and Resources

Berkin, Carol. *Revolutionary Mothers: Women in the Struggle for America's Independence*. New York: Knopf, 2006.

Blecki, Catherine La Courreye and Kain A. Wulf. *Milcah Martha Moore's Book: A Commonplace Book from Revolutionary America*. University Park: Pennsylvania State University Press, 1997.

Block, Sharon. *Rape and Sexual Power in Early America*. Chapel Hill: University of North Carolina Press, 2006.

Brown, Kathleen M. *Foul Bodies: Cleanliness in Early America*. New Haven, CT: Yale University Press, 2009.

Buel, Joy Day and Richard Buel, Jr. *The Way of Duty: A Woman and Her Family in Revolutionary America*. New York: W.W. Norton, 1984.

Cleary, Patricia. *Elizabeth Murray: A Woman's Pursuit of Independence in Eighteenth-Century America*. Amherst, MA: University of Massachusetts Press, 2003.

Crane, Elaine Forman., ed. *The Diary of Elizabeth Drinker*. Boston: Northeastern University Press, 1991.

Dayton, Cornelia Hughes. *Women Before the Bar: Gender, Law, and Society in Connecticut, 1639–1789*. Chapel Hill: University of North Carolina Press, 1995.

Demos, John. *The Unredeemed Captive: A Family Story from Early America*. New York: Vintage Books, 1995.

Diner, Hasia R. and Beryl Lieff Benderly. *Her Works Praise Her: A History of Jewish Women in America from Colonial Times to the Present*. New York: Basic Books, 2002.

Godbeer, Richard. *Sexual Revolution in Early America*. Baltimore: Johns Hopkins University Press, 2002.

Gunderson, Joan R. *To Be Useful to the World: Women in Revolutionary America, 1740–1790*, rev. ed. Chapel Hill: University of North Carolina Press, 2006.

Hatley, Tom. *The Dividing Paths: Cherokees and South Carolinians through the Revolutionary Era*. New York: Oxford University Press, 1995.

Haulman, Kate. "Fashion and the Culture Wars of Revolutionary Philadelphia," *William and Mary Quarterly* LXII(October 2005):625–662.

Hogan, Margaret A. and C. James Taylor. *My Dearest Friend: Letters of Abigail and John Adams.* Cambridge, MA: Harvard University Press, 2007.

Horne, Field, ed. *The Diary of Mary Cooper: Life on a Long Island Farm, 1768–1773.* Oyster Bay, NY: Oyster Bay Historical Society, 1981.

Jensen, Joan M. *Loosening the Bonds: Mid-Atlantic Farm Women, 1750–1850.* New Haven, CT: Yale University Press, 1986.

Karlsen, Carol F. and Laurie Crumpacker, eds. *The Journal of Esther Edwards Burr, 1754–1757.* New Haven, CT: Yale University Press, 1984.

Kerber, Linda K. "The Paradox of Women's Citizenship in the Early Republic: The Case of *Martin vs. Massachusetts,* 1805," *American Historical Review* 97 (April 1992): 349–378.

Kerber, Linda K. *Women of the Republic: Intellect and Ideology in Revolutionary America.* Chapel Hill: University of North Carolina Press, 1980.

Levy, Barry. *Quakers and the American Family: British Settlement in the Delaware Valley.* New York: Oxford University Press, 1988.

Lewis, Jan. "The Republican Wife: Virtue and Seduction in the Early Republic." *William and Mary Quarterly* XLIV (October 1987): 689–721.

Little, Ann M. *Abraham in Arms: War and Gender in Colonial New England.* Philadelphia: University of Pennsylvania Press, 2007.

Lyons, Clare A. *Sex Among the Rabble: An Intimate History of Gender and Power in the Age of Revolution, Philadelphia, 1730–1830.* Chapel Hill: University of North Carolina Press, 2006.

Marcus, Jacob R. *The American Jewish Woman: A Documentary History.* New York: Ktav Publishing, 1981.

Merritt, Jane T. *At the Crossroads: Indians and Empires on a Mid-Atlantic Frontier, 1700–1763.* Chapel Hill: University of North Carolina Press, 2003.

Miller, Marla R. *The Needle's Eye: Women and Work in the Age of Revolution.* Amherst: University of Massachusetts Press, 2006.

Monaghan, E. Jennifer. *Learning to Read and Write in Colonial America.* Amherst: University of Massachusetts Press, 2005.

Norton, Mary Beth. *Liberty's Daughters: The Revolutionary Experience of American Women, 1750–1800.* Ithaca, NY: Cornell University Press, 1996.

Nylander, Jane C. *Our Own Snug Fireside: Images of the New England Home, 1760–1860.* New Haven, CT: Yale University Press, 1994.

Pinckney, Elise. *The Letterbook of Eliza Lucas Pinckney, 1739–1762.* With a new introduction. Columbia: University of South Carolina Press, 1997.

Plane, Ann Marie. *Colonial Intimacies: Indian Marriage in Early New England.* Ithaca, NY: Cornell University Press, 2000.

Roark, Elizabeth L. *Artists of Colonial America.* Westport, CT: Greenwood Press, 2003.

Smith, Merril D. *Breaking the Bonds: Marital Discord in Pennsylvania, 1730–1830.* New York: New York University Press, 1991.

Soderlund, Jean R. "Women's Authority in Pennsylvania and New Jersey Quaker Meetings, 1680–1760." *William and Mary Quarterly,* XLIV (October 1987): 722–749.

Ulrich, Laurel Thatcher. *Good Wives: Image and Reality in the Lives of Women in Northern New England, 1650–1750.* New York: Oxford University Press, 1982.

Ulrich, Laurel Thatcher. *A Midwife's Tale: The Life of Martha Ballard Based on Her Diary, 1785–1812.* New York: Knopf, 1990.

Westlake, Marilyn J. *Women and Religion in Early America, 1600–1850: The Puritan and Evangelical Traditions.* New York: Routledge, 1999.

Wilson, Lisa. *Life After Death: Widows in Pennsylvania, 1750–1850.* Philadelphia: Temple University Press, 1992.

FILMS

John Adams (2008). Based on David McCullough's Pulitzer Prize-winning book. This HBO miniseries stars Paul Giametti as John Adams and Laura Linney as Abigail Adams.

Mary Silliman's War (1994). Based on part of Joy Day Buel and Richard Buel, Jr.'s book, *The Way of Duty* (1984). The story concerns the Revolutionary War experiences of Connecticut's Mary Fish Silliman.

A Midwife's Tale (1997). This movie documents the writing of Laurel Thatcher Ulrich's *A Midwife's Tale*, and dramatizes the experiences of Martha Ballard. Directed by Richard P. Rogers.

WEB SITES

Adams Family Papers

The correspondence of John and Abigail Adams is available online at the Adams Family Papers: An Electronic Archive, hosted by the Massachusetts Historical Society. The site includes other Adams family documents as well. http://www.masshist.org/digitaladams/aea/.

Colonial Williamsburg

The Web site has a historical research section with articles, reports, and links to other features. http://research.history.org/Historical_Research.cfm.

DoHistory

This site uses Maine midwife Martha Ballard as a historical case study. The site includes excerpts from Laurel Ulrich's book, *A Midwife's Tale*, and clips from the movie. It also has other primary documents and links to other Web sites. www.DoHistory.org.

Raid on Deerfield, the Many Stories of 1704

This site, created by the Pocumtuck Valley Memorial Association/Memorial Hall Museum, chronicles the Deerfield raid by examining the cultures of all the groups involved and tells their stories. http://1704.deerfield.history.museum/home.do.

Index

Note: An italicized page number indicates an illustration. Page numbers followed by an "n" and a second number indicate that the reference is to a note on the designated page. For example, 52n58 refers to note 58 on page 52.

About the Author

MERRIL D. SMITH is an independent scholar and editor of *Encyclopedia of Rape* (Greenwood, 2004) among other works and author of *Women's Roles in Seventeenth-Century America* (Greenwood, 2008).